THE FRENCH INVASION OF BRITAIN AND IRELAND, 1792–1815

THE FRENCH INVASION OF BRITAIN AND IRELAND, 1792–1815

THE REVOLUTIONARIES AND SPIES WHO SOUGHT TO TOPPLE THE GOVERNMENT OF KING GEORGE

PAUL DAWSON

FRONTLINE
BOOKS

First published in Great Britain in 2023 by
Pen & Sword Frontline Books
An imprint of
Pen & Sword Books Ltd
Yorkshire – Philadelphia

ISBN 978-1-39906-808-6

A CIP catalogue record for this book is
available from the British Library.

Typeset by Lapiz Digital
Printed and bound by CPI UK

Pen & Sword Books Ltd incorporates the imprints of Pen & Sword Archaeology,
Atlas, Aviation, Battleground, Discovery, Family History, History, Maritime,
Military, Naval, Politics, Social History, Transport, True Crime, Claymore Press,
Frontline Books, Praetorian Press, Seaforth Publishing and White Owl

For a complete list of Pen & Sword titles please contact:

PEN & SWORD BOOKS LTD
47 Church Street, Barnsley, South Yorkshire, S70 2AS, England
E-mail: enquiries@pen-and-sword.co.uk
Website: www.pen-and-sword.co.uk

or

PEN AND SWORD BOOKS
1950 Lawrence Rd, Havertown, PA 19083, USA
E-mail: Uspen-and-sword@casematepublishers.com
Website: www.penandswordbooks.com

CONTENTS

ACKNOWLEDGEMENTS

This is the first major piece of research I have undertaken since suffering a severe traumatic brain injury on 22 June 2016. The injury has left me with a speech impediment, reduced movement in my left side and cognitive impairment. I thank James Tozer for helping me to assemble a coherent text from a jumbled mass of notes, jottings and paragraphs and proofreading the final version. I am eternally grateful.

This story tracks the hopes and aspirations of British subjects living in England, Scotland, Ireland and Wales who asked the French to invade their own country and overturn the monarchy and government.

In writing this story, I must thank Sally Fairweather for accompanying me to archives across Europe, and for her help in taking countless hundreds of photographs of archive papers. I am also grateful to Robert Cooper for his company during visits to archives in France.

I am grateful to Nicholas Dunne-Lynch for his friendship, provision of research material and enjoyable discussion about the United Irishmen and the Irish Legion. I thank Dr Mathieu Ferradou for giving his time generously to discuss the United Irishmen in France. I am grateful to Cécile Déjardin for her thoughts on the Irish émigré in Paris following the 1798 rebellion. I thank Martijn Wink, my friend and research colleague, for pointing me in the direction of the Netherlands National Archives and the Dutch evidence for the preparations at Texel to aid Ireland.

I am grateful to the staff at the National Archives Kew, National Library of Ireland, the National Records of Scotland, Helen Walker of the West Yorkshire Archive Service, the librarian of Leeds University Special Collection, staff at the Service Historique de la Défense in Paris as well as the Archives Diplomatique, Archives de la Marine and Archives Nationales in France for allowing me access to records in their holdings and for permission to quote their material.

PROLOGUE

News of the opening events of the French Revolution was greeted with widespread enthusiasm by British observers, and this was most potent among those championing domestic political reform, men such as John Horne Tooke, the Revd Dr Richard Price and his numerous colleagues in the Unitarian clergy, and congregation members such as Benjamin Vaughan, John Hurford Stone and Mary Wollstonecraft. For these groups and their associated literary, scientific and political circles, events in France signified a much deeper change in government that needed to happen in England, and many were prepared to do what ever was necessary – including taking up arms against the British Crown – to achieve this goal. The French Republic declared that the 'natural and imprescriptible rights of man' were to be defined as 'liberty, property, security and resistance to oppression'. The Republic demanded the destruction of aristocratic privileges by proclaiming an end to feudalism and exemptions from taxation. It also called for freedom and equal rights for all human beings (referred to as 'Men') and access to public office based on talent. The monarchy was restricted and all citizens had the right to take part in the legislative process. Freedom of speech and press was declared and arbitrary arrests outlawed. The Declaration also asserted the principles of popular sovereignty, in contrast to the divine right of kings that characterized the French monarchy, and social equality among citizens, eliminating the special rights of the nobility and clergy. This new ideology attempted to marry the Rousseauist civic humanist focus on public virtue and political liberty with the rational empiricism of the Enlightenment.[1]

On 19 October 1792, in the dining room of White's Hotel, Paris, members of the British Club, or Society for the Rights of Man, gathered for their first meeting. The society was dedicated to 'the cause'. The 'cause' was the French Republic, and the declaration of the rights of man.

Sat around the table were John Hurford Stone, newspaper editor Sampson Perry, poet and playwright Robert Merry, lawyer John

Frost as well as the Scottish pamphleteer John Oswald, former MP Sir Robert Smith, Lord Edward Fitzgerald, George Edwards and some no less equally radical women, including Helen Maria Williams and Charlotte Smith. They had come from the English-speaking world – Ireland, England, America, Scotland – to bask in Paris' atmosphere of cosmopolitan hope. They came from the 'middling sort' to aristocracy. Here was a cross section of society, all revelling in the new world created by the revolution in France. Many were linked by a shared religion: Thomas Walker, Thomas Chrisite, the Wordsworths, John Hurford Stone, Benjamin Vaughan, Mary Wollstonecraft and others such as John Milnes aka 'Jack Milnes the Democrat' were all Unitarians. They followed a proscribed religion that treated the adherents as second-class citizens in their own country. Irish Catholics such as John and Henry Sheares were also second-class citizens in their own country. The Anglican Ascendancy following the Restoration of the monarchy in 1660 placed legal impediments on all non-Anglicans in revenge, by and large, for the attempts by Puritans and Presbyterians to dis-stablish the Church of England during the Commonwealth. Dissent from Anglicanism was seen as politically and socially dangerous. Indeed, the newly resurgent Anglican Church expelled 2,000 clergy in summer 1662 over matters of doctrine, theology and church governance, and enabled Parliament to pass restrictive laws against Dissenters and Catholics.

Unsurprisingly for those men and women who faced legal repression of their faith, and by and large lacked the right to vote and have a say in the governance of their country, the primary topic of conversation at the dinner was undoubtedly the French Republic. The French Revolution laid aside any test on family lineage and religion Unitarians like Catholics lacked the same civil rights as communicants in the Church of England. Of those who dined that evening, many wondered if a new social order could be achieved in France, why not England? Radical ideology combined the British traditions of liberalism, Whigism and constitutionalism and aligned with Franco-American principles of rights, equality, republicanism and democracy to foster a desire to export revolution, if needs be backed by French bayonets.

Irish peer Lord Edward Fitzgerald, writing from the hotel on 30 October 1792, described his own sociable routine: 'I lodge with my friend Paine, – we breakfast, dine, and sup together.' Fitzgerald basked in the atmosphere of fraternity and embraced the egalitarianism of republican citizenship. He ostentatiously preferred walking, eschewed the use of carriages, and sported a republican cropped haircut, *à la romaine*, playing the part of the French citizen. Prior to the dinner at White's, he had even publicly renounced his aristocratic title, calling himself *'citoyen Edouard Fitzgerald'*, an attitude that was celebrated with a toast.[2] Thomas Paine, a founding father of the American Republic and the author of the *Rights of Man* (1791–2) who was prosecuted in England for seditious writings and was considered a threat to the political stability of the English monarchy, came to France in September 1792. Paine had broad interests and politics and had been a friend of Edmund Burke, although by this point they were mortal enemies, as Paine resolutely believed the British Crown and Parliament were nothing more than self-interested institutions run for the benefit of a land-owning elite and called for values based on reason, tolerance and understanding rather than institutions. He was a pioneer, along with Mary Wollstonecraft, of the concept of basic human rights, whereas men like Burke openly rejected and ridiculed such ideals.

The 'patriotic feast' gathered about a hundred guests from the entire Atlantic revolutionary galaxy to celebrate the recent French military victories at Valmy and Jemappes. Toasts were drunk to the abolition of slavery, universal suffrage for all men and women and religious tolerance. All the members present pledged their attachment to liberty and equality as exemplified by France and urged the 'victorious troops of liberty to lay down their arms only when there are no more tyrants or slaves'.[3] On 28 November, an address to the National Convention prepared by residents at the hotel was presented to the Convention. The document had been signed on 24 November by the president John Hurford Stone and by other men who will be examined in this book – the Revd William Jackson, Edward Fitzgerald, William Duckett, Henry and John Sheares, Bernard MacSheehy and lastly Nicholas Madgett.[4] The French Republic declared that the 'natural and imprescriptible rights of man' were to be defined as 'liberty, property, security and resistance to oppression'. The Revolution laid aside any test on family lineage and religion. If this could be achieved in France, the idea that this could be replicated in England was rapidly gaining ground, and many who sat at the dinner table planned to do just that.

Chapter 1

THE ROAD TO REVOLUTION

Prior to the Act of Union, Ireland was a kingdom in its own right, but under the rule of the British Crown. Executive power was largely in the hands of the Lord Lieutenant and the Chief Secretary, appointed by the British prime minister. However, Ireland also had its own Parliament, which throughout the eighteenth century had lobbied for greater control over trade and law-making in Ireland. The Irish Parliament was subservient to the British Parliament at Westminster, but increasingly, as the century wore on, agitated for greater autonomy.

The Parliament was however supremely exclusionary: the majority of the population was barred from political participation on the grounds of religious and ownership of property. Membership of the Parliament was confined to members of the Anglican Church of Ireland, which, allowing for some conversions, was overwhelmingly composed of descendants of English settlers. The Parliament was not a democratic body; elections were relatively infrequent, seats could be purchased and the number of voters was small and confined to wealthy, property owning Protestants. As in England, Dissenters, who were primarily Presbyterians and Unitarians, and were mostly descendants of Scottish immigrants, while not excluded as rigorously as Catholics from public life also suffered from discrimination – marriages performed by their clergy were not legally recognized, for example.

Under the Penal Laws, enacted after the Catholic defeat in the Jacobite-Williamite War of the 1690s, all those who refused to acknowledge the English king as head of the Church – therefore Catholics and Presbyterians – were barred not only from Parliament but from any public position or service in the army. Catholic-owned lands were also confiscated for alleged political disloyalty throughout the seventeenth century. Catholics, to a large extent the descendants of the pre-seventeenth-century Irish population, also suffered from restrictions on landholding, inheritance, entering the professions and the right to bear arms.

Although some of the Penal Laws were relaxed in 1782, allowing new Catholic churches and schools to open, and allowing Catholics into the professions and to purchase land. However, the great majority of the Irish population was still excluded from political power, and to a large degree from wealth and landholding also, as the last decade of the eighteenth century dawned. Discontent among Catholics was exacerbated by economic hardship and by tithes, compulsory taxes that people of all religions had to pay, for the upkeep of the established Protestant Church of Ireland. It cemented into power the 'Protestant Ascendancy' which made Catholics and Dissenters second-class citizens.

As in Ireland, in England the 'Protestant Ascendancy', or more correctly the ascendency of the Church of England, ensured that Catholics and Dissenters were disenfranchised from participating in state affairs. More radical Dissenters such as Unitarians – those who denied the Trinity – also fell foul of the blasphemy laws, and, like all non-Anglicans, found that the Test and Corporation Acts blocked them from local and national administrative functions if they did not take Communion in the local parish church. According to the Test and Corporation Acts, if a non-Anglican took a Crown or municipal office, without taking the sacrament in an Anglican church, then under the law the Unitarian had to pay a fine of £500 and had no recourse to legal defence against the charge. The Acts also stated that non-Anglicans could not act as a guardian or executor under terms of a will or even inherit a legacy if they transgressed the law, and the estate was forfeited to the Crown. These Acts made perhaps 20 per cent of the population in 1780 second-class citizens. Since the Stamp Act protests of 1768, and increasingly so from 1774 with the outbreak of war with the American Colonies – this is explored in the author's companion volume *Fighting Napoleon at Home* also published by Frontline – English radical groups such as the Yorkshire Association, Society for Constitutional Information and London Corresponding Society all campaigned for political reform, religious toleration and the creation of a new constitutional framework. These ideas were fostered from the pulpit of politically active ministers – such as the Revd Dr Richard Price, who openly approved of rebellion when undertaken on behalf of liberty against authoritarian power.[1] For Price the Test and Corporation Acts were just one example of the executive impacting on personal liberty and interfering with personal conscience. Price's influence would figure large in both England, Scotland and Ireland. One of Price's colleagues, the Revd Dr Joseph Priestley, Unitarian minister at Mill Hill Chapel in Leeds, did not hesitate to justify tyrannicide as 'the generous attack of the noble and daring patriot' in his publication *An Essay on the First Principles of Government* (1768).[2] For English radicals such as John Cartwright and religious Dissenters the desire for political reform and the perceived injustices of the Test and Corporation Acts led to an upsurge in opposition to the status quo: when Americans began to speak out against injustices meted out to them by English tyranny, the Dissenters understood their rhetoric, and took up the cause as their own. These views of a reformed constitution were promoted through associations formed to debate radical ideas, disseminate literature and link like-minded people, as well as through flourishing academies such as that in Warrington in Cheshire. This was called 'the cradle of Unitarianism' by Arthur Aikin Brodribb, writing in the *Dictionary of National Biography*, who went on to say that it: 'formed during the twenty-nine years of its existence the centre of the liberal politics and the literary taste of the county of Lancashire'.[3] It opened in 1757 and closed in 1782. Tutors included the Revd Dr Priestley and Gilbert Wakefield. The academy drew many luminaries of the day, and came to be known as 'the Athens of the North' for its stimulating intellectual atmosphere. Its former pupils included Benjamin Vaughan and Archibald Hamilton Rowan who are prominent in the story told in this book.

On 26 August 1789, the French National Assembly adopted the Declaration of the Rights of Man and of the Citizen. The declaration directly challenged the authority of Louis XVI and set out a series of individual rights protected by law, and removed any religious test on civic participation. If this could happen in France, why not in England and Ireland many thought. To mark this momentous moment, the veteran political radical the Revd Dr Richard Price gave a sermon on 4 November 1789 to the Revolution Society hailing events in France as the dawn of a new era:

> Behold all ye friends of freedom ... behold the light you have struck out, after setting America free, reflected to France and there kindled into a blaze that lays despotism in ashes and warms and illuminates Europe. I see the ardour for liberty catching and spreading; ... the dominion of kings changed for the dominion of laws, and the dominion of priests giving way to the dominion of reason and conscience.[4]

Price, filled with the heady and buoyant optimism that the Revolution in France offered, declared that: 'The representatives of France work for the world and not for themselves only, and the whole world has an interest in their success.' He added:

> The Society for commemorating the revolution in Great Britain, disdaining national partialities, and rejoicing in every triumph of liberty and justice over arbitrary power ... cannot help ... expressing the particular satisfaction with which they reflect on the tendency of the glorious example given in France, to encourage other nations to assert the unalienable rights of mankind, and thereby to introduce a general reformation in the governments of Europe, and to make the world free and happy.[5]

The sermon reinterpreted the principles of 1688–9 in a more equal and democratic form and praised the French Revolution. The Revolution Society called for correspondence with similar groups across Britain and accepted a motion by Price to send the French National Assembly a congratulatory letter in which the society 'disdaining national partialities' expressed the hope that people whose liberty was repressed by 'a tyrannical government' might imitate the French and regain their liberty. The letter was signed by society president Lord Stanhope and the Revd Price sent it to the duc de La Rochefoucauld, who read it to the French National Assembly. The president of the assembly, Jean de Boisgelin, Archbishop of Aix, sent a reply to Lord Stanhope, applauding the spirit of 'humanity and universal benevolence' that characterized the London Revolution Society. The exchange of two letters initiated an extensive correspondence between the Revolution Society and the French National Assembly as well as with various Jacobin clubs in France. One of the first letters received was a congratulatory note from a patriotic society in Dijon, which arrived on 30 November 1789.

Chapter 2

THE REVOLUTIONARIES

Support for the ideals of the French Revolution in England and Ireland was most potent among those championing domestic political reform, none more so than members of the United Irishmen, and as has been discussed, the London Revolution Society. The society was formed to commemorate the English Revolution of 1688. Membership included Unitarians and high-profile Whigs, though dissenting merchants and tradesmen formed the bulk of the society's membership. Many prominent reformers, such as John Horne Tooke, Thomas Brand Hollis, Capel Lofft and John Cartwright, belonged to both the Revolution Society and the Society for Constitutional Information; these members provided a vital link between the two societies, which were similar in terms of social composition, ideology and campaigning methods. The Revolution Society was also in touch with the Whig Club through the good offices of Whig MP and playwright Richard Brinsley Sheridan. It is notable, however, that Charles James Fox, another Whig Club member, distanced himself from the new group.

The society was international in its outlook. On 9 December 1789 the society set up a 'committee of correspondence' to answer letters received from French sources. This eight-man sub-group included Richard Price and met in Clements Lane at the house of the society's secretary, Benjamin Cooper, who played an increasingly prominent role in the group's activities as its correspondence increased.[1]

As could be expected, the London Revolution Society advocated change to the current political system, with a particular focus on parliamentary reform, the repeal of the Test and Corporation Acts and the abolition of the slave trade. With the attempt in 1789/90 to repeal the Test and Corporation Acts, the only hope for abolition came through political reform: Unitarian clergy and their circles now took the lead in this. Thanks to prompting from John Horne Tooke, the society worked with the Society of Constitutional Information to draft and sponsor Henry Flood's programme of moderate parliamentary reform in the Commons during March and April 1790.[2]

The duc de La Rochefoucauld invited Price to the Fête de la Fédération on 14 July 1790 and the Jacobins of Bordeaux invited an English delegation the following year; the Fête de la Fédération was held on the first anniversary of the storming of the Bastille and celebrated the events of the Revolution.[3] Though neither of these visits took place, members of the Jacobin Société des Amis de la Constitution de Nantes did travel to London in 1790, where they were feted by the society on 29 October, attended the anniversary dinner on 4 November and discussed French and British politics with Lord Stanhope.[4]

Price and like-minded reformist groups were promoting the rights of man and international revolution. Members of the good Revd's congregation in Hackney included John Hurford Stone and his brother, Mary Wollstonecraft, Helen Maria Williams and Benjamin Vaughan; both Stone and Vaughan were members of the London Revolution Society. These people came to be known as 'Citizens of the World' and 'Friends of Liberty'. It was only natural that Price would send a message of congratulations to Paris. Indeed, Price corresponded with those directly involved in the events in France such as Turgot and Rabaut Saint-Étienne, the leader of French Protestants through his sponsor, former prime minister Lord Shelburne, ennobled further as Marquess of Lansdowne. Lansdowne was at the centre of a circle comprising both industrialists, commercial entrepreneurs and Dissenters and featured Price and his Unitarian colleague the Revd Dr Joseph Priestley. Both men believed that government was for the happiness and benefit of all people and that the people had the right to overthrow the government if it acted for a narrow section of society. Similar views were expressed by one of Price's congregation, Benjamin Vaughan, who was also part of the circle. From 1788 Vaughan edited his own radical newspaper, *The Repository*, which espoused the political ideology formulated around Lansdowne. Others in the circle were Jeremy Bentham and Étienne Dumont, speech writer for Mirabeau and editor of Mirabeau's radical paper, the *Courrier de Provence*. On the edge of this circle of largely Unitarian clergy and intellectuals were men such as John Milnes of Wakefield, who was known throughout his life as 'Jack Milnes the Democrat' for his forthright Jacobinism and had travelled to Paris to imbibe the heady spirit of the Revolution at first hand. When Price spoke in favour of the Revolution, he was doing so on behalf of the 'Lansdowne circle' and for all those seeking liberty. The structural change to English politics occasioned by the French Revolution and the

6

development of clear party politics changed everything.[5] As enthusiasm for the ideals of the Republic in France gained momentum, Price became a central figure in both the Lansdowne circle and Unitarianism.

As could be expected, when Richard Price died in April 1791 a wave of letters of condolence was sent from France. He was spared the heartbreak of the Terror and the idealism of the Revolution itself.

The public debate over the controversial ideals of the French Revolution gave renewed energy to metropolitan reform societies such as the Society for Constitutional Information, one of the most famous and most influential radical societies of the later eighteenth century. In the north of England the society grew rapidly via the Nonconformist, principally Unitarian political currents in the rapidly growing un-enfranchised mill towns and manufacturing centres, organized by ordinary working people who declined the patronage and control of the wealthy. Following the publication of the new French Constitution on 3 September, which for the first time granted universal male suffrage, the Revolution Society declared:

> As some gentlemen had industriously laboured to throw an ODIUM on the FRENCH REVOLUTION, and endeavoured to persuade people here, that is in the interest and ought to be the business of Britons to reprobate it; it is therefore judged advisable, in order to remove all unfounded apprehensions ... We rejoice in the glorious events of the French Revolution ... and for erecting a government on the Hereditary rights of man – rights which appertain to ALL, and not to any ONE more than the other ... We say and repeat it, that the French Revolution opens to the world an opportunity in which all good citizens rejoice, that of promoting the general happiness of Man ...[6]

Every year since 1788 the society had held a formal dinner to mark the anniversary of the Glorious Revolution on 4 November. In 1788, the Revd Andrew Kippis had presided, in 1789 the Revd Dr Price and in 1791 to mark the anniversary the London Revolution Society proclaimed that:

> This truly patriotic Society uninfluenced by party, or sinister views, met on this day to commemorate the Anniversary of the Revolution, and with zeal for the cause of Freedom and welfare of Mankind in every part of the World; seem unanimously disposed to assert with proper dignity, the rights of their fellow men in this, and every nation on the face of the earth – Let every man heartily join them until oppression, arbitrary power, and tyranny is rooted out from amongst every enlightened people in the world.[7]

The Mayor of Paris, Jérôme Pétion de Villeneuve, who arrived in London on 30 October, was guest of honour. In his diary Pétion noted that the meal was attended by about 350 people and he as guest of honour was sat next to the president, Thomas Walker of Manchester. It was here that Pétion met the bluff-spoken Yorkshire man the Revd Dr Joseph Priestley – whose chapel, home and library had been destroyed by fire by supporters of Edmund Burke earlier in the year because of his championing of 'French principles' – as well as Thomas Paine. Many wore the French tricolour cockade and the orchestra punctuated the proceedings by playing the revolutionary anthem '*Ça Ira*', an emblematic song of the era. The Revd Theophilus Lindsey, nominal leader of the Unitarian denomination, remarked that 'the music being happily intermixed with the toast and some excellent songs. ... seemed to inspire the whole company'.[8] The meal engendered brotherhood and solidarity between English and French revolutionaries, and provided a direct means of contact between revolutionary groups in England and the French state.[9] Patriotic toasts were drunk to the king, and others declared 'the sovereignty of the people, acting by a just and equal representation'. Another toast celebrated 'The Glorious Revolution in France – May it serve as a lesson to the oppressor and an example to the oppressed' and another opined that 'the wisdom, courage, and virtue which distinguished the late National Assembly in France be conspicuous in the Present'.[10]

A few days after the London gathering, the Revolution Club of Manchester assembled to celebrate the events in France. The meeting was chaired by notable radical Thomas Walker, with toasts drunk in the hope that 'the nations of Europe awake from their lethargy, and assert their birth-right, in daring to be free', while another toast was made in anticipation that 'every commemoration of the Revolution find the people of England better acquainted with the principles of Liberty, and more firmly determined to support them'.[11] Similarly, at a meal organized by the Bath Revolution Club, the club wished 'the whole world be one City, and is inhabitants presented with their freedom'.[12] A prominent member of the Bath group was Hannah Milnes, sister to Jack Milnes from Wakefield. Similar events had been held in Sheffield and Wakefield and the Leeds Constitutional Society published its own declaration on 17 November 1791:

I am convinced that the end of society is common happiness – that government is instituted to secure to man his natural rights, which are equality, Liberty, Safety; and Prosperity, – and that ALL men are equal by nature; And I am convinced that the PEOPLE have no part in the government of this County; the Parliamentary Representation as it is called, being inadequate, imperfect and corrupt; I, therefore, will by every constitutional means in my power promote thorough reform in the Commons House of Parliament, namely, universal Right of Suffrage and annual elections.[13]

Across the Irish Sea, the events of the French Revolution had awakened the desire in the Irish to reform their Parliament and work towards Home Rule. To this end reformist groups were founded, the Catholic Committee to fight for Catholic emancipation and the United Irishmen for political reform. Initially the United Irishmen, founded mainly by non-subscribing Presbyterians in Belfast in 1791 – notably the Unitarian Dr William Drennan and his co-religionist Archibald Hamilton Rowan – campaigned for reform, lobbying for the vote to be extended to Catholics and to non-property holders. Simon Butler chaired a meeting in Dublin on 9 November 1791 that declared that the Irish nation was in a:

> … state of abject slavery, no hope remains for us but in the sincere and hearty Union of All the People, for a complete and radical reform of Parliament; because it is obvious, that one party alone, have ever been unable to obtain a single Blessing for their country; and the policy of our Rulers has always been such, as to keep the different sects at variance, in which they have been but too well seconded by our own folly.
>
> For the attainment then of this great and important object – for the removal of absurd and ruinous distinctions – and for promoting a complete coalition of the People – a Club has been formed, composed of all religious persuasions, who have adopted for their name – THE SOCIETY OF UNITED IRISHMEN OF DUBLIN.[14]

Butler probably owed his position as chairman as much to his lineage, being son of 10th Viscount Mountgarret, as to his ability as a public speaker, and chaired most subsequent meetings. Butler often acted as legal adviser to the society and the Catholic Committee; on 21 January 1792 he produced a report for the United Irishmen detailing the severity of the remaining restrictions on Catholics under the Penal Laws. He acted as counsel for James Napper Tandy in June 1792, and wrote a number of addresses for the United Irishmen. In the 1770s and 1780s, Napper Tandy was the best known of the middle-class radicals who pressed more vigorously for reform than the moderate, deferential 'patriots' and enthusiastically welcomed the Revolution in France and was eager that Ireland should emulate it. It was Napper Tandy who, at the request of Theobald Wolfe Tone and Thomas Russell, convened the first meeting of the Dublin Society of United Irishmen. Concurrently in Belfast, radicals led by James Napper Tandy declared:

IN the present great era of reform, when unjust governments are falling in every quarter of Europe; when religious persecution is Compelled to abjure her tyranny over conscience; when the rights of men are ascertained in theory, and that theory substantiated by practice; when antiquity can no longer defend absurd and oppressive forms against the common sense and common interests of mankind; when all government is acknowledged to originate from the people, and to be so far only obligatory as it protects their rights and promotes their welfare; we think it our duty, as Irishmen, to come forward and state what we feel to be our heavy grievance and what we know to be its effectual remedy ... IMPRESSED with these sentiments we have agreed to form an Association, to be called, THE SOCIETY OF UNITED IRISHMEN; and we do pledge ourselves to our Country, and mutually to each other, that we will readily support, and endeavour by all due means to carry into effect the following resolutions:

RESOLVED, That the weight of English Influence in the Government of this Country is so great, as to require a Cordial Union among ALL THE PEOPLE OF IRELAND, to maintain that balance which is essential to the preservation of our Liberties and the extension of our Commerce.

THAT the sole constitutional mode by which this influence can be opposed, is by a complete and radical reform of the Representation of the People in Parliament.

THAT no reform is practicable, efficacious, or just, which does not include Irishmen of every Religious Persuasion.

SATISFIED as we are that the internecine divisions among Irishmen have too often given encouragement, and Impunity to profligate, audacious and corrupt administrations, in measures which, but for these divisions, they durst not have attempted; we submit our Resolutions to the Nation as the basis of our Political Faith.

WE have gone to what we conceive to be the root of the evil; we have stated what we conceive to be the remedy. – With a Parliament thus reformed, everything is easy; without it, nothing can be done: And we do call on and most earnestly exhort our Countrymen in general to follow our example, and to form similar Societies in every quarter of the kingdom for the promotion of Constitutional knowledge, the abolition of bigotry in religion and policies, and the equal distribution of the Rights of Man through all Sects and Denominations of Irishmen.

THE people, when thus collected, will feel their own weight, and secure that power which theory has already admitted as their portion, and to which, if they be not aroused by their present provocations to vindicate it, they deserve to forfeit their pretensions FOR EVER.[15]

A wave of revolutionary ardour was rising across England, Ireland and Scotland. Letters from the Revolution Society circulated among Jacobin clubs in France and, by spring 1792, some fifty-two clubs, from all parts of France, had entered into correspondence with the London Revolution Society, which they took to be a semi-official organ for the celebration of the French Revolution. In May 1792 the society published its 'complete' correspondence, though some letters from and to correspondents in Britain, Germany and France – present in the letter book of the society — were not included for obvious political reasons. In its early stages, the correspondence was characterized on both sides by enthusiasm and confidence that an open and friendly exchange between the respective peoples would diminish national prejudice, leading to an alliance between Britain and France and, ultimately, to universal peace. Conflicting visions of how society should change and develop emerged.[16] The debate rapidly became an escalating battle of political rhetoric and mobilization of public opinion through media and public rallies. The British Crown viewed the emergence of these radical groups with alarm. The Crown and the Tories believed that the British system of a parliamentary monarchy and the rule of law, combined with a property based on social order and the established church, were the bastions which guaranteed British liberties and commercial prosperity. The existing 'natural order of things' was to be maintained at all costs; religious tolerance was unacceptable; political reform and giving the middle class and working men the vote was to be stemmed. The war of ideology against France was also a war against the people of the United Kingdom. The rich elites wanted to retain their power and repress the grievances of all those men and women who wanted political reform and to obtain universal suffrage, or at the very least to allow all tax payers to vote, all those who made a commitment to intellectual improvement and the demand for respect regardless of rank or wealth: freedom, reason and tolerance were markers of discrete Jacobin identity. To achieve this the state resorted to acts of terror and intimidation. Unlike the 1780s when compromise was possible, in the heated atmosphere of the 1790s, the middle ground was lost, as both sides rapidly polarized into opposing camps. Those seeking reform and a greater participation in politics were no longer tolerated by the elite: reform was seen as irresponsible revolution.[17] This was a war of ideology.[18] The governing elites believed themselves to be under direct threat from France as much as from radical activity at home, and argued that if property and social order was to be maintained in England, nothing short of exterminating anti-revolutionary sentiment at the point of a bayonet would do.[19]

The London Corresponding Society

So far, reform had largely been the preserve of the 'middling sort'. However, the accelerating pace of industrialization and urbanization at the end of the eighteenth century was a great driver of social change in Britain in this period. It witnessed the creation of the urban working class. As ever more steam-powered factories were built in towns such as Birmingham, Manchester, Sheffield, Leeds and of course London, so the need for a labour force to work in the new factories increased as the Industrial Revolution began to gather pace (this is explored in a companion volume on Luddism). The labour force was created through an unprecedented shift of labour from agrarian jobs in the countryside to urban jobs in the town and city. Suddenly new urban areas were flooded with an eclectic mix of social and economic classes, including those from other countries – notably Ireland, looking for work in these new industries. The common thread for many of these men was that the social and economic constructs they were so accustomed to had been severely disrupted by relocating to new urban areas which by and large tended to fuel the engines of associations, clubs and societies. The formation of these organizations, whether for political, cultural or other reasons, served to connect people of similar interests, but not necessarily the same backgrounds. It was among these urban centres that the ideas of equality and the 'rights of man' had the largest impact. The desire for equality as well as political representation drove reform. It was to these people that Thomas Hardy, a Scottish shoemaker living in London, convinced of the need for political reform by the ideals of the Revd Dr Richard Price, appealed to in founding his reformist club: the London Corresponding Society.

Among the papers and pamphlets handed to Hardy by John Cartwright from the library of the Society for Constitutional Information was a proposal from the Correspondence Committee of the Irish Volunteer movement to restore 'the purity and vigour' of the Irish constitution through parliamentary reform.[20] Buoyed by the ideals of the French Revolution, Thomas Paine's *Rights of Man*, Part 1, as well as the politics of the Revd Richard Price and John Cartwright, Hardy formed the London Corresponding Society. At the first meeting of the society on 25 January 1792, Hardy led seven friends in a discussion that determined that 'gross ignorance and prejudice in the bulk of the nation was the greatest obstacle to obtaining redress' from the 'defects and abuses that have crept into the administration of our Government' and that to remove that obstacle it should be the aim of those subscribing 'to instil into [the public] in a legal and constitutional way by means of the press, a sense of their rights as freemen, and of their duty to themselves and their posterity, as good citizens, and hereditary guardians of the liberties transmitted to them by their forefathers'.[21] In contrast to some of Whig-establishment reform clubs, the organization allowed all subscribers to participate in open debate and to elect members to leadership positions such as tithing-man, divisional secretary, sub-delegate and delegate and by May 1792 comprised nine separate divisions. Membership cost a penny a week, which made working-class mass participation possible. High-profile members included John Gales Jones, Olaudah Equiano, Joseph Gerrald, William Skirving, John Towgood and John Hurford Stone. Equiano, drawing on abolitionist networks, brokered connections with the United Irishmen. Stone was the link with France and Talleyrand. Veteran reformer John Horne Tooke became central to the development of the society and its links with other reformist groups.

Chapter 3

THE RIGHTS OF MAN

On 16 February 1792, the second part of Thomas Paine's *Rights of Man* was published in which he advocated, among other things, the right of the people to replace their government if they thought it appropriate. Paine gave the go-ahead for reformists to consider taking direct action. An impassioned supporter of Paine's ideals, Thomas Erskine MP stood up in the House of Commons on 30 April 1792 and declared:

> THE rights of man are the foundation of all government, and to secure them is the only reason of men's submitting to be governed; – it shall not be fastened upon the unfortunate prisoner at the bar, nor upon any other man, that because these natural rights were asserted in France, by the destruction of a government which oppressed and subverted them … The rights of men, that is to say, the natural rights of mankind, are indeed sacred things; and if any public measure is proved mischievously to affect them, the objection ought to be fatal to that measure, even if no charter at all could be set up against it.[1]

The Crown believed itself to be under existential threat from the ideals encapsulated in the *Rights of Man*, and on 21 May 1792, the king issued a proclamation against seditious writings in which he commanded all magistrates to 'make diligent inquiry in order to discover the authors and printers of such wicked and seditious writings'.[2] Originally aimed at prohibiting the publication of any work by Paine, the bill allowed the censoring and banning of all material that the Crown considered seditious: no more could one satire the Crown, Parliament or support reform in print. It amounted to the end of a free press: freedom of speech was now under threat. In order to root out 'traitors' the newly developing Post Office also played an active role in gathering information. Local postmasters were tasked with the collection and reporting of information on all manner of topics and activities within their respective areas, though again their zeal and efficiency in completing these functions varied from office to office. Reports were sent to the head office in London for examination. The post of 'suspects' was intercepted by the postmasters and officials and turned over to government spies. Official encouragement of spying and informing spread rapidly, resulting in the largest number of trials for sedition and treason in British history. The reaction of the Crown drove moderate reformers into the arms of the radicals, and increased the growing urge 'to do away with Kings and princes' and men like Burke. As anger at the Crown's heavy handed tactics developed among moderates and radicals, as if on cue, an emissary from revolutionary Paris arrived in London, around whom a circle of radicals rapidly grew.

The Bishop of Autun

Walking with a stick, in consequence of his club foot, and standing at a little over 5ft 3in in height, his grey hair curled meticulously every day with iron tongs, Charles Maurice de Talleyrand, former Bishop of Autun, enters the story. It was into an increasingly turbulent London political scene that Talleyrand – a man described as 'shit in silk stockings' by Napoléon – stepped. Talleyrand excited extreme emotions: you either hated him or loved him. Yet, it is undeniable that he had considerable charm.

Along with Adelaide de Flahaut and Stéphanie-Félicité, comtesse de Genlis, he entered the murky waters of Irish and British politics upon his arrival in London during January 1792. The former bishop was seeking an alliance or pact of neutrality between Britain and France, and was aided in his task by a group of largely Unitarian radicals which included John Hurford Stone and Thomas Christie. Talleyrand became the focus of a clique of English radicals. In February 1792 John Hurford Stone introduced Talleyrand to the Revd Dr Joseph Priestley, Charles James Fox and the radical Richard Brinsley Sheridan.[3] Stone explained to Jérôme Pétion, Mayor of Paris, on 12 February 1792, that:

> In the Birmingham affair, when the house of Dr. Priestly [sic] was sacked, my letters were found and given to the Secretary of State, and were found to contain material of a criminal nature such as perhaps, as I don't remember, that we always [? think] tyrants when those who are persecuted or abused speak the truth. I was threatened, but I [? am not concerned], it interferes however with my ability to serve in this negotiation, moreover I will be extremely flattered to give back to M. Talleyrand all compliments that me and my patriotic friends are able to give.[4]

15

Despite having garnered support from Stone and other like-minded reformists both inside and outside Parliament, Talleyrand returned to Paris in March without a definite answer from the British. In his own lifetime John Hurford Stone was considered highly intelligent and cultured, his Unitarianism having evolved to embrace the deism of Paine. His private life was as 'colourful' as his public life. He lived in an open relationship with Helen Maria Williams and did not feel the need to divorce his wife for several years. In October 1790 he presided at a dinner given by the Society of Friends of the Revolution to a French deputation from Nantes. In September 1792, he had been in Paris and presided at a dinner of British residents at White's Hotel to celebrate French victories. It was here that Lord Edward Fitzgerald was introduced to his future wife, Pamela, by Stone. It was alleged that Lady Edward Fitzgerald, born Stephanie Caroline Anne Syms, also known as Pamela, was a natural daughter of the duc d'Orléans and comtessse de Genlis. Also present was the aforementioned William Jackson. Stone, his wife, Rachel Coupe, and mistress, Helen Maria Williams, were arrested as 'spies' following the decree of 9 October 1793, but were released on 30 October. Stone immediately plunged back into radical politics: a week later he had returned to London and was talking to radical groups.[5] During the reign of terror, Stone paid 12,000 francs to help the comtesse de Genlis' husband escape from prison, but she later refused to pay this debt back. In April 1794 Stone was denounced as an agent of William Pitt and he and his wife were arrested again, but released on the condition that they left the country. They fled to Switzerland, where Helen Maria Williams was staying. In June, Stone was allowed to return to France to obtain a divorce and plunged back into radical politics. Indeed, such was his enthusiasm for the ideals of the French Republic that Stone had written to 'Citizen' the Revd Dr Joseph Priestley in March 1790 forecasting that he would live to see 'the Empire of falsehood, religious and political, overthrown and the world free and happy'.[6] He was now actively engaged in exporting revolution.

On returning to France. Talleyrand persuaded the new foreign minister to appoint the young marquis de Chauvelin as ambassador to London and returned there as his assistant. The two men arrived, officially, in London on 29 April, just after France had declared war on Austria, with whom Prussia then allied itself. Through skilful negotiation Talleyrand secured a declaration of neutrality from the British government on 25 May. A person of interest, 'Madame de Dion', accompanied him and was established in a grand mansion on Piccadilly.[7] But all was not as it seemed.

Following Talleyrand's arrival in London, a group known as the Irish Association had emerged from the shadows to organize along with the Catholic Committee of Ireland the liberation of Ireland and was, it seems, centred in London or at least had a 'safe house' in the city. From this group evolved what the French would term the 'Revolutionary Committee'. Its appearance in London is only known through the French Royalists who had escaped from the September massacres and arrived in London. One such émigré was Jean-Bertrand de Cruchent, who offered his services to the British Crown to report on the hated Talleyrand's activities.

Cruchent informed the Home Office with some concern that Talleyrand had arrived in London before the ambassador, and 'had been in London since the 25th or before', adding that that 'the Bishop of Autun [Talleyrand] and a secretary might be in London incognito, plotting with ill-intentioned Irishmen'. Cruchent closed his letter with the warning that 'zealots' were gathering to discuss a revolution in Ireland and England, and that 'Madame Dion' was sending secret messages to the French.[8]

According to Cruchent, the Irish Association that Talleyrand was working with seems to have been organized in the same manner as the London Corresponding Society and was formed into eight 'cells' headed by a 'chief'. Cruchent further noted that the 'chiefs' met as a committee and informed their 'cells' of deliberations, adding that the meeting of the 'chiefs' was overseen by a central directory: clearly the organization of the United Irishmen that was to appear in England from 1795 was already well established. Cruchent reported that the 'chiefs' communicated with the French via messages sent through Amsterdam or The Hague, and were in contact with 'a long-established' movement in Ireland centred in Dublin: one would assume this to be the Catholic Committee encountered earlier. Cruchent furthermore noted that leaders travelled to and from London to Ireland. The assignation between the association and Talleyrand took place in the Albion public house on James Street, where the landlord allowed them to meet in secret. The goal of the association was to establish a republic based on the French constitution.[9] Clearly, Talleyrand was promoting both revolution in England and Ireland. Is it a surprise that Talleyrand was 'playing politics? Of course not: Talleyrand was 'making sure' that Britain remained neutral by covertly working with an underground, radicalized, militant movement. Officially, Talleyrand was assisting the French government to negotiate British neutrality in any war that might occur: the charm offensive through lavish meals, balls and receptions was just one modus operandi. In case traditional diplomacy failed, Talleyrand was hoping that by promoting social and sectarian division in England, Ireland and Scotland, British troops would be tied down at home and unable to wage war on the continent. If that insurgent activity resulted in Ireland being liberated from the British Crown, as sought by the United Irishmen, then France would have a new ally. If the disturbances in England caused sufficient chaos, then Pitt would fall and Charles James Fox would become prime minister, and no war would break out. Such a strategy would become the official policy for the course of 1792.

As winter turned to spring, Cruchent, in a letter of 3 May, sent to the Home Office copies of the letters received in France from radical cells in London. Cruchent highlighted that 'on the night of the 23 a treaty was signed' between the French and eight Irish chiefs in a public house on Throckmorton Street, London. He reported that the plan agreed in London had already been passed by leaders in Dublin.

Cruchent noted that under the terms of the treaty the French would give £4 million to the Irish to buy muskets and pay 'their army', and that Talleyrand was giving 18 guineas to each member of the radical groups. Twenty-five ships of the line and fifty transports would bring French reinforcements to Ireland once the revolution had commenced.[10] These muskets were probably destined to arm the Volunteers that were being mobilized by James Napper Tandy. In a further letter, Cruchent reported that the primary objectives of the new French envoys to Ireland and England were 'to be the conclusion by the Bishop of Autun of a treaty with Irish interests and the fomenting of an insurrection in London on 14 July next'.[11]

On 15 May, Cruchent reported to the Home Office information he had received from his agent in Maastricht, an émigré called Botereau. Botereau was a merchant in Amsterdam who noted that a revolution in Ireland was being openly spoken of by Jacobins in Amsterdam and Rotterdam, adding that it was hoped that the Irish albeit with French military support would rise in revolution. Worryingly, Cruchent commented that communication was centred on agents in The Hague, who were in direct contact with France, and also Dublin and Edinburgh as well as transmitting letters to London regarding the importance to the French regime of the attempt of 'the bishop' (Talleyrand) to separate Ireland from Great Britain.[12] It seems undeniable that Talleyrand was at the centre of an underground network that was actively promoting Irish revolution.

On 22 May, Talleyrand was reported to be travelling to the Midlands, to Birmingham in particular. The day before 'seditious' handbills had been stuck up on walls in the town and a 'tumult' had taken place between loyalists and radicals.[13] Talleyrand, it is assumed, was heading to the Midlands to meet a group of radicals based there. An informant reported that 'John Hurford Stone, of London Fields, Hackney, had gone to Paris with John Towgood as a deputation from the Constitutional Society.' He was perfectly correct in this observation. The informer, furthermore, drew the Home Office's attention to the fact that Stone and Towgood were congregation 'members of that arch traitor Dr Priestley, whose conventicle is contagious to many houses at Hackney, whose seditious tenants are well known'. He also stated that Ambassador Chauvelin and the Bishop of Autun, Talleyrand, were in correspondence with some of Priestley's congregation.[14] Who these people were is not known. Priestley had arrived in Hackney in 1791 when he became principal of the New College. Members of Gravel Pitt Lane Unitarian Chapel were John Hurford Stone and his brother William and the Revd Dr Richard Price had been minister there from 1770–91 and Priestley from summer 1791. Talleyrand was not alone in London in finding willing accomplices to undermine the British Crown.

Events in France now intervened in the planned Irish rebellion. The storming of the Tuileries palace by the Paris mob on 20 June made Talleyrand's position in London untenable, and he officially left the city on 7 July. The Irish revolt was delayed. To mark Bastille Day, James Napper Tandy paraded through Dublin with his Volunteers, dressed in red coats and bearing green cockades, the men no doubt carrying muskets that Talleyrand had helped them to obtain. Before he left London, Talleyrand, in a letter dated 2 July 1792, reported that:

One of my English patriots, just returned from Paris, has this instant left me. If all his patriotic countrymen possessed the same enthusiasm which he does, a Republican fraternity would soon be established between France and England, and the Channel exist no longer, or be dried up. He speaks with rapture of what he has seen and experienced, and is confident of bringing about a revolution here, as soon as a republic is proclaimed in France ... Being ordered by the insurrection committee at Paris on an expedition to Yorkshire and to Scotland, I was obliged to advance him one hundred and fifty guineas, though I'm thoroughly convinced that he was paid all his expenses before he left France. He showed with ecstasy his red cap, and the tricoloured cockade, and intends to buy and distribute many dozens of them during his journey, which will probably extend as far as Ireland, as I want a trusty and active person there; and he has obtained the entire confidence of our principal patriots. Inform Pétion of these particulars, but let nobody else know that I have written to you.[15]

Talleyrand's mission, as Cruchent had uncovered, was linked to radical groups in Scotland and also in Yorkshire, and it is assumed Lancashire as well as Ireland. It is also clear that Talleyrand was working for Jérôme Pétion de Villeneuve, who would become the first president of the National Convention on 20 September 1792 and was mentioned earlier. Had Pétion's visit to London in October 1791 been to help establish the network that Talleyrand was engaged with? It seems a very reasonable suggestion indeed. Certainly, as Mayor of Paris, Pétion was officially responsible for maintaining order within the capital and, as he acknowledged in summer 1792, the investigation of and suppression of counter-revolutionary activity. The mayor was de facto head of operations concerning counter-espionage operations in Paris and his remit seems to have extended beyond the walls of Paris; one suspects through the phenomenon now known as 'mission creep'.[16]

In a letter of 21 July, written while at Dover – where had he been since leaving London more than ten days earlier? Who had he met? What had he agreed? – Talleyrand explains that he had being giving money to reformist and radical groups, exactly as Cruchent had informed the British Crown:

> They have numerous adherents in this country who approve of all the late changes, who support their cause, and who are ready to imitate their example, but also advantageous, in making the patriots here know their friends from their enemies, many persons having come forward who, from their affluent situation in life and high rank in society, were never thought friendly to a reform which must subvert all unnatural property as well as level all unnatural distinctions. It disseminates a desire and spirit of innovation among the lower classes, and diverts the attention of ministers from more serious and dangerous undertakings ripening for sudden explosion ... I, therefore, did not hesitate to advance to each patriot who waited on me, a smaller or larger sum, according to the recommendation of the executive committee, which he previously presented ... When I say these patriots, I mean the Scotch and Irish as well as the English. Although they disagree on account of national prejudices, in the chapter of rapacity they are truly brothers.[17]

For the radical leaders, it seemed France would incite revolution and bring their long-held hopes and ambition for a reformed Parliament to fruition, as well as the abolition of the national church. For the Irish Catholics, an Ireland free from the English yoke seemed to be within 'touching distance'.

Chapter 4

AGENT PROVOCATEURS

During Talleyrand's tenure in London French Foreign Minister Lebrun engaged the services of his secret service to link with radical groups in Ireland and England. Lebrun's goal was seemingly the same as Talleyrand's.

To this end, Irish émigré John Francis O'Neil, who had Gallicized his name to Jean François Noël, was to report on the state of affairs in London as the replacement for Chauvelin, the chief agent in London who was made ambassador. Noël was a defrocked Irish priest, who had entered the Foreign Ministry in April 1792 as a secretary in the department concerned with German and Belgian affairs. He was a confidant of Georges Danton and also Condorcet. Noël was charged with spreading revolutionary turmoil in Britain either in concert with the *orateurs* of the radical clubs such as the Society for Constitutional Information and also to network with the Roman Catholics in Ireland with the view to an uprising there.[1] He was under strict orders, however, not to engage with Richard Sheridan or Charles Grey and the now defunct 'Friends of the People', as Chauvelin had done. Lebrun instructed Noël that his actions in London could in no way undermine Talleyrand and the endeavour to keep Pitt to his policy of neutrality.[2] Indeed, the former Bishop of Autun had returned to London on 18 September. Talleyrand was still engaged on Pétion's business, and it seems beyond reasonable doubt that he was directly funding reform groups in England, Ireland and Scotland.[3]

After spending the summer in England, Noël had travelled to Ireland and informed Paris that Ireland was on the verge of insurrection. He returned to England in early autumn and wrote in October from London the good news 'that England is not ready to go to war with France' because 'Ireland is extremely agitated'. Talleyrand and Lebrun's scheming had it seemed worked: Pitt was afraid that if the country went to war, he would face civil war in England and Ireland.[4]

To support Noël, a second agent was dispatched from Paris. Pierre Vincent Benoist d'Angers arrived in London in September 1792 and met with the shadowy Revolutionary Committee of Ireland: this seems to be the same organization as the Irish Association that had met with Talleyrand earlier in the year, before returning to Paris to rendezvous with Danton and Lebrun. According to Benoist, this 'very secret Committee' sought to trigger a general uprising all over Ireland, organized in conjunction with the Volunteers and with the democratic movements in Scotland and England.[5]

Benoist did not name any members of the committee, but their names are listed in reports from émigré Cruchent dated 'Sunday 1 September 1792. Cruchent noted that he had come into the possession of a letter dated 23 August which contained 'news about Ireland' and added 'M. Payne, seconded by Hamilton, Tandy, Simon Butler, Germa [?] and Sharman' who were united in the cause of Ireland.[6] This placed Archibald Hamilton Rowan, James Napper Tandy and the United Irishmen leadership centre stage. Cruchent reported that it was important that a spy was to be sent to Dublin to discover the truth of the planned rebellion.[7] William Sharman was a founder of a Reform Club created to revitalise the campaign for parliamentary reform (20 May 1786), and it is not a surprise that he was a member of the Northern Whig Club founded in Belfast in March 1790.[4] At the Volunteer review held in Belfast in July 1791 to celebrate the fall of the Bastille he presided at a dinner for over 300 Volunteers held that evening in the Linenhall. The Volunteers were headed by James Napper Tandy who hoped to form a paramilitary organization in imitation of the French National Guard which was allied to the aims of the United Irishmen. Sharman it is recalled, had written a year earlier on the need to bring about political reform, aided by Simon Butler, president of the United Irishmen. Sharman was directly connected to leading English reform groups.

Born on May Day 1751, Archibald Hamilton Rowan had spent his early years living in London. He was a Unitarian, as were other militant Irish republicans Oliver Bond, Samuel Neilson, John Binns and Dr William Drennan. As could be expected, he was educated at the famous and influential Warrington Academy, a Unitarian institution, and then at Cambridge alongside his friend and co-religionist Benjamin Vaughan.[8] As a Unitarian he could attend the university but was not permitted to graduate. Having left London and returned to Ireland, he joined the Dublin Society of United Irishmen at its formation or shortly after (November–December 1791) and, along with his father, was a founder member of the aforementioned Northern Whig Club (March 1790) and presided over a meeting at which the French Revolutionary Army was congratulated on its victories at Valmy and Jemappes (5 November 1792).[9]

Hamilton Rowan became a leading figure in Irish radicalism, both in Ireland and France where he met the Committee of Public Safety which was followed up with audiences with influential figures in the government, notably Robespierre and Jeanbon, who were both eager to progress an Irish invasion.[10] The Irish were taking the first steps towards transforming a reformist association into a underground radical movement, the aim of which was the overthrow of the British Crown in Ireland. Veteran reformer James Napper Tandy features heavily in this account as was Thomas Paine, and both were involved in directly planning revolution in Ireland.

In September, Cruchent sent the Home Office a letter dated 23 August from a correspondent in Liège, forecasting revolution in Ireland on 20 September. In the letter from the informant, Butler and Sharman are mentioned as ringleaders. The letter also told the Home Office that 400–500 Jacobites, i.e., Catholic supporters of James II who was deposed in 1688 and in favour of Irish independence from England and Catholic emancipation, were in Brabant and Holland. Worryingly, Cruchent noted that the Jacobites had set off for the north of Ireland hoping to aid the revolution.[11] On 1 October Cruchent reported that his agent in Liège had during the previous month uncovered letters containing references to Ireland, the Bishop of Autun (Talleyrand) and a suspicious contract placed at Rotterdam for 80,000 firearms.[12] Revolution seemed imminent.

Colonel Sharman and James Napper Tandy, in forming the Volunteers in 1780, looked outside Ireland for support. They found willing assistance from the Revd Christopher Wyvill, leader of the Yorkshire Association created in 1780 to agitate for political reform In his crusade for reform, he also embraced repeal of restrictive legislation against Unitarians and Catholics. The Revd Dr John Jebb, a notable Unitarian and former Anglican, and his colleague the Revd Dr Richard Price campaigned passionately for Irish Catholics to have the vote. Wyvill's letters to Sharman are housed in York City Library. It is no surprise therefore that Irish radicals – both Unitarian and Catholic – were aware of broader support from England, especially Yorkshire, and this may well explain the sudden appearance of an emissary from Ireland in Wakefield, the home town of the Milnes family, de facto leaders of the Yorkshire Association in the West Riding. Popular social movements tracked across national boundaries on both sides of the Irish Sea and into France. Indeed, the Revd Dr Richard Price wrote to Sharman in July 1782, 'A native of England, but a Citizen of the World, and a warm friend to universal liberty.'

Chapter 5

THOMAS ATTWOOD DIGGES

As well as dealing with the Irish Committee and John Hurford Stone, Talleyrand employed his own secret agents to link with radicalized group in England and Ireland. One of the most notable of these was Thomas Attwood Digges.

Born a Catholic in Maryland, Virginia in 1742, Digges was living in Lisbon by 1770 and in London by 1775. He acted under a number of aliases during the American Revolution, supplying gossip and intelligence to John Adams and Benjamin Franklin among others He used his contacts to smuggle cloth and other supplies to the revolutionary troops via Spain. Digges and David Hartley, Unitarian MP for Hull – at the 1780 General Election, 'Jack Milnes the Democrat' aka John Milnes of Wakefield was Hartley's agent and funder[1] – conducted a secret peace treaty, which ultimately failed in 1778, and a second peace plan was drafted between John Adams and the government of Lord North in 1782. Always in debt, due to profligate spending and making bad decisions, Digges was imprisoned in Dublin in 1785. Therefore, in order to raise money – this is one of the main reasons why otherwise upright citizens get involved in crime and become informants – Digges became engaged in the illegal smuggling of textile machinery to America. He was seemingly a member of a group organized by Benjamin Franklin called the Deistic Society and Club, whose members in the period 1781–3 included the Revd Dr Richard Price, the Revd Dr Priestley, Benjamin Vaughan, Josiah Wedgwood, Thomas Day[2] as well as Thomas Paine and David Hartley. These men were united by republican politics and rational religious dissent: all were Unitarians. Italian radical Giovanni Fabbroni was an intimate friend of Price, Digges, Jefferson, Franklin, Priestley and Vaughan.[3]

Vaughan was a member of the Revd Dr Richard Price's congregation at Newington Green, London, and worshipped alongside Mary Wollstonecraft. He was a vocal champion of the 'Rights of Man' who was on the one hand a Jacobin[4] and on the other a slave owner.[5] Jefferson, Franklin and Digges were at the centre of a radical group of Unitarians, who shared the same vision of liberty, equality and fraternity.

Why Wakefield?

In October 1792, Digges appears in Wakefield taking lodgings at the Strafford Arms Hotel. On the evidence of an informant, the magistrates' bench in Wakefield reported to the Home Office that Digges was in Wakefield purporting to sell 'some estates in America'.[6] This seems to be a legitimate cover story, as Digges confirms this in a letter he wrote to Thomas Jefferson: 'Birmingham, 10 March 1793. ... I am at present engaged in this central part of England trying to get Leasehold or annual Tenants for my Lands fronting the Presidents on Potowmac, and adjoining the new Federal City and Bladensburgh, and I expect to Embark for America in May or June.'[7] But behind this facade far more was going on. Digges was an agent for Jefferson, and also for France: Wolfe Tone describes Digges as being of 'Maryland, lately of London and Paris.'[8] What brought him to Wakefield? Without a shadow of a doubt the Milnes family.

Solicitor John Henry Maw and John Milnes were heading to Paris from Wakefield. Maw lived in a large town house on Westgate, Wakefield, a neighbour of co-religionist Harper Soulby. Maw, it is believed, had travelled with John Milnes aka 'Jack Milnes the democrat' to Paris in 1790–1. Maw and Milnes were members of the same Masonic lodge as Jack Milnes' cousin and co-religionist, Richard Slater Milnes, who was provincial grand master of Yorkshire from 1784–1804. According to Wakefield historian Dr John William Walker, so strong was Maw's republican sentiment, it is said that he 'dipped his handkerchief' in the blood of executed King Louis on 21 January 1793. Milnes was in Paris in 1790, when he met and married Catherine Carr. Their son, Anckerstrom – later changed to Alfred – Mirabeau Washington was born in Paris on 21 April 1792. The comte de Mirabeau was a close friend – via the Revd Dr Price and the Lansdowne circle – and was supposedly godfather of his namesake. Educated at Warrington Academy – like Archibald Hamilton Rowan who it is suspected he knew – by Dr Joseph Priestley and Jean-Paul Marat, and had come into contact with other firebrands such as Anna Laetitia Barbauld, it is not a shock to learn that Milnes was a self-professed Jacobin. It is also worth noting that Milnes was a friend of Thomas Paine. Little wonder he earned his 'democrat' sobriquet as he supported the Americans in their conflict with the Crown and fought for political reform and Unitarian emancipation. Therefore, it is no surprise that he was a resident at White's Hotel. Milnes was in Wakefield again by the end of 1792, but Maw did not return until summer 1793 via Naples. Jack and Catherine were eventually married in England for the sake of respectability on 9 September 1802 at St Paul's Parish Church, Canterbury. After the subsequent Peace of Amiens was signed in March 1802, he and his family returned to Paris and then made their way to Canada. In Canada Milnes lived with his reputable elder brother Sir Robert Shore Milnes, the Deputy Governor General of Lower Canada. Jack resided in Quebec for two years before returning to Wakefield in 1806.[9] Jack Milnes and his sister, Hannah, are recorded as spending time in Bath, where Hannah distributed republican and Jacobin propaganda, celebrating the Batavian and Swedish revolutions.[10]

Milnes' cousins in Wakefield – James and Richard Slater Milnes, the latter being MP for York – as well as their minister the Revd Thomas Johnstone – gaoled for his opposition to the seditious writing Acts – were the leaders of the Wakefield Constitutional Society and diametrically opposed to the politics of William Pitt. Digges had been in Paris and it can only be supposed that he had met Milnes and told him of the support for reform in his home town and by his kinsmen. It is also known that Digges was in contact with the radical Sheffield Constitutional Society. Digges, the magistrates were informed, visited 'some respectable houses in the Town & Neighbourhood of Wakefield, & is not reserved in professing his opinion relative to Pain [sic Thomas Paine] nay even in the support of the murderous proceedings in France'.[11] Almost certainly this would have included the homes of James Milnes and Richard Slater Milnes, and we suppose the parsonage home of the Revd Thomas Johnstone and that of Robert Bakewell.

Who was Digges Working For?

It seems that Digges was in Wakefield perhaps on nothing more than the strength of a recommendation from an émigré in Paris. So, what was he planning? Digges, the magistrates noted:

> dispersed the seditionous [sic] resolutions from Stockport by himself & Agents. The above-mentioned Lockwood & his sons have been assiduous in making converts & going amongst the colliers & others in the Neighbourhood. An engraver[12] was supposed to have been the secretary to one or more of the clubs, was frequently with Digges at his lodgings in Wakefield.[13]

Clearly Digges was working for persons unknown, collaborating 'hand in glove' with radical groups and active in promoting revolution. Interestingly, colliers would become highly militant as the eighteenth century ended and the nineteenth century began, taking part in food riots in 1800[14] and actively participating in the Luddite violence in 1812.[15] Clearly, Digges found fertile ground among the colliers and other working-class communities. After his arrest in Dublin 1785, Digges was in Belfast by 1790, and here he befriended Theobald Wolfe Tone and Thomas Russell, co-organizers of the United Irishmen in 1791, who were seeking Irish independence. In October 1791, before he left Belfast for England, Digges assured the Belfast United Irishmen that revolutionary France would come to Ireland's aid to spread liberty, and that should religious divisions be overcome and Ireland emerge with a good system of government and free from debt, 'she would in arts, commerce and manufactures spring up like an air balloon and leave English behind her at an immense distance'.[16] Digges was clearly connected to France, and knew well enough the mood of the Irish émigrés in Paris and their dealings with the French government. Digges also it seems knew James Napper Tandy and the more militant of the Irish such as Thomas and William Putnam McCabe, who feature later in this story. Digges had been present when the Society of United Irishmen had agreed their manifesto on 18 October 1791, and it seems involved in developing the more radical nature of the movement. In England, Digges appears to have been both raising funds for the United Irishmen as well as disseminating propaganda. In 1792, printed handbills of resolutions dated 9 November 1791 from both the Dublin and Belfast societies were seized in Sheffield, and the magistrates stated that Digges was responsible for distributing these.[17] Digges it is assumed had left Belfast and landed in Liverpool and travelled to Glasgow – most probably to meet Thomas Muir – and had travelled via Manchester. Indeed, radicals in Manchester led by Thomas Walker toasted 'The intrepid Volunteers of Belfast, who have nobly stood forward in the cause of Liberty' on 14 July 1792 when copies of the United Irishmen manifesto were also discovered.[18] This suggests some form of underground network between English, Scottish and Irish radicals existed as early as 1792, and would later coalesce into the United Irishmen network. In Paris Thomas Paine presented copies of the United Irishmen's declaration to Minister Lebrun:

> I enclose an Irish newspaper which has been sent me from Belfast. It is the Address of the Society of United Irishmen of Dublin (of which I am a member) to the Volunteers of Ireland. None of the English newspapers that I have seen have ventured to publish this address, and as there is no

other copy of it than this which I send you, I request you not to let it go out of your possession.[19]

The courier it seems was non-other than Digges. This comes as no surprise as Digges was engaged in industrial espionage of a highly criminal nature and at the same time was deeply involved with the United Irishmen and English radicalism. Digges subscribed to former slave Olaudah Equiano's autobiography *An Interesting Narrative*, then entering its 5th edition, printed in 1792 in London and also by Joseph Gales in Sheffield. The Dublin edition of Equiano's work sold an impressive 1,900 copies: James Napper Tandy was one of the subscribers and it seems knew Equiano, and backed abolitionism: thus connecting Napper Tandy and Digges through radical politics and abolitionism. Unsurprisingly, Equiano was also linked to English radicals and was a friend of Thomas Hardy, the first secretary of the radical London Corresponding Society, and it was Equiano who brokered connections between Hardy and the radical movement in Sheffield, drawing on abolitionist associations and networks. Equiano was connected with both key United Irish radicals and the London Corresponding Society, and it seems likely that both he and Digges were instrumental in the formation of the United Irishmen and branch groups. Digges it seems acted as an agent provocateur for Theobald Wolfe Tone's campaign, and was clearly a complex character and also very much a 'key player' in radical politics. The legacy of Olaudah Equiano in Ireland reflects the complex union between Irish nationalism and the anti-slavery movement. It would be a gross over-simplification to insist that Irish radical separatism and the cause of abolitionism have always gone hand in hand. But history teaches us that there was a connection between the two, bounded by anti-colonial sentiments and a shared sense of oppression. Digges had been in London at about the same time as the Bishop of Autun: was Digges part of the Revolutionary Committee? It would seem so.

As noted earlier in the magistrate's letter, as well as linking Wakefield radicals to a wider, international network, Digges was distributing the tracts of the Stockport Corresponding Society. The Stockport resolution was printed on 25 August 1792 by the 'Swinish Multitude'. It was a phrase used by conservative politician Edmund Burke in his *Reflections on the Revolution in France* to suggest that it was futile to try to reduce inequality and educate the working class: breathtaking arrogance from a man who never did a day's labour or felt the pangs of hunger. In consequence of Burke's derogatory and inflammatory rhetoric, the phrase was seized on by English radicals as a symbol of loyalist arrogance and was used ironically in a great number of literary works and images that lampooned Burke. The Stockport resolution declared:

1. That all men are born free and equal with respect to their rights.
2. That the sovereignty of every nation ought to be vested in the people; it is their birth right; all power is derived from them; and every attempt, to govern without their consent, is as wicked as it is unjust.
3. That the people of Great Britain are not fully, fairly and adequately represented in Parliament; and that a speedy and effectual reform is necessary.
4. That every man in Great Britain who pays taxes, has undoubted right to be an elector.
5. That it is necessary that some peaceable and effectual method to collect the votes of the people be adopted; and the elections annual.
6. That war is the height of wickedness and barbarity; and that if Governments were rightly instructed, its existence would be annihilated.
7. That religion is a private right of the mind; therefore, there ought to be neither Test Laws nor Toleration but UNIVERSAL LIBERTY of CONSCIENCE.
8. That the rules of Morality are indispensably necessary to every nation on the globe; but we embrace as brothers and as friends (provided that their morals be good) all the human race, without distinction of country, religion, sect or party.
9. That the liberty of the press ought to be held inviolable in all manners.
10. That the tribute of our warmest thanks is due to those great writers who have signalized themselves in the important cause of Liberty: – who by their writings have extended political science far beyond what the most illustrious sages of Greece and Rome could ever attain – they do honour to human nature; we earnestly commend them to the profit of our fellow citizens.
11. That it is with the greatest pleasure and satisfaction we behold the increasing number of Societies in this nation to obtain Parliamentary reform.[20]

The Stockport resolution contained nothing that had not been said in 1774 by the Feathers Tavern Petition, which sought to remove legal impediments to Dissenters and supported political reform led by the Revd Christopher Wyvill, or by the Yorkshire Association in 1783, but now in 1792, to the British Crown and Prime Minister Pitt it smacked of Jacobinism, revolution and sedition. It is extremely likely that the Stockport resolution would have been avidly read and agreed with by the societies in Leeds, Sheffield, Wakefield, Almondbury and Halifax.

To counteract the spread of the *Rights of Man* across the north, Francis Russell, secretary to the Duchy of Lancaster, informed the Home Office of his readiness to use under-bailiffs to promulgate loyalist publications in Lancashire and the West Riding of Yorkshire, where he noted that the circulation of Paine's books was strong and many clubs had been formed.[21] In returning to Digges' activities in Wakefield, the landlord of the Strafford Arms, Jonathan Gledhill, acting on his suspicions about Digges' erratic behaviour and the company he kept, spied on him and uncovered an underground radical network centred on Digges and his hotel.

Gledhill informed the Wakefield magistrates on 13 December 1792, and noted in his evidence that Joseph Lockwood, the chairman of the Wakefield Constitutional Society and a 'Painesman', frequently called on Digges.[22] Gledhill stated that Digges only ate breakfast at the Strafford Arms and dined out 'in the town or neighbourhood'. Suspicious of the company Digges was keeping, Gledhill sent his 14-year-old schoolboy son, Timothy, to enter Digges' lodgings to read his papers and go through his belongings while Digges was out seeing friends. Timothy noted that in late October when Digges had first become a resident he had copied a letter for Digges 'dated Alexandria, Octr – signed Charles Wallis', and that other documents in his dressing table mentioned 'Emigrant or French Emigrants' and he had been paid 2*s.* to copy three letters. Gledhill senior said furthermore: 'That Digges went away for three or four days, but where to it was not known.' One such journey was to Cannon Hall, near Barnsley, but this may have been a code word, as Gledhill recounts in his evidence to the magistrates that upon Digges leaving for Cannon Hall, a stranger asked for Digges who had, he reported, come from Cannon Hall. Digges left for Sheffield in December, sending his luggage via the stagecoach 'to be left at Mr Peaches',[23] but did not take the stagecoach himself and instead set off walking to Newmillerdam. If Digges was heading to Sheffield, he would indeed head through Newmillerdam, a journey of about 24 miles which would take roughly 9 hours on foot. This suggests that he felt he was already a wanted man or was meeting someone en route. It is certain he intended to arrive in Sheffield as Dr Richardson, the postmaster for Wakefield, and provide the magistrates with a letter containing instructions to re-direct Digges' mail from Wakefield to Sheffield.[24] Sadly, that letter is lost to history.

Given Digges' background in Ireland, the fact that Irish republican literature was found pasted up in Yorkshire and Lancashire should come as no surprise. Wolfe Tone, as secretary of the Catholic Committee, had toured Ulster in the summer with Samuel Neilson (the founder of the United Irish newspaper, the *Northern Star*) and John Keogh (a member of the Steering Committee of the Catholic Committee), cementing local alliances and making sure that the revolution did not happen prematurely. Digges, it is reasonable to suppose, was part of this operation, as were members of the democratic societies across England.

One such man was Joseph Lockwood, a member of the Wakefield Constitutional Socety and a Unitarian who attended Westgate Chapel, Wakefield, where the Revd Johnstone was minister and the Bakewell and Milnes families worshipped. Indeed, the Lockwood family attended and worshipped at the chapel until the early 2000s: the family attended in three different centuries. Gledhill senior, the informant for the Wakefield magistrates' bench, tells us: 'Lockwood is sometimes sent for by Digges, on pretence of wanting something doing about his shoe.'[25] Clearly Lockwood was a key member of the reformist Jacobin grouping that was centred around the chapel. The 'respectable houses' that Digges visited in Wakefield were surely those of the Milnes and Bakewell families and the Revd Johnstone.

Digges was one of the key people recruiting Irish, Scots and English radicals from 'the democratic movements' to rise in revolution funded by Lebrun and secret agent Benoist. Benoist believed the conspiracy that was developing would benefit from the support of members of Parliament, who frustratingly he does not name in his report. He adds that a man was reportedly sent to recruit officers into Irish regiments in the Netherlands and Germany before going to Spain.[26]

Yet, all was not as it seems. Digges' activities as a secret agent were far more complex than working for France. At the same time Digges was working for Thomas Jefferson and involved in obtaining machinery and technicians to establish the American mint through industrial espionage in Birmingham and Sheffield in 1792–3.[27] That he was an agent for Jefferson is not in any doubt. How he was connected to English and Irish Jacobinism is harder to ascertain. On the evidence of the Wakefield magistrates, Digges was distributing radical propaganda, overseeing the printing of handbills and other material and its distribution, and was seemingly a key player in an underground network as an agent provocateur, but is it possible he was a double agent? Winnifred Gales, who certainly knew Digges when she had settled in America, suggested that she and her husband, a radical newspaper editor who is discussed in a later chapter, 'had sold hundreds of Paine's works previous to Mr Digges's warning voice, and had printed thousands by order of the Constitutional Society!'.[28] This is either retrospective wishful thinking by Mrs Gales, as it is known that John Crome printed over 1,000 copies of the *Rights of Man*, or Digges was 'tipping off' the Gales not to hold on to the copies of Paine's work they had. The inference being Digges knew that the Gales' premises might be raided. Was this guess work on his part or based on information he had supplied? It is impossible to prove either hypothesis. Indeed, Digges is totally absent in the Sheffield historical records aside from the information sent to the Wakefield magistrates. It is known that he was in Birmingham by spring 1793 and had headed home by the end of 1798, but his whereabouts in between these dates is totally unknown.

Clandestine Book Distribution

Thanks largely to the state's bests efforts to ban the book, the *Rights of Man* became the most read book of the era. It lit the 'blue touch paper' that sparked Luddism and working-class solidarity through the United Englishmen. Distribution of reformist material was one of the key objectives of the Society for Constitutional Information and the London Corresponding Society. The *Rights of Man* and works of John Locke, the seventeenth-century moral philosopher, were key texts in the underground movement.

As the works of Thomas Paine had been banned, copies had to be printed clandestinely, and one of the main activities of the radical groups was the distribution of the *Rights of Man*. This involved a number of processes, and central among them was setting the page and subsequent printing. The books were distributed by an underground network between radical groups in the West Riding and further afield. In this David Martin and John Crome were prominent.

It is known that Digges was actively engaged in distributing copies of seditious material and producing illegal copies of the *Rights of Man* on behalf of the Sheffield Constitutional Society, both of which had been printed by John Crome in Sheffield. Indeed, Earl Fitzwilliam's steward, Charles Bowns, informed the earl on 12 January 1792 that: 'there are now in Crome's Press 1500 Copies of Mr Paine's Pamphlet which are to be sold at 3d each'.[29]

Crome had come to Sheffield in the 1780s as a bookbinder and was a known associate of the radical Joseph Gales and Henry Redhead Yorke. Indeed, history tells us Crome had been a committee member of the Sheffield Society for Constitutional Information, and in his Waingate pressroom gathered like-minded individuals from across the town. He was bold enough to print handbills that were posted in Sheffield and nearby villages denouncing the government. Crome issued a weekly intellectual journal, *The Spy*, which sought to fill the gap in radical news distribution after the collapse of the *Sheffield Patriot* and the flight of Joseph Gales to America in 1794.[30]

Chapter 6

TOM'S 'TRUTH'

Meanwhile, across the Channel, General Kellerman had led the French Revolutionary Army into battle against the Prussian Army headed up by the Duke of Brunswick. Against all expectations, Kellerman defeated the Prussians at the Battle of Valmy on 20 September 1792. Among radical groups a new wave of Gallic euphoria spread across the country: French freedom was extolled as being 'far superior' to British and toasts were raised to 'the Virtue of Revolutions'. On 15 October, 5,000–6,000 supporters paraded through the streets of Sheffield as part of a mass rally and displayed a banner condemning Burke's contempt for popular radicalism and the government's prosecution of Paine.[1] In London two radical societies burnt in effigy George III's brother-in-law, the Duke of Brunswick. On 27 September the Manchester Constitutional Society represented by Thomas Walker and Samuel Jackson, the Manchester Reformation Society, Norwich Revolution Society, the Friends of the People and the London Corresponding Society sent a message of congratulations to the French government.[2] From Newington Green on 31 October came a separate address in support of the Republic, with the Sheffield Constitutional Society following suit as well as the London Revolution Society on 5 December, the Nottingham Constitutional Society and the Derby Constitutional Society having done the same a few days earlier at the end of November.[3]

Talleyrand was well aware of the public mood, and almost simultaneous with the festivities in Sheffield reported to Pétion that:

Permit me to request the favour of you to communicate to the other members of the Executive Council some remarks concerning the real and relative situation of Great Britain and Ireland ... in the British nation the far greater part of the inhabitants call loudly for a reform, and desire

33

a revolution which may establish a commonwealth, is undeniable; but the British patriots possess neither our activity, our disinterestedness, nor our energy, philosophy, or elevated views; and they have not yet been able to acquire, for a support and rallying point, the majority in the Legislature. They may, however, and they certainly do, intend to resort to arms in support of their petitions for reform and their attempt to recover their lost liberties. But as long as the strength and sources of the present Government continue unimpaired, they may distress it, and even shake it, but I fear, without aid from France, they will be unable to change or to crush it. The ministers even expect to be reinforced with the interest and talents of all those violent alarmists, terrified or seduced by the eloquent sophistry of the fanatic Edmund Burke ... We have it this moment in our power to command not only the neutrality of Great Britain and Ireland, but, if it be thought politic, to form an offensive and defensive alliance with the English, Scotch and Irish commonwealths, established by our arms ... by the last official return from the executive committee, you see that England alone contains 166,000 registered patriots, of whom 33,600 may be provided with firearms from our dépôts, and the remainder in four days armed with pikes. Our travelling agents assure us that, besides these, as many more are ready to declare themselves in our favour were once landed and able to support them effectually. ... I am, however, not too sanguine in my expressions or expectations when I assert that at this period, even in England and Scotland, we shall meet with less resistance and fewer obstacles than many may suppose, if we are only discreet, prudent, and, above all, expeditious. ... in forty-eight hours, we may, without opposition, land 50,000 or 60,000 men in twenty or thirty different points, under the names of emigrants, and seize on the principal dockyards, arsenals and naval stations. With the assistance of our numerous secret adherents, we may even occupy London itself, and, what is certain and may be depended upon, our landing will be the signal for a general revolt. The Government, terrified by invaders from abroad and harassed by insurgents in the bosom of the country, without confidence in its troops or reliance on the fidelity of the people, would never, with its trifling forces, be able at the same time to repel an enemy and quash rebellion ... Should, Citizen Minister, this plan obtain the approbation of the Executive Council, no time is to be lost in carrying it into execution and in informing me of its determination, that the patriots here may be prepared to rise at a moment's warning and unite with us in our glorious undertaking.[4]

Talleyrand was clearly in buoyant mood about the hopes of success.

On 4 November, the London Revolution Society sat down to dine and mark the Revolution in France. For this occasion, Lebrun, the French Foreign Minister, sent copies of the 'Marseillaise', which was sung heartily by the 500 guests. On this occasion the Revolution

Society toasted the political and military achievements of France and praised the future French constitution as 'a model for all nations'.[5] On 27 November, a procession marched through Sheffield. French republican banners were displayed, the tricolour cockade was distributed and the bells of the parish church peeled in support of the French Revolution.[6]

Minister Lebrun in Paris rejoiced at the news being sent back to him from his agents across the country. Lebrun's ambitious propaganda campaign had been so successful in winning over 'hearts and minds' to the Republic, that by late October he saw no need to carry this on: Lebrun was convinced from the reports he had received 'that revolutionary principles' were now 'snowballing out of control' in England. He was furthermore of the belief that any attempts by the British Crown to 'repress self-generating irresistible Jacobin Revolutionary sentiment' would result in revolution.[7]

This was perfectly true. The ring leaders – if such a term is appropriate – were gathered at White's Hotel in Paris. Noël argued that an insurrection in Ireland and possibly also the North of England, would keep England out of the war: England and France were at peace, albeit uneasily in winter 1792.[8] Noël reported to Lebrun on 2 November that 'Ireland was ripe for Revolution' and that Scotland and England were on the verge of revolution, adding that Jacobinism and French principles were spreading rapidly in England, Scotland and Ireland. He concluded that Pitt's government was 'now suspended on a volcano' that was ready to erupt.[9] For Lebrun it seemed almost certain that Pitt would not declare war on France, and that the time was ripe to take advantage of the British Crown's weakness.

Yet, for the instigator of the underground network between France and the radical groups in England and Ireland the future looked bleak. On 15 November, Talleyrand requested an answer from Minister Lebrun as to why his plan had not been adopted.[10] Clearly, Lebrun was side-lining Talleyrand, and he had taken direct charge of the plot. In-fighting between the various political factions in Paris undermined efforts to co-ordinate any plan of operations. Indeed, Talleyrand never received a reply to his question, and the National Convention issued a warrant for his arrest in December 1792. He was now trapped in England. Talleyrand remained living as an English 'milord' until William Pitt expelled him in January 1794, and he embarked for America in March. He remained there for two years, engaging in profitable financial speculations that enabled him to rebuild his finances.

The noisy demonstrations in favour of revolution and reform, as well as the activities of French agents such as Achille Viart, Noël and Benoist, convinced the Home Office of the existence of a French

Jacobin plot to revolutionize the capital in concert with radicals.[11] The Crown now took the first steps to declare war on its own citizens to stem rebellion at home.

White's Hotel

The scene now returns to where our prologue began: White's Hotel in Paris. The British Crown's conviction that a French-led Jacobin plot existed was perfectly true. Across the Channel in Paris, Thomas Paine, 'Citizen' Edward Fitzgerald, the Sheares brothers and Scottish poet and soldier John Oswald were actively plotting an armed insurrection in England and Ireland. Indeed, this group was trying to force Jean-Jacques Brissot and the Girondins – at that time the leading group in the Convention – away from their declared policy of neutrality toward England. The greatest hope of the republicans in England, Ireland and France lay in Ireland, where they were optimistic that the Catholic Convention which was to be held in Dublin during December 1792 would be a powerful vehicle for rebellion. It was almost guaranteed that demands made by the Irish Catholics for emancipation would not be accepted by the British Crown – despite many of the hoped-for concessions being made in 1791 to English Catholics – and that the refusal of these demands would induce discontent and spark a revolution spearheaded by the revived Volunteers, supported by French funds. Napper Tandy in Ireland, Wolfe Tone in Paris, along with Paine, and their allies in England seemingly had a common goal: to export revolution and the creation of a new political order.[12] In this context, the dinner held at White's Hotel on 18 November 1792 was a significant event. As stated in the Prologue, it was here that Thomas Paine and John Hurford Stone along with a hundred other patriots from the English-speaking world dined with French revolutionaries to celebrate the French military victories, the survival of the young Republic in the face of its enemies and, above all, the hope the Revolution gave to the exiles in Paris and in Ireland and England. Several French deputies, including Henri Grégoire, attended and the next day, under the latter's presidency, the Convention voted for the famous decree of 19 November promising 'fraternity and relief to all peoples who want to regain their freedom'.[13]

On 28 November, in Paris the Society for Constitutional Information, represented by the American Joel Barlow and John Frost (also secretary of the London Corresponding Society), along with twenty delegates from the Society for the Rights of Man, each presented an address of congratulations to the President of the French National Convention. Grégoire addressed the delegates as 'co-citizens of the world':

Nature and principles bring England, Scotland and Ireland closer to us; may this cry of friendship resound in both republics.

The vows you make for the deliverance of peoples will come true. [...] Royalty is either destroyed, or dying on feudal rubble: and the Bill of Rights placed next to the thrones, is a devouring fire that will consume them (Applause.)[14]

Grégoire made it clear, it was a moral duty to export revolution to all those who were oppressed. Benoist was sent back to London and Ireland to aid the Irish.

Pitt's Response

The activities at White's Hotel did not go unnoticed. British loyalist Captain George Monro documented the activities of British radicals in Paris in late 1792 and early 1793 for the British Crown and believed that Paine, Fitzgerald and others were 'up to no good'. He reported that: 'The party of Conspirators have now formed themselves into a Society, the principles of which I have the honour of inclosing.'[15] Monro was convinced of their guilt in planning sedition or worse:

I here beg leave to remark that the people concern'd in these addresses extend their views in the most culpable degree far beyond simply a mere reform in the [more?] equal representation in Parliament; they extend their damnable ideas to the tottal [sic] subversion of Royalty, and the entire overthrow of the present British Constitution on which they mean to form a Republic. There are people in power in France now backing them in their diabolical schemes, and I dare say will gladly give them every assistance in their power to carry them into execution.[16]

On 21 December 1792 Monro wrote to Lord Grenville at the Foreign Office about the group at White's, and disclosed that: 'Their dispositions are such that I am sure they would, with the assistance of France, put anything in execution that could injure their country', adding that 'England ought to be on their guard against such parties.'[17] At the end of the month, Monro noted that the group at White's Hotel 'would stand at nothing to ruin their country'.[18] He was correct.

The British Crown was now aware of the French plans and the threat from 'the enemy within'. Yet, the plot had spread further than Monro could have realized, nor for that matter William Pitt. Monro's reports from December accentuated the conspiratorial streak in British radical politics in France and confirmed in the mind of William Pitt that the group in Paris was an ultra-violent fringe in the radical underworld whose members had little sense of loyalty to their country. It is undeniable that the intermixing of British and Irish radicals in the French capital caused concern to the British Crown as it marked the beginning of an ultra-violent culture of more organized Irish resistance to the British, which in turn influenced the British radical movement and the shadowy Revolutionary Committee that Lebrun and Talleyrand had engaged with.

On 1 December 1792, the government issued a royal proclamation mobilizing the militia to meet the 'radical invasion'. The Painite claim to the right of mass participation in politics and society at large had to be crushed.[19] A week earlier John Reeves had announced the formation of a loyalist association to counteract the groundswell of sedition and encouraged like-minded souls to do the same. Within months his call, assisted by the government's press network, was answered by 1,500 local societies, creating a movement of prodigious proportions. Reeves was backed by Pitt and his government, who had conceived a programme of deliberate persecution of the voice of opposition.[20] The public stirred by Reeves' populism for 'Church and King' and 'John Bull and England' roused opposition against political reform and 'the other', i.e., Unitarians, Jews, Catholics and nascent trade-union ideas. Reeves declared that the king could rule without the Lords or Commons.[21] This was a step too far for many, even loyalists, who sought to preserve the constitution from reform and above all else to defend inequality of rank and religion and preserve wealth. On 18 December 1792, Paine was on trial in absentia for sedition: the result was a foregone conclusion. It is undeniable that the noisy demonstrations by the reformist and Jacobin groups in support of the French Revolution and the ideals of Thomas Paine as well as their addresses of loyalty to the French government provoked an overwhelming conservative reaction. Tom's 'truth' had become 'libel' at the hands of the Crown. Paine answered the sedition and libel charges as follows: 'If, to expose the fraud and imposition of monarchy ... to promote universal peace, civilization, and commerce, and to break the chains of political superstition, and raise degraded man to his proper rank; if these things be libellous ... let the name of libeller be engraved on my tomb'.[22] Pitt's administration took the guilty verdict in Paine's trial as a sign that further prosecutions for sedition were possible and duly undertook to prosecute radical groups into submission. In the seventeen months following the trial, eleven publishers of the *Rights of Man* were prosecuted, receiving prison sentences of up to four years.[23] The trial also unleashed unprecedented acts of violence and public displays of loyalism. The public were faced with a stark choice: either support the mob or face the consequences.

In response to the trials, loyalist associations organized the burning of effigies, spectacles witnessed by hundreds of thousands of Englishmen and women. Even allowing for journalistic exaggeration, the numbers reported in the press are impressive: 5,000 in Marlborough, Wiltshire; 3,000 in Leeds; 2,000 in Changford, Dukinfield and Nettlebed in Cheshire; 1,000 in Bridport and Croydon; and 300 in the Hampshire village of Cosham, just outside Portsmouth on the south coast of England. However, very few newspaper reports give any figures, but of the thirteen reports that do, the average attendance at each burning was 1,500 people at over 200 burnings, with therefore in the region of 302,432 people involved nationwide. It is, however, misleading to regard these events as 'spontaneous demonstrations of loyalty'. Such occasions took time to organize: the bonfire had to be built, the 'guy' made, the fireworks purchased, beer and food obtained. These events – street theatre designed to gather a diverse section of community to foster a sense of 'we are in this together' – were highly ritualized imitation trials with the punishment the loyalists felt Paine deserved being meted out, had he been present at his actual trial.[24] The burnings were part of a highly co-ordinated campaign against reform and the supporters of human rights and democracy and instigated by loyalist groups headed by John Reeves, who is discussed later.

None of these events went unnoticed in France. The propaganda campaign of Reeves had a remarkable effect on public mood. Noël reported to Lebrun at the end of November, commenting that the reformist Duke of Richmond was leading the reactionary party to the events taking place in England, in much the same way as the Comte d'Artois had done in France in 1789. Tellingly, Noël noted that Pitt was a weak leader, who was 'on the back foot' politically and using 'populism' to cement himself in power, supported by the Reevite associations, which Noël acidly compared to the Club Monarchique in France from 1788–92. He concluded in late November that 'all symptoms indicate that revolutionary moments cannot be far off'.[25] He was wrong: in the wake of the public burnings of Paine both Chauvelin and Noël reported in the last week of December that Pitt had rallied the country behind him, and that revolution was now impossible.[26]

Chapter 7

INVADING IRELAND

Aware of Catholic discontent in Ireland, and in an attempt to diffuse the 'ticking bomb' that could ignite revolution, in Dublin, the Irish Parliament began to make concessions to Catholics. The Relief Act of 1791 undoubtedly marked a great step forward in the removal of Catholic grievances in England, but both Pitt and Fox felt, along with the Catholic body, that much more was required. Remarkably despite their polticial differences, both men pledged themselves to support Catholic emancipation, but they were both thwarted by the obstinacy of King George III, who insisted that to agree to any such measure would be a violation of his coronation oath. In Ireland, naturally enough, the Irish Catholics desired the same legal status. The Catholic Relief Act (1793) enabled Catholics to take degrees but not to have full standing, and also gave Catholics meeting the property requirement of 40s. the right to vote but not to sit as members of Parliament. To benefit from the legislation, Catholics had to take the oath of allegiance, which many republicans and nationalists refused to do. Catholic schools had been legal since the 1780s but had to be licensed by the Protestant Church of Ireland. Far from diffusing the situation, the Act made matters worse: the newly enfranchised Irish Catholics could only vote for Protestants. In Ireland and England, Unitarians and non-subscribing Presbyterians were not granted any concession to their faith, which was still illegal. At the same time, it was made illegal to import gun powder to Ireland and to hold 'seditious meetings'. It was against this background that more radical ideas were formulated.

Thomas Paine

Attempts to foment revolution in England had failed, largely thanks to the loyalist backlash led by Reeves and Pitt. If revolution in England was 'off the cards', encouragingly François Noël reported in a letter to

Lebrun dated 2 November 1792: 'Ireland is ripe for a revolution. It is merely waiting for the time to strike and the first cannon shot fired by Great Britain would surely be the signal for a general uprising and a definitive division.' He added:

> ... the people of Ireland sigh after a new order ... It is extremely likely that this year will be marked by very pronounced steps on the part of the Irish. They are brave, oppressed for a long time and have weapons without the British government noticing, they have found a way to [import] more than 50 thousand muskets from Birmingham.[1]

Strengthening the picture that Ireland rather than England was a better target for French aid, agent Benoist added that the French would be: 'Breaking an unsupportable yoke, freeing a great people from oppression, in a word, <u>making Ireland a Republic and separating it from England</u>: this is the ultimate aim of six or seven men [the Revolutionary Committee] filled with courage, enlightenment and dedication.'[2]

It was now that Thomas Paine, John Oswald, Edward Fitzgerald and John Hurford Stone began to actively encourage and aide a foreign power to invade England and Ireland to realize the social, economic and political reforms that they had failed to bring to fruition through the only lawful means available via petitioning the Crown. If revolution was to be achieved in England Thomas Paine presciently remarked: 'the best way is not to arm a fleet against England ... but to look at Ireland as the most interesting theatre where the whole game must be played out'.[3]

As Paine was writing these words, agent Benoist reported that the Revolutionary Committee in Ireland had asked to send a delegate to France.[4] This was Richard Ferris, a former Irish priest who had worked for many years in France. Ferris met the French authorities on 20 December 'at the request of Minister Le Brun on behalf of the Executive Council'. Ferris continues that 'Minister Le Brun appeared to grasp avidly the proposals' he had made 'and he asked him to draft them in a memorandum to be presented to the Executive Council and to the committee then occupied with that part'.[5] Ferris detailed this project in four points: 3.5 million Irish Catholics were 'resolved to shake off the yoke under which they groan'; 80,000 Volunteers were armed and ready to rise up; the Irish Revolutionary Committee coordinating the two movements was asking for the support of France, to organize a landing of French troops to provide additional soldiers and also artillery; that he, Ferris, would recruit Irish officers and men serving in the British, French and German armies.

Born on 10 February 1754 at Ballymalis, Ferris went to France in 1769 at the age of just 16, and enlisted in the Irish Brigade. By 1778 he had become a priest, a doctor of civil and canon law, a lawyer for the *parlement* of Paris and an administrator at the Collège de Montaigu at the Sorbonne. In 1788 he received two further lucrative offices, most notably as canon of Amiens cathedral. Upon refusing to take the clerical oath in 1790, he returned to the army with the rank of captain. He then 'drops off the radar' until he appears at White's Hotel in November 1792. It was here he met Paine and others. With the knowledge that Ireland (with some prompting from the French) was ready to rise in rebellion, Paine recognized that a revolution in Ireland 'would make things very difficult for the English government' and perhaps precipitate a change in government. He added that he had spoken to 'Mr [name blanked out] who is in Paris on this subject'.[6] In a document from 1793 the identity of the mystery man is revealed: Lord Edward Fitzgerald. Indeed, Fitzgerald had requested the French government give 'the 40,000 volunteers', pay and arms for three months, and if this was done a 'revolution would be inevitable'.[7]

In a memorandum concerning supporting a revolution in Ireland, Paine noted that the Irish Volunteers needed 40,000 muskets, adding that these troops were the backbone of the revolutionary force in Ireland. The Convention – presumably the Catholic Convention – desired independence for Ireland 'in the manner of America', i.e., a republic and the abolition of seignorial duties and tythes 'paid to the clergy of the Anglican church'. The independence of Ireland was only possible if the garrison of 15,000 to 16,000 Crown forces were overcome: the Volunteers needed arms and money. Paine requested 200,000 francs and 40,000 muskets be sent to Ireland to pay the Volunteers to be on active service for 100 days and noted that as soon as the revolution had succeeded the sum would be paid back. Paine also commented that 12,000 French soldiers would be needed to 'ensure Ireland was detached from England'.[8]

Paine had graduated from political theorist and writer to advocating rebellion: never to return to his native country, with nothing left to lose, Paine embarked on an ambitious plan to invade the country that had turned him into a national enemy. Paine, like others in his circle, crossed the line into treason, to bring about radical and immediate change. Paine presented this information to Lebrun during a meeting on 4 January 1793.[9] In response, Lebrun expressed his concerns about sponsoring revolution in Ireland, remarking that:

We have to make sure beforehand if everything we are told about Ireland is true; if the Revolutionary Committee exists; if there are 80 thousand men ready to run to arms; to ask if all minds all disposed to insurrection. Above all, we must not lose sight of the view that most of those who speak about Freedom in Ireland are enthusiasts of the Catholic Religion. Can we hope that such fanatics will want to confide in us and prefer our system, our indifference to Religion [...]?

We must certainly help all Peoples to break the chains of slavery; we must make war on all tyrants; but in this moment we have so much to do at home, that the outside must occupy us very little. [...] I saw samples of this famous Irish committee at Whites Hotel [...]. I have had the opportunity to deal with many of these individuals ...When the inhabitants of North America separated from the Metropolis it was not grounds of Religion that made them act; the word Religion was never uttered in Boston or Philadelphia![10]

The American Revolution, as Lebrun notes, was fought over political ideology and not religious sectarianism. The ideological backgrounds of the American and French revolutions were markedly different to England and Ireland which was driven by religion as well as political ideology. As noted earlier, in England, Unitarians and other Dissenters made up 20 per cent of the population: and perhaps also reflected the strength of radical feeling in the country. The English revolution lacked sufficient grass-roots support, as it was primarily backed by a narrow religious group. In Ireland, the desire was more for Catholic supremacy than political reform. As could be easily grasped, Lebrun was worried that the French were getting drawn into sectarian violence, and replacing the British Crown's oppression with that of fanatical Catholics. The French had other reasons to be wary about an expedition to Ireland. France and England were still engaged in a 'phony war' and any plotting with Irish republicans could lead to war, which France could ill afford. The British Crown had known of the Catholic Convention and hopes that it would be a catalyst for Revolution for several months by the dawn of 1793, as a letter by Edmund Burke reveals:

This morning I received a message from Hussey. [...] [Irish] Catholics are determined to hold a rally as soon as possible. [...] It is expected that steps will be taken by the government to interrupt their procedures [...]. If this were to happen, [...] as most Catholics are armed, and ready to defend what they call their rights, the consequences would be terrible.[11]

The letter reveals that the British Crown took the threat of insurrection seriously.

The Mission of Colonel Oswald

If the French were to land in Ireland, the French needed up-to-date information about the public mood regarding an invasion and revolution. Recognizing that it was now many months since first-hand information had been received from Ireland, and in order to liaise with the Irish leadership, 'Thomas Paine ... Sent American Oswald to Lord Edward Fitzgerald with an offer of 20,000men, arms munitions and money ... to help the Irish shake off the English yoke and to establish their independence.'[12] Colonel Eleazer Oswald was born in Falmouth in 1755, but emigrated to America and during the Revolutionary Wars backed the Americans against the British Crown. In 1792 he went to France and was named Colonel of Artillery by General Charles François Dumouriez on 18 September 1792, and under his orders served at Jemappes on 6 November 1792.

Oswald set out on 20 February 1793, but due to passport issues 'embarked on 2 April' and discovered he could not sail direct from Dunkirk to Ostend. Arriving at Christianland on 14 April thanks to a passage on a Danish ship, he set out for Scotland ten days later aboard a smuggler's boat. He landed at Largs, and six days later passed through Leith, Edinburgh and Glasgow. In Glasgow he found passage to Port Patrick and finally arrived in Belfast on 5 May, and on the 8th reached Dublin, where he remained for two weeks. Oswald carried 'two letters written by Paine to influential Irish Men'. These unknown Irishmen were, it is supposed, Fitzgerald and Archibald Hamilton Rowan.

During his journey across Scotland and from this time in Ireland, he reported that the British economy was stagnant with a record number of bankruptcies and increasing levels of unemployment and disaffection with the British Crown. He noted the 'people' blamed the hardships they were enduring on the war with France. Concerning the mood in Ireland, he informed the French that the Volunteers had been fully disarmed on the orders of the British Crown and had also been totally intimidated. He also noted that the Crown had withdrawn regular troops and sought to replace them with a militia 'which was an extremely unpopular measure and generally disapproved of'. Oswald tells us he met the 'influential Irishmen' he carried letters for and discussed fomenting a rebellion in Ireland fuelled by the discontent towards the Crown. Oswald left Dublin fourteen days later aboard an American sloop bound for Bordeaux, where he landed on 1 June, arriving back in Paris on the 8th.[13] This was perfectly true as in February 1793, the Irish Parliament in an attempt to prevent the Catholic Convention had ordered that the Defenders – a Catholic oath-bound secret society that took part in paramilitary activities – and Napper Tandy's Volunteers were to be disarmed and legislation passed to hinder any future gatherings.[14] It was reported that twenty-one Defenders, portrayed by the British Crown as anti-Protestant and pro-French fanatics, were sentenced to death and a further thirty-seven to transportation. The Crown also pursued the Irish republican leadership: Napper Tandy fled and Bond, Neilson and Archibald Hamilton Rowan were prosecuted for seditious libel for having published and distributed the address calling the Volunteers to arms. The Volunteers that did assemble called only for reform.[15] Oswald returned to America in 1795 and died of yellow fever in New York on 30 September of that year.

Enter William Duckett

The execution of King Louis led to the breaking of diplomatic ties between Britain and France: war was declared on 1 February 1793. John Hurford Stone reported that if revolution was to be fomented in England, then it was to be religious Nonconformists that the French were to look to for support. Stone – a Unitarian – informed Lebrun that Dissenters were zealous defenders of liberty despite being persecuted by the Crown, and would do so even if it meant risking their lives.[16] Communication between English radical groups and the French was essential if the French were to intervene successfully in fomenting revolution. Direct communication had been lost with the recall of Lebrun's agents in December 1793, and to re-initiate conact, William Empden Duckett and other former students of the Irish College in Paris were commissioned by the French foreign minister, the aforementioned Pierre Lebrun, to go to Ireland and England to disseminate propaganda (March–April 1793).

Duckett was born in 1768 in Killarney, County Kerry, in 1768. By 1784 he was studying for the priesthood at the Irish College, Paris, leaving in July 1789. He also studied at the Collège Sainte-Barbe and may have paid occasional visits to Ireland. When, on 10 August 1792 (the day of Louis XVI's arrest), the Irish College was attacked by revolutionaries, Duckett supported them. In doing so he came to the attention of the Montagnard politician Léonard Bourdon. Another who came to Bourdon's attention was the administrator of the college, Nicholas Madgett. He was born in 1740 in Kerry and went to France (in or before 1760), where he studied for the Catholic priesthood at the Irish College, Toulouse in 1764 and was ordained a priest there on 4 April 1767. He served as a *curé* in provincial France until pressures of the Revolution made him switch to a secular career. He was employed in the mid-1790s under the Convention and Directory as a translator in the department of foreign affairs with the rank of *sous-chef* overseeing nearly everything relating to Ireland. On 29 October elections were held for the position of *proviseur* of the Irish College by the scholars:

> Murry [*sic* Murray], Duckett, J Oneil, Mac Sheehi [*sic* MacSheehy] senior, Mac Sheehi [*sic* MacSheehy] junior, Curtayne, Blackwell, Ferris MacMahon; and on counting the ballot, MacMahon received votes and Citizen Duckett five votes, and considering that Citizen Duckett had five votes which are the majority of nine, the number of voters, he was nominally elected ... the voters then proceeded to choose an administrator of the temporalities of the said establishment ... the count revealed the name of Citizen Nicholas Madgett.[17]

Duckett and his students attended the Society for the Rights of Man held at White's Hotel, where they became integral to subversive activities in England and Ireland.

The operation was planned by Nicholas Madgett.[18]

Duckett was placed at the head of the group to be sent to Ireland which comprised Edward Ferris, Jeremy Curtayne, Bernard MacSheehy and Bartholomew Murray, who were to disseminate propaganda. As could perhaps have been predicted by sending a group of young men with no experience of clandestine operations, the group was arrested on arrival in London. On hearing no word from the group, three weeks after their departure Madgett wrote on 13 March that 'one can hardly doubt' that the agents had informed the British Crown of their actions.[19] Madgett was of course wrong, and the mission had been given away thanks to information passed to the British Crown by former Irish priest Charles Somers, who, while in Paris, had become aware of the activities of the former college students.[20]

Ferris seems to have remained in Ireland, but the others did make their way back to France and were sent on a new mission. Ferris was replaced by a man called Sidderson, who travelled with Curtayne and Duckett to Ireland. An informant for the British Crown wrote:

> Three Jacobin emissaries were sent over to Ireland in the spring ... one Duckett aged about 22 years of age & two others of the same age – they embarked in a Danish vessel at Dunkirk ostensibly bound for America – were most liberally supplied by the late guillotined minister LeBrun, and there is very reason to suppose that they landed at Dingle on the S.W. coast of Ireland & brought over arms and ammunition for – as it is known the insurrections that broke out in the neighbourhood of that town, of which place said Duckett is known to be a native. There appears sufficient reason to believe that the troubles were solely owing to the influence of Duckett & his associates.[21]

The 'troubles' alluded to here were the Militia Riots that began in May. The riots marked a crucial stage in the breakdown of social and political relations within Ireland and the increasing radicalisation of the United Englishmen and the Defenders. Exploiting the discontent could have led to a broader rebellion. The rioting at Dingle reached a climax on 24 June when a crowd of about 4,000 from the rural resistance movement known as the 'Whiteboys' gathered on the peninsula driven by opposition to the Militia Act, taxes and paying tithes to the Anglican Church. The press reported 'a vast multitude of these frantic wretches assembled in the town of Dingle' and attacked the houses of establishment figures and 'burned all the tithe notes and papers they could get'.[22] The Crown forces opened fire and fourteen protestors were shot dead, one of whom was a woman. Mr Cooke, Government Under Secretary at Dublin Castle, declared: 'Militia may be the pretext but something deeper is at the bottom'. Nor was the rioting at Dingle isolated: nineteen were killed near Ballinafad and twenty-six at Bruff.[23] Cooke was it seems quite correct. Soaring food prices combined with famine led to civil unrest which the French and United Irish leadership hoped to profit from.

From Ireland, Duckett seems to have travelled to London, some time during autumn 1793, and fostered links with the London Corresponding Society.

Nicholas Madgett junior, cousin of Nicholas Madgett, now enters the story. Nicholas Madgett junior was born in 1758 and trained for the priesthood in France, where he was ordained and became the *curé* at Blaignan in the Médoc. On refusing to take the oath required by the civil constitution of the clergy (November 1790) he was expelled from his parish, and by late spring 1793 was in Ireland working for Dublin Castle. He informed the British Crown that Duckett was 'a violent republican, the object of his mission was to prepare the minds of the people for insurrection'. Madgett junior tells us that under the name Junius Redivivus, Duckett contributed two articles to the radical *Morning Chronicle* (published on 17 November and 3 December 1793) and to the radical Irish press. Duckett became a committed United Irish militant.[24]

Whilst Duckett was in Ireland, the French Revolution began its downward spiral to terror. The Revolution began to consume the revolutionaries. In Paris, Minister Lebrun was suspected of complicity with General Charles François Dumouriez and was arrested on 2 June 1793 with twenty-nine fellow Girondins, including Étienne Clavière. He was guillotined on 28 December. His arrest and death plunged the Irish and English émigrés in France into chaos as they had backed the now toppled Girondins. It seemed that any hope of convincing France to invade was 'dead in the water'. Or was it?

The Mission of Richard Ferris

Independent of Duckett, in July Richard Ferris dispatched a *mémoire* of events in Ireland to the French National Convention, noting that Ireland was ready for revolution and also that in Scotland disaffection was such that the people were waiting for Ireland to revolt before the people would rise.[25] With Lebrun under arrest, the French did not seem interested in Ireland, yet beyond reasonable doubt Ireland was a tinder box ready to explode, which could be harnessed into a revolutionary moment. That moment did not come, despite Duckett's prompting, and the Militia Riots had by and large ended by August and had resulted in 200 dead. At the height of the troubles Ferris left Ireland and arrived in France in August.[26] Days later he reported to the Minister for Foreign Affairs about the rising tide of dissent in London regarding the war – Britain and France had been at war since February 1793 – and added that 'the people of Ireland could profit from the discontent against the British Crown and the inequitudes of its actions'.[27]

Since hostilities had begun in the new year, the British Army under the command of the Duke of York crossed the Channel and by summer 1793 the French were losing the campaign. However, the action at Hondschoote, on 6–8 September, turned everything in France's favour.

With the French Army having the upper hand, thoughts turned once more to fomenting revolution in England. Public opinion was turning against the war and government. To exploit this situation, the Committee of Public Safety on 22 September instructed the Ministère de la Marine to formulate plans to land troops on the coast of England.[28] At the end of September, the Ministère de la Marine reported that plans were being prepared to land 100,000 troops.[29] Contiguously, in Cherbourg a plan was formulated to invade 'the Norman Islands' – Jersey, Guernsey and Sark – in a diversionary attack to draw the British Army and more importantly the Royal Navy out of the Channel while a French landing in Ireland took place. The dates for the invasion were set for 19 and 20 February 1794.[30] This plan had been partially put into operation in 1781, and had succeeded to some degree, so no doubt many had 'high hopes' of success as long as one forgot the invasion of Jersey had actually failed.

As well as facing the British Army in the Low Countries, the French Republic had to contend with the British in France too. In February, the National Convention had voted to approve a levy of 300,000 men, to be chosen by lot among the unmarried men in each commune. Thus, the arrival of recruiters reminded locals of the methods of the monarchy, aroused resistance in the countryside and set in motion the first serious signs of civil war, particularly in the Vendée. Outright rebellion broke out in March. The British Crown sent money, arms and gunpowder to bolster the Catholic Royalist Army.

In retaliation for the British involvement in the Vendée, part of the French government's event planning to land in Ireland centred on fomenting revolution in England and Ireland. It was hoped that English radicals based in London and major towns and cities would cause a diversionary rebellion which would draw the British Army away from the south coast, allowing the French to land in force to take London. An invasion would also mean that the British Army would have to end all operations on the continent. If Ireland could be prompted to rise in rebellion, then the British Army was sure to be stretched too thinly to oppose the French. The plan was conceived to draw the British troops under the Duke of York back to the mainland, and in the process cause as much havoc as possible to bring down the government and thus end the war.[31] These plans originated with a then relatively unknown and young general, Lazare Hoche.[32] If the French were to invade, they needed to be sure of the public mood, and to that end Ferris was finally authorized to travel on his mission to Ireland in October 1793, taking with him 13,200 livres.[33] His objective was to make his way to London and report back to Paris on the public mood and situation before heading to Ireland where it was hoped he would be able to incite new troubles.[34] Since August, Ferris had been critical of the delays between his first discussion with the French government in December 1792 and the eventual planning over six months, and remarked 'precious time passed; this is how we lost (I dare to say it) the most infallible means of consolidating the revolution'.[35] Ferris' disaffection with the French helps explains his later actions.

Madgett junior, now working for the British Crown, enters the story once more, his handler being William Huskisson MP – he was killed by Stephenson's *Rocket* at the opening of the Liverpool and Manchester Railway in 1830. In January 1793, Lord Dundas had appointed him to oversee the execution of the Aliens Act, in which capacity he was: 'a sort of extra clerk to read and digest French documents and to see the numerous French emigrants who then swarmed to that office, and with whom neither the minister [Dundas] nor his two under secretaries Nepean and King, could hold any direct intercourse from their ignorance of the language'.[36] Thanks to his undoubted linguistic skills he became the point of contact between French émigrés working for the British Crown and Lord Dundas, and in this role manifested such ability that in 1795 he was appointed Under Secretary at War.

Madgett junior reported that on arriving in England Richard Ferris offered his services to the Crown 'as a sure way of aborting the plans of the Jacobins'.[37] Thanks to Madgett junior's inducement, Ferries betrayed a plan that was never going to 'get off the drawing board', but it caused a tidal wave of panic in the British government: maybe that was the idea all along? Was Ferris not defecting but actually fulfilling his mission objective to confirm the French were going to land? The Crown had already learned about some of the planning being carried out in France, and Ferris confirmed it, which was rather convenient. While it is unclear whether his spying activities produced any great results for either side, both the British and the French handed Ferris a lot of money to fund his espionage. Ferris returned to Ireland in 1796 during the build up to the Bantry Bay landing, when Madgett junior denounced his presence, and thereafter he disappears from history for five years. His past caught up with him when in 1799 he was arrested and charged with spying by the French. However, through his pre-Revolution connections to Talleyrand, then foreign minister, Ferris managed to get himself released and soon established himself as a successful lawyer in France.[38]

In May 1795, Huskisson obtained an American passport for Madgett junior, and the latter returned to France under the alias of William S. Burns, an American businessman. He had in his pocket £100 in cash which was no doubt intended to 'grease palms' in uncovering information about French interests against Britain. Arrested for espionage, he was placed on trial for being a spy, but the case ended in acquittal on 22 July. He was not released until 25 November 1795, when he made for England, from where he was sent to Ireland to report on the activities of the United Irishmen.[39] The careers of Madgett junior and senior have become largely intermingled, with Madgett senior often quite understandably confused with his younger namesake.[40]

Madgett senior's plan had failed, and the British Crown knew what was being planned. Clearly, Madgett or Lebrun had been hugely naïve judges of character or they had been 'hoodwinked'. As we shall see, naïve judgement and outright incompetence would become a hallmark of the French secret-service dealings with Ireland.

A Scottish Republic

As Colonel Oswald had noted, Scotland was starting to embrace the polemic of Thomas Paine. In April 1792, a group of young Whigs founded the Society of the People, Associated for the Purpose of

Obtaining a Parliamentary Reform. Its purpose was the extension of the right to vote as well as parliamentary reform through the abolition of rotten boroughs and redistribution of seats to rapidly growing industrial towns. In July 1792, the Friends of the People Society of Edinburgh came into being. This group set its subscription rates lower than its English counterparts and as a result had a far wider membership base. Members came from a broad spectrum of trades which included shopkeepers, artisans, weavers, tailors, cobblers, brewers, bakers, tanners, butchers and hairdressers. Soon other groups were set up in Scotland. Branches of the Friends of the People operated independently but came together in conventions. It was one of these groups that was in communication with France by summer 1792. The de facto leader of the Scottish movement was Thomas Muir of Huntershill.

Muir was born in 1765 and attended the University of Glasgow from the tender age of 10, graduating in 1782 with an MA at the age of 17. A child prodigy, in politics he was a Whig and backed parliamentary reform and as early as September 1792, acting upon his own initiative, he began corresponding with Archibald Hamilton Rowan, Dublin secretary of the Society of United Irishmen. In his communications Muir detailed the aims and objectives of the association and explained that he wished to forge an alliance between Irish and Scottish radicals.[41] Such was the strength of Scottish republicanism that in Perth on 26 November 1792, 'A Tree of Liberty' was erected in the town and demonstrators cried for 'Equality and Liberty' and for the end of monarchy and aristocracy. Following this came demands from some elements of the membership to buy arms and to demand political reform by force. Making his way to Edinburgh on the morning of 2 January 1793 to attend Tytler's trial, Muir was himself arrested on a charge of sedition and completed the journey under guard. After interrogation before the sheriff and refusing to answer any questions, Muir was released on bail. He headed to London and then on to Paris, where he had interviews with members of the National Convention including Condorcet, Brissot, Mirabeau and Madame Roland. Muir also met Paine. He travelled to Ireland in March.

In response to the disarming of the Volunteers and crackdown by the British Crown, on 5 April 1793, the Society for Constitutional Information wrote to Simon Butler and Oliver Bond of the Dublin United Irishmen, stating that: 'as the freedom of one continent has already spread its influence to Europe, so on the other hand we are persuaded that the establishment of despotism in Ireland must end in the slavery of Great Britain'.[42] Similar letters of support were received from the

Scottish radicals, in reply to which, Archibald Hamilton Rowan wrote to the Scotsmen's spokesperson Norman Macleod in a letter dated 25 July 1793 – which was carried from Ireland to Scotland by Thomas Muir – stating that: 'The votary's of liberty are of no country, or rather of every country, and ... the destruction or establishment of the rights of mankind in one Nation conduces a similar consequence in its neighbouring state'.[43] Rowan argued that the extreme danger posed by the government's repressive measures to the liberties of both countries necessitated closer co-operation between the two reform movements and the adoption of bold measures.[44]

Thus, it comes as no surprise that in May 1793 the United Irishmen sent letters to the National Convention of the Friends of the People in Edinburgh. Ireland's voice, the address stated, 'shall be heard, Irishmen have willed it, and they must be free'. The Belfast United Irishmen went on to express their pleasure at the political awakening of Scotland and urged the Scots to persevere in championing reform. 'Nor can we suppose for a Moment,' the address continued, 'that you will ever suffer the Whisper of Malice, or the Frowns of Office to deter you from your pursuit. It is worthy of Men – worthy of you. And ye will not abandon it! We know the Conflict is arduous, But where the public Good is the End – Success is sure.'[45]

There can be little doubt that Muir concurred with Rowan and there is every possibility that he saw in himself just the man to persuade the Scots to co-operate with the Irish in resisting the rise of despotism, resulting in the 'pike plots', which are discussed later. Muir spent a week with Hamilton Rowan at Rathcoffey, and then decided to return to Scotland armed with masses of literature and letters for Scottish republicans at the start of August. Landing in Portpatrick on 24 August 1793, he was immediately arrested for treason. Fellow radical Fyshe Palmer, who was called by the prosecutor at this trial 'the most determined rebel in Scotland', was also arrested at the same time. Palmer was educated at Eton College and Queens' College, Cambridge from 1765 with the aim of taking holy orders in the Church of England. He graduated with a BA in 1769, MA in 1772 and BD in 1781. On encountering the works of the Revd Dr Priestley, Palmer became a Unitarian. Naturally enough, he plunged into radical politics and was ultimately found guilty of treason. For this crime of wanting religious freedom and political reform he was sentenced to seven years' transportation, along with Thomas Muir, William Skirving and Maurice Margarot.

Chapter 8

THE FATAL NAÏVETY OF THE REVD WILLIAM FRANCIS JACKSON

With the Ferris mission ending in failure, a new agent was sent to England and Ireland to gauge the public mood. William Empden Duckett was now based in London and an ardent member of the London Corresponding Society according to at least one informant to the Crown, he was involved in what happened next.[1]

The Revd William Jackson was dispatched to England and Ireland via Hamburg where he met Benjamin Beresford – Archibald Hamilton Rohan's brother-in-law – to liaise with radical groups. He carried letters to John Horne Tooke and Yorkshire radical Dr Crossfield. Jackson, an Irish Presbyterian minister who had been in exile in Paris since late 1791, was allied politically with the Jacobins and in response to the English declaration of war against France he published 'An Answer to the Declaration of the King of England Respecting his Motives for Carrying on the Present War' (1793). He was arrested in October 1793 along with John Hurford Stone and become a French agent to gain his release. An informant told the Crown that: 'Stone from Paris was over last November and his brother-in-law drove him about (always by night) to different houses in the West end of the town'.[2] Stone was perhaps now too well known to return to London, so in his place he sent the Revd Jackson, and it was Stone who provided Jackson's introduction to his brother William living in London, Benjamin Vaughan and William Smith MP. Jackson was 'to sound out' opposition political groups on their support of invasion as well as the probable reception the French could expect: crucially he was to assess the level of collaboration the French would receive from radical groups.[3] Stone, in a letter written to John Horne Tooke that was taken to England by Jackson, expressed the view that France continued to be the champion of all mankind:

> And now my Patriotic Friend let me offer you my warmest and most heartfelt Congratulations at the immense Prospect of Public Happiness which is opening before Us. You are amongst the small Number of those who in the Worst of Times have never despaired of the Cause of Liberty [...]. I look forward with Joy to the Moment when [...] the barriers, parties of Ministerialists & Oppositionists, Dissenters, Churchmen, Nobles, Priests & Kings shall [give way] to the divine Reign of Equality without which there may be a Confederation but not Society, a Government but no People.[4]

This letter provides a glimpse into Stone's ideology: it is clear he was fighting for the freedom of all those oppressed by the state and links Tooke – and inter alia the radical groups in England – directly with Jackson's mission.

On 26 January 1794, Jackson landed in Hull to assess the possibility of a French invasion and how it would be received. He travelled immediately to London where he joined William Stone and Horne Tooke. William assured Jackson that the population was without doubt anti-French, and it seems contacted the authorities with his concerns. Jackson received a more sympathetic response from Benjamin Vaughan MP, who wrote a paper detailing the strength of oppositional groups in England. Vaughan stated that in the event of French invasion, the British people would instinctively rally to the Crown to 'defend hearth and home' and categorically stated that: 'if France were to invade England, everyman would turn out, from good will or fear, and the few who are discontented would be quelled with ease as the French citizens were by La Fayette at the Champ de Mars'. Co-religionist William Smith MP agreed with Vaughan's sentiments, and told Jackson that: 'we should only wrap our cloak tighter around us, like the man in the storm, and refuse every offer of fraternity that came to use'. Jackson approached Richard Sheridan and the Revd Dr Priestley and met the same response. His dispatches containing the depressing news were sent John Hurford Stone in Paris via Hamburg on 18 March. They were intercepted and sent to Evan Nepean at the Home Office.[5] From the information Jackson had received from men who had two years earlier been at White's Hotel or vocal champions of the Revolution, Pitt's propaganda drive starting in December 1792 had cooled any mass support for the French. Yet, it does seem that some elements of the radical underground in England were indeed preparing arms to support the French, but the strength of support for an invasion is almost impossible to gauge.

Jackson's dispatches about the lack of English support for an invasion never reached France, where planning continued for an invasion. On 4 March, a new scheme of operations was agreed upon: the Isle of Wight was to be captured to blockade Portsmouth and Southampton.[6] French agents were active in preparing for a rebellion along the south coast. A French spy was reported as travelling from Exeter to Bridport linking with the English underground radical network and endeavouring to 'seduce' dockyard workers in Plymouth.[7]

Jackson left Chester on 30 March and arrived in Dublin on 3 April.[8] It was here he met Wolfe Tone, Edward Lewines (a French-educated Irish lawyer) and others who belonged to the Society of United Irishmen. Lewines, born in Dublin in 1756, studied at a seminary, but rather than being ordained he became a Dublin attorney. He joined the Society of United Irishmen and owing to his knowledge of the French language was sent to Paris in summer 1793, by which time Henry Sheares was president and he, Lewines, was secretary of the United Irishmen in Dublin. Lord Edward Fitzgerald refused to meet Jackson, and prominent United Irish leaders Simon Butler and Leonard McNally expressed scepticism that the French were planning to land troops. It was Lewines who organized Jackson's introduction to the gaoled Archibald Hamilton Rowan. Rowan gave Jackson an idea of the strength of the United movement in Ireland as well as the desire for revolution there. He offered Jackson the support of the United Irish for any French invasion of Ireland.[9]

Wolfe Tone gave Jackson a document prepared on the state of Ireland for the Committee of Public Safety. Three copies were made by Hamilton Rowan, dated 24 April 1794, one copy of which was sent to the Hamburg merchant house of Chapeaurouge to be handed to French Minister Reinhard and a second copy was sent to the French minister at The Hague. Jackson had put these 'top-secret' letters in the open post, where they were found by the postmaster. Was this the action of a double agent hoping to 'tip off' the British Crown, or did urgency override confidentiality, or was he simply naïve in believing the post was not monitored? The true reason for his actions will never be known, but much to his surprise, Jackson was arrested on 28 April.[10] Some in Ireland felt that Jackson was not operating alone: 'Duckett & his associates lay as it were perdues, waiting a more favourable opportunity. There scarce appears room to doubt if among Jackson's papers the names of Ferris, Curtin, Madgett are found.'[11]

The secret negotiations between Paris and English radicals had been infiltrated. A Home Office informant – John Cockayne, who travelled with Jackson – identified John Hurford Stone as linking English radicals with the French government in a 'project, idea or plan' to orchestrate a French-based invasion of the British mainland. The account of the plan detailed the precise location of the intended landing and the way in which the French forces would enter the country:

> The plan stated, and the statement was supported by a Drawing, that at, or near the Spits, there is a passage where the water is shallow, or from some other local cause which I know not, but the sinking one or two hulks of seventy-four gunships, would prevent the British fleet, when in the harbour, from coming out.[12]

The report also gave details of how boats would be sunk and troops landed on the Isle of Wight before heading for the mainland at Southampton. Men from the northern port towns of Calais, Boulogne, Dunkirk and Dieppe, who could converse in English, would be called upon to take part in the invasion. The author concluded: 'This is the only thing like a systematic plan of home attack on England, that I ever heard, nor do I believe that any other was seriously entertained.'[13] The plan that the Crown had uncovered, and linked directly to Stone, was exactly what had been planned for in France. The similarities between the French plan and that uncovered in the Revd Jackson's papers demonstrates the reality of the intent of Paris to attempt an invasion.

One of Huskisson's spies operating in the Ministère de la Marine reported that 16,000 French troops were ready to embark from Dunkirk, Le Havre and Cherbourg on 6 March. To assess the threat, a squadron of four British frigates appeared at Cherbourg on the 8th, and this threw the French into chaos. The French government, correctly as it turns out, believed that the invasion plans had been 'leaked' and called off the operation on 29 March.[14] In addition to this force, 20,000 men were assembled at Brest, supported by 300 cavalry troopers, a battery of 8 field guns and 12 howitzers along with 80 days of rations. General Laborde was to lead the right wing to attack Jersey and General Vezu the left wing to attack Guernsey. In addition there were 5,800 men from L'Armée de l'ouest, 5,300 men from L'Armée du Cherbourg and 8,800 men from L'Armée du Brest. Once 'the Norman Islands' had been secured, the Isle of Wight was the next objective.[15] The threat of invasion was taken so seriously by the British Crown that Pitt authorized the formation of Volunteer infantry and yeomanry cavalry for the internal defence of Britain and Ireland.

The French placed reliance on radical groups in England to rise up in support, and contrary to what Vaughan told Jackson, an underground movement *was* on the march. A spy working for Evan Nepean in the Home Office reported that the Sheffield Constitutional Society had armed themselves with pikes and spears.[16] Following the tip-off, special constables uncovered a cache of spears, pikes and caltrops 'to be thrown in the lane to lame the horses' in Sheffield.[17] Another spy reported that pikes were being made in Birmingham to arm the London Corresponding Society.[18] In Hampshire Josiah Webb of Pamber was reported as being 'a dissenter and a Francophile with 3 brothers in London whom he visits' by neighbours. He was arrested for the illegal manufacture of weapons which were destined to arm the revolution. An informant reported that: 'thousands of pike handles have been made by Josiah and conveyed to Newbury in George Webb's waggons, and from thence to London'.[19] North of the border in Scotland the 'Pike Plot' (a plan to stage a revolutionary coup in Edinburgh as the start of a general insurrection) was uncovered and its architect, Robert Watt (a former government spy), was hanged and suffered the ignominy of post-mortem decapitation after twelve pike heads were discovered in his house. Co-conspirator David Downie was tried but pardoned.[20] The Crown was now understandably convinced that reform societies and religious Dissenters were colluding with France to bring about revolution.

However real the invasion threat was, John Hurford Stone's plan had been given away by a 'comedy of errors'. William Stone informed the Crown of his brother's plan, and Jackson's colleague, Cockayne, had immediately told Prime Minister Pitt of Jackson's plan, through fear of being implicated in the plot himself. Jackson, through his inept and naïve actions, was in prison for more than a year before his trial at his own request so he could build his defence. Wolfe Tone and Rowan fled Ireland. Wolfe Tone went to America. One thankful loyalist wrote: 'this is a most <u>horrid</u> conspiracy against both church and state, under the pretence of reform … it is a mercy the plot is discovered'.[21]

The Treason Trials
Realizing he faced a charge of high treason which carried with it the sentence of being hung, drawn and quartered, Archibald Hamilton Rowan knew he was 'a dead man' and it was only a matter of time before charges were brought and his life terminated. Rowan, locked up in Newgate Prison, Dublin, persuaded his gaoler to allow him to spend his wedding anniversary at home, which was a major error. Rowan broke his parole and made his way to the south coast. On 5 May, he

escaped to Brittany in a small fishing boat manned by three sailors. He landed at Roscoff and was gaoled – quite reasonably – by the French authorities as a British spy. John Sullivan, a French secret agent and Irish émigré – he was the nephew of Nicholas Madgett, the former college administrator – organized his release.[22] Sullivan had arrived in France in 1783 and was employed as an English and mathematics teacher at La Flèche until 1793, when he joined the Republican forces in the Vendée and from the Vendée he became a secret agent working for Madgett.[23] Following Rowan's release, he headed to Paris, where he met Robespierre.[24] Rowan, according to Benjamin Vaughan, was ill when he arrived in Paris during June, and confined to his bed. Vaughan remarked that he visited him twice a day owing to their friendship from school days in Lancashire and time together at Cambridge.[25] What the pair discussed is lost to history. Rowan remained in Paris for a year, but with Robespierre's fall, however, he was 'on the wanted list' and obtained a passport from Nicholas Madgett to sail for America, leaving Paris on 17 April 1795. There was a £1,000 bounty for Rowan's capture.[26]

In April 1794, when the debacle that had foiled the invasion attempt became known in France, Stone was denounced as an agent of William Pitt and he and his wife were arrested again, but let go on the condition that they leave the country. He could not safely return to England, and the couple fled to Switzerland where they joined Helen Maria Williams.

Despite being arrested in 1794, Jackson was not placed on trial for treason until 23 April 1795. Rather than face trial and interrogation, he killed himself a week later, taking the secrets of the plot to his grave.[27]

Benjamin Vaughan, a close friend of both Stone brothers and William Jackson, knew he would face arrest for treason through implication and fled to France where he was arrested as a spy. He informed London friends: 'that after 8 or 9 days confinement to my room in Cherbourg, and 4 weeks solitary imprisonment at Paris, I am going to Switzerland without delay'.[28] He left for Switzerland on 3 July.[29] William Stone was gaoled and had to wait until 1796 to be tried for: 'treacherously conspiring with his brother, John Hurford Stone, then in revolutionary France, to destroy the life of the King and to raise a rebellion in his realms'. He was acquitted due to lack of evidence.[30] During this period the law of conspiracy was developed rapidly by the judges, and in Stone's 1796 trial justices Sir Nash Grose and Sir Soulden Lawrence persuaded Chief Justice Lord Kenyon to accept evidence of conspiracy that he was at first inclined to exclude. William was acquitted and Thomas Erskin, his defence lawyer, pithily commented: 'if promoting an invasion was treason, warding it off must be the reverse'.[31] Despite telling the Home Office of his brother's 'treason', by November 1796 William had moved to France, as public opinion concluded he was a traitor like his brother.

Arrests in Ireland and England confirmed the Crown's suspicion that all reforming societies were traitors and working to overthrow the government. The threat to the Crown was very real. Tens of thousands of working-class radicals wanted their voices heard across England, in Ireland Catholics wanted the same rights as members of the Church of Ireland: high on their list of demands was the right to vote, the right to participate in society, political reform and Home Rule. The plan was simple: create an underground army which would rise up when the French landed.

The British Crown embarked on a campaign of repression: all radicals and reformists were to be rounded up. With evidence to hand of a planned invasion supported by British radicals, at 6:30am on Monday, 12 May 1794, Hardy, the secretary of the London Corresponding Society, and Daniel Adams, the secretary of the Society for Constitutional Information, were arrested in their respective homes and charged with treasonous practices. Thomas Walker in Manchester was also arrested along with the leadership of both national bodies and regional affiliated societies.

Following the arrests in London, the British Crown formed two secret committees to study the papers they had seized from the radicals' houses. After the first committee reported its findings, the government introduced a bill to the House of Commons to suspend habeas corpus; thus, those arrested could be held without bail or charge until February 1795. Furthermore, the committee asserted that on the evidence they had uncovered the radical societies had been planning at least to 'over-awe' the king and Parliament by the show of 'a great Body of the People' and install a French-style republic. Irish Jacobins and republicans were brutally repressed: in April twenty-one defenders, presented by the Irish and British state as anti-Protestant and pro-French fanatics, were sentenced to death and thirty-seven to deportation. The leaders of the United Irish were hunted down: Napper Tandy fled and Neilson was prosecuted for seditious libel for publishing and distributing the address calling the Irish to arms.[32] Simon Butler was arrested along with Oliver Bond. Their trial resulted in acquittal, yet it was unwise for them to remain in Ireland. In response to the trial of William Jackson, one of those caught up in the proceedings was Theobald Wolfe Tone. A spy working for Lord Camden noted that Wolfe Tone and Thomas Russell were heading to France funded by £1,500 raised by the sixteen different societies of United Irishmen in Belfast.[33] This was incorrect and Wolfe Tone sailed for America on 17 April 1795. He met Nicholas Madgett senior in August of that year. Edward Fitzgerald, Arthur O'Connor, Thomas Addis Emmet, Dr William MacNeven and Olivier Bond headed from Ireland to France. The new leadership in Ireland transformed the movement into an ever more militant republican revolutionary force. In the wake of the trials and diaspora of the existing leadership the key players in what happened next were John and Henry Sheares (the first of whom was a lawyer), Samuel Neilson, the Russell brothers, the Simm brothers, Dr William MacNeven, Roger O'Connor (brother of Arthur), the brothers Charles and Barthelemy Teeling, Michel Byrne, John Swetman, Edward Lewines, Mathieu Dowling, John Chambers, Hugh Wilson and Joseph Cormick. Most of these individuals would find themselves reunited in Scotland four years later, imprisoned in Fort St George.

As E.P. Thompson comments, the trials, although they were not government victories, served the purpose for which they were intended – radical politics collapsed, fearful of governmental retribution.[34] Despite this victory, Pitt's own oppressive legislation against reform, freedom of speech and the press created a situation whereby English Jacobins had an ever increasing array of grievances against the Crown that they wanted redressed. Pitt's own actions in denying political reform and the legalization of Catholicism and Unitarianism, not abolishing the Test and Corporation Acts and the seditious writing and meeting Acts and suspending habeas corpus empowered the radical and turned simmering anger into burning rage. Pitt, far more than France, created the conditions that allowed the United Englishmen to emerge from the shadows.

Chapter 9

EXPORTING REVOLUTION

The arrests of 1794 were a defining moment for 'the children of the revolution', which many of the émigré radicals gathered in France considered themselves to be. They were orphans in the storm who had been expelled from their native countries and now sought retribution. As well as seeing a shift in the leadership in Ireland and England, the treason trials far from stamping out radicalism drove it to new extremes. It marked a withdrawal of the middle-class idealists and their replacement with an altogether more radicalized and violent working class. For the British Crown the threat of invasion and from 'home-grown terrorists', which is how Pitt and others viewed members of the London Corresponding Society and similar august bodies, had been defeated.

Mother Nature now intervened: a wet summer in 1794 meant famine. Wheat that in 1790 had cost about £2 10s. per quarter rose to about £3 in 1794 and by 1795 was selling at anything from £4 to almost £5 per quarter, while in the same year a 4lb loaf of bread cost a shilling, almost double its price twelve months previously.[1] A loaf of bread cost the same as the average workman's daily pay. Cut off from imports of grain from Russian ports in the Baltic, prices rose from 52s. a quarter in April to 80s. by July, and then reached 150s. a quarter by August. Food riots broke out in towns and cities, including in the Midlands Leicester, Dudley and Wolverhampton.[2] There were also riots in Chester and Shropshire.[3] During food riots in Birmingham the militia opened fire and killed protesters. Nottingham, Newcastle, Bristol and Leicester erupted in violence at the cost of food and all across the country famine drove a wave of violence. In London at the height of rioting on 14 August, the High Sherriff of Surrey reported that a carefully prepared handbill was passed to soldiers policing protests in St George's Fields which contained a persuasive call to the cause of 'liberty', as well as an attempt to seduce the soldiery from their duty, 'let soldiers protect the Rights of Citizens and Citizens will avenge the wrongs of soldiers'.[4] On the same day, Downing Street was attacked and several of Pitt's windows were smashed, leaving one under secretary in fear of bloody revolution.[5]

Paris

The events taking place in England did not go unnoticed in Paris. A French secret agent, Louis Monneron, had been in England since late summer 1795 and had witnessed the famine and anger on the streets first hand. He reported back to the French Directory on 17 November 1795 about the public mood and the British Crown's actions in silencing dissent. After stones were thrown at the king's coach at the opening of Parliament on 29 October 1795, the government responded by introducing the 'gagging acts' on 6 November (consisting of the Seditious Meetings Act and the Treasonable Practices Act). This body of legislation worked to place further restrictions on the movement for radical reform in Britain. Monneron was also tasked with assembling data on the British economy, as well as the strength of both the British Army and the recently raised volunteer forces in England and Ireland.[6]

The Scottish group Monneron met included those who had gathered around Thomas Muir. What had started as reformist groups now became revolutionary movements in England, Ireland and Scotland: by the end of 1795 a nationally co-ordinated network had emerged that was in contact with radicals in Ireland and France and seeking to liberate Ireland and establish a Jacobin-style republic. To achieve this the United Irishmen and their English counterparts completed their transformation into an armed insurrectionary movement to aid the French.

The failure of the Jackson mission does not seem to have affected the Directory's plans to send agents to Ireland, England and Scotland. The Directory sought to land a mortal blow against England with the minimum amount of effort and engaged in 'little wars' and 'war by other means': if the radical groups and disaffected could be prompted to rebel against the Crown through the proffering of gold and muskets, then it was a win-win situation for France. Ensuring the English, Scots and Irish could be induced to liberate themselves without major French investment was the goal. The policy was driven by Director Lazare Carnot, whose Anglophobia, like that of General Hoche, had been fashioned by their experiences of the counter-revolution in the west of France. Carnot sought to export back to England with interest the civil war that the English had begun in France. Duckett informed

Tallien and by inference Abbé Sieyès that: 'To establish freedom, you must destroy the British government.'[7] Emmanuel-Joseph Sieyès was a French Roman Catholic abbé, clergyman and political writer who was the chief political theorist of the French Revolution. He held office as president of the Senate in 1799 and was in office with Bonaparte and Roger Ducros as Consul of France. Before this, during 1795 he went on a diplomatic mission on the orders of Jean-Lambert Tallien, who had been president of the National Convention from 21 March 1794–5 April 1794 and deputy in the Council of Five Hundred from 2 November 1795–10 November 1799, to The Hague, and was instrumental in drawing up a treaty between the French and Batavian republics. Part of this treaty placed the Batavian fleet at Texel at the disposal of the French, and it was this fleet which would come to prominence in the months ahead.

The United Threat

The British Crown's elimination of peaceful methods of agitating for reform and the prospect of French assistance encouraged the remaining members of provincial and metropolitan reform societies to achieve their goal of universal male suffrage and annual parliaments by physical force. Living in squalor, made increasingly 'economically redundant' thanks to the Industrial Revolution, starving and seeing family and friends die of typhoid from drinking contaminated water, is it any wonder that the working class erupted against the elite and bourgeois? Protest meetings and food riots had been a common feature of class conflicts in the eighteenth century but now, at the dawn of the nineteenth, the events that started in winter 1795 represented a different phenomenon – a national movement, formulating its propaganda with a clear political ideology and agitating for resistance against ruling class and state. In the wake of the treason trials, the moderate members of the remaining constitutional societies began to withdraw: the reformist movement was splintering into those who wanted to continue to press for reform via constitutional means and those who sought direct action: a working-class protest movement emerged.

In the documents created by the United Englishmen, sections of the 'Declarations, Resolutions, and Constitution of the Society of United Englishmen', printed by the Manchester radical William Cowdray, reflect the reformist ideology of the democratic movement of the early 1790s, presenting the United Englishmen as a network of 'societies in every quarter of the kingdom, for the promotion of constitutional knowledge, the abolition of bigotry in religion and politics, and the equal distribution of the rights of man throughout all sects and denominations of Englishmen'. This agenda makes it difficult to distinguish the official line of United Englishmen and the politics of the London Corresponding Society, and its sister groups in Manchester, Sheffield and Leeds, led by the erstwhile Major Cartwright. Maybe that was the point.[8]

Since the 1770s, legal means of protest against the state to enact political reform via petition had failed. It was clear to many that if legitimate lines of protest would not make the Crown listen to the voice of the people, then direct action was seen, quite logically, as the only way of achieving reform. One historian, Jenny Graham, asserts that: 'the fundamental ideology of the United Englishmen ... and even their personnel, can arguably be interpreted as a further development of a movement wholly frustrated in all its previous attempts to alter the political system by means other than force'.[9] The appeal to knowledge and education was not hollow rhetoric. National schools were identified as an objective in the society's constitution, so too old-age pensions.

The United Englishmen directly modelled its strategic aims and organization on the United Irishmen: members of the new group were sworn in and given a membership card bearing the motto 'Liberty, Justice and Humanity' and a small eight-page pamphlet outlining the aims of the organization and its constitution. Each group was to be organized on a cell system where members were known only to the 'conductor' of the organization, one conductor managing a group of ten. The organization was clearly inspired by the London Corresponding Society, as noted earlier, and the membership was probably largely the same, especially in London and the industrializing towns of the north of England.

The London groups rapidly made contact with groups across the country, which emerged mostly in the north of England and the Midlands. In Manchester, one of the earliest United Englishmen cells was established in late 1795 or early 1796. The first English use of the United Irish branch system was in Manchester. Each branch comprised a minimum of fifteen members. When a branch had grown to thirty-six members, it divided into two divisions. Each division elected a treasurer and secretary. Linking the divisions was what was termed a baronial committee, to which each division sent its secretary and two other divisional members. An elaborate network of baronial, county, provincial and national committees provided a nationwide organization which was underpinned by a code of secrecy to ensure the names of committee members were not known to persons other than those who elected them. The divisional structure was later reduced to ten members to further hamper governmental interference and detection of meetings. So that members could identify one another, secret signs were taught to members by their Irish compeers, while immigrants from Ireland, such as James Dixon, were responsible for distributing Irish oaths and radical literature to English democrats. The Manchester Branch aimed to abolished taxes, the Test and Corporation Acts – the long-hoped dream of Unitarians and Presbyterians – and reform Parliament with equal and fair representation by giving every man the vote. In addition, the United Englishmen were 'to learn their exercise and joined the French when they invaded this country and make it a free nation'. Membership of the United Englishmen was by swearing an oath of allegiance.[10] The regicidal nature of some branches was given expression at Stirling, where members referred to George III as 'George Whelps' and toasted 'The Old Dog's head cut off, the Bitch hanged, and all the Whelps drowned.'[11]

Run in secret, very little is known about the United movement. Consequently, how far this was a cohesive coordinated organization was (and consequently still is) difficult to ascertain. How far this was influenced and driven by the French secret service or the United Irishmen (or indeed both) is almost impossible to judge. But it is known that the French were in direct dialogue with the United Englishmen from summer 1796.

United Colombia

As well as the desire to export revolution to England and Ireland, other more audacious plans were formulated. Edmond-Charles Genêt, the French Ambassador to the United States, worked openly in the United States to foment rebellion and in a rousing pamphlet, 'The Free French to their brothers in Canada', printed in 1793, he called on the French Canadians to rebel against the British:

> Man was born free. By which fate did he become the subject of his own brother? ... Everything around you invites you to freedom; The country in which you live was conquered by your fathers. It owes its prosperity solely to their care and to yours, this land belongs to you, it must be independent.
>
> Break away from a government which degenerates day by day and has become the cruelest enemy of people's freedom. Everywhere one finds traces of the despotism, the greed, the cruelties of the king of England. It is time to overthrow a throne onto which hypocrisy and imposture has been sitting for too a long time, that the vile courtiers who surrounded it be punished for their crimes or that dispersed all over the

65

Earth the opprobrium of which they will be covered attests to the world, that a late but bright revenge has taken place in favour of humanity.

This necessary revolution, this inevitable punishment prepares quickly in England. Every day the republican principles make sharp progress there and the number of the friends of liberty and France increases in a significant way; but do not wait the outcome of this event to reclaim your rights, work for yourselves, for your glory, do not fear anything of George III, of his soldiers, in too small a number to successfully oppose your value, his weak army is retained in England around him by the murmurs of the English, and by the immense preparations of France, which do not allow him to increase the number of your torturers. The moment is favourable, and the insurrection is for you the holiest of duties.[12]

Genêt's effective propaganda led to a groundswell of anger against the British Crown.

Ira Allen was instrumental in the founding of Vermont and was the state's first treasurer, 1778–86, and co-founded the state university. On 25 October 1790, Allen was commissioned major general of the Third Division of the Vermont State Militia by Governor Thomas Chittenden. In 1795, he promulgated the idea of seizing Canada. He was in Paris in July 1796 with a letter of recommendation from the governor, who described him as a 'man of honour, merit and distinction'. He had sailed from London with £2,000 in coin and landed at Deal from where he gained passage to Le Havre. He was charged by the governor in letters dated 27 October 1796 'to search for arms and other munitions of war for the use of the militia'.[13] Allen presented a plan to the Directory for raising a rebellion in Canada and using irregular American troops to invade.[14] Allan hoped – in rehashing his vision of the American Revolutionary Wars – to unite Vermont and Canada as an independent republic of 'United Columbia'. He hoped that the uprising would trigger the French Canadians to rise and force the British out of North America. He drew heavily from Genêt when stating that the new republic was to abolish feudalism, tenants would be allowed to buy their land, Crown Property would be nationalized and distributed to the poor and the electoral franchise would be extended to all those who could read and write. Allen also noted that France would have the satisfaction 'of Bringing Liberty to the unfortunate French oppressed by kings and priests'.[15] The rebellion would also remove British troops from a European war and draw the Royal Navy away from guarding Ireland, allowing a French invasion. Allen hoped that the loss of Canada and the increase in the

English national debt would lead to revolution in England and that France and 'reunited Columbia will be masters of the seas. The rights of man will be extended with advantage and the republics will soon enjoy repose.'[16] Allen provided the Directory with strength returns for the British garrison in Canada, noting the garrison was about 5,000 men, of which 2,000 were in Quebec, which he remarked was the sole defensible location. He reported that the citadel was armed with thirty-two cannon and its walls were 20ft high. To liberate Canada, Allen proposed to arm 20,000 partisans which he would recruit in Lower Canada. After securing Lower Canada, he proposed that his victorious army would invade New Brunswick, Nova Scotia and Newfoundland.[17] To ensure success, Allen requested military aid from France in the form of arms as well as experienced officers to take command of the Vermont Militia. To that end, he asked the Directory to send 3,000 troops, as well as arms and uniforms for a further 4,000 men.[18] The Directory seemingly agreed with Allen's proposal and he was granted permission to buy 20,000 muskets and bayonets at the end of July.[19] One suspects the Directory felt the hard cash on offer was sufficient incentive to sell the arms, rather than back the revolutionary plans. If the revolution succeeded, then the French would have a new ally and could bask in the shared glory, if the plans failed, the Directory had 'big pile of gold' which always comes in useful.

At the end of September, Allen, now going by the alias of John Bates, was in Dunkirk asking General Henri Clarke head of the Topographical Department at the Ministry of War for nautical charts of Canada.[20] By October Allen was in Ostend buying arms.[21] In a second letter written in October Allen informed General Clarke of the importance of rallying America to the cause of France.[22] Allen also recommended to the Directory that in order to hasten internal disorder in England and therefore aid the establishment of a republic in Ireland and England, France should close her ports to English shipping, and enforce the blockade in the Netherlands, Spain and Italy. Allen argued that the collapse in trade would result in increased unemployment and therefore disaffection from which the French would benefit. Finally, he added that if the war continued despite the blockade, the tax rises the British Crown would have to levy to meet the national debt would cause revolution.[23] In essence, Allen had predicted the Continental System and its effects on England a decade before such a blockade was implemented by Napoléon.

By summer 1796, the British Crown faced the triple threat of invasion in Canada, Ireland and England.

Chapter 10

ORDER FROM CHAOS?

The actions of the British Crown in Ireland created the perfect conditions for revolution. Earl Fitzwilliam, appointed Lord Lieutenant on 10 August 1794, believed that the 'Protestant Ascendancy' in Ireland alienated Catholics from British rule which would drive them into supporting Jacobinism and a French invasion of Ireland; the loss of Ireland in such an event would weaken British sea power and make possible an invasion of England. Fitzwilliam aimed to reconcile Catholics to British rule by delivering Catholic emancipation and ending the 'Protestant Ascendancy'. Fitzwilliam arrived in Balbriggan, Ireland on 4 January 1795. On 10 January, he wrote to the Duke of Portland: 'not one day has passed since my arrival without intelligence being received of violences committed in Westmeath, Meath, Longford and Cavan: Defenderism is there in its greatest force ... I find the texture of government very weak and chaotic'. On 15 January, he again wrote to Portland, claiming that the violence committed by peasants was not political but 'merely the outrages of banditti' and could be eliminated by helping Catholics of rank to preserve law and order. This could only be done by emancipation: 'No time is to be lost, the business will presently be at hand, and the first step I take is of infinite importance'. However, he 'endeavoured to keep clear of any engagement whatever' on emancipation but that 'there is nothing in my answer that they can construe into a rejection of what they are all looking forward to, the repeal of the remaining restrictive and Penal Laws', adding:

> I shall not do my duty if I do not distinctly state it as my opinion that not to grant cheerfully on the part of government all the Catholics wish will not only be exceedingly impolitick, but perhaps dangerous. ... If I receive no very peremptory directions to the contrary, I shall acquiesce with a good grace, in order to avoid the manifest ill effect of a doubt or

the appearance of hesitation; for in my opinion even the appearance of hesitation may be mischievous to a degree beyond all calculation.[1]

Earl Fitzwilliam's reform attempt in January–February 1795 revived hopes held by the Catholic Committee (founded in 1759) of putting an end to the Penal Laws that made Irish Catholics non-citizens in their own country, but failed due to opposition by George III who declared that Fitzwilliam was: 'venturing to condemn the labours of ages ... [which] every friend to the Protestant religion must feel diametrically contrary to those he has imbibed from his earliest youth'.[2] Writing on 10 February to the Duke of Portland, Fitzwilliam believed that: 'emancipation would have a good effect on the spirit and loyalty of the Catholics of Ireland, and Catholics of rank would be reconciled to British rule and put down disturbances'. He also proposed the formation of an Irish yeomanry officered by Catholic gentry which would enable the British Army garrison to be deployed against the French.[3] Four days later Fitzwilliam repeated his views arguing that such radical change was needed in support of national security, noting: 'the disaffection amongst Catholics was so great and only such a change in direction could retain Ireland'.[4] Fitzwilliam was perfectly correct. However, where the king led, Pitt followed, as did the Protestant Irish Parliament. George III now took a direct hand in government: he had brought down the government in 1783 to oust Charles James Fox from power, and was prepared to be a 'hands on monarch' in government when policies were enacted he despised. The king was appalled by any idea of concessions to Catholics. The Duke of Portland wrote to Fitzwilliam on 16 February, in a letter approved by the Cabinet, and stated that: 'the Bill for Catholic Emancipation in Ireland ... [would] produce such a change in the present constitution of the House of Commons as will overturn that, and with it the present ecclesiastical establishment'. The Anglican ascendancy was in danger, and therefore any chance of reform was 'off the cards'. Fitzwilliam was recalled in disgrace on 20 February.[5] As Fitzwilliam quite rightly predicted, the British Crown's failure to enact reform resulted in rising tensions in Ireland. A spy working for Lord Camden reported on 4 July that a meeting of the United Irishmen in Dublin had discussed a letter from the 'Friends of the People', London and made resolutions to support London.[6] The spy wrote to Camden on 7 July informing him that the United Irishmen planned a rising in 'the north for about 20 July with attacks on Carrickfergus and Charlemont'.[7] Sectarian violence broke out, and witnessed the formation of the 'The Orange Order' to cement the 'Protestant Ascendancy': Catholics and New Light

Presbyterians – Unitarians – had no place in Irish affairs. The sectarian violence commonly known as the 'Armagh outrages' committed by the newly founded Orange Order in the summer of 1795 cemented an alliance between the Volunteers and the United Irishmen.

The Mission of Eugene Aherne

A witness to these events was Eugene Aherne, who had travelled to Ireland in late summer from Paris and had met with the United Irish leadership as it then was.

Eugene Aherne was born in Kerry in 1748, the family name being O'Heren. He was educated at the Irish College in Paris alongside MacSheehy, Duckett, Murray and others, and embraced the revolution. In 1794, he gained employment with the French government and was sent on a secret mission to Scotland, and two years later he undertook a similar mission to his native country where he was to interview John Keogh and other national leaders. Whether Keogh was a member of the Dublin Society of United Irishmen is unclear. Certainly, no record has been found of his admission or of his participation in its affairs, yet the suspicion remains given his involvement with the Catholic Committee. Aherne would become a friend of Wolfe Tone when he arrived in France and was prominent among the Irish exiles in France who were making renewed efforts to obtain French aid. He later held the rank of captain in the Irish Legion, which was established in 1803 by Napoléon. Miles Byrne noted: 'he spoke French fluently, and had the gay manners of a well-bred Irishman; he was a good patriot, and could not fail to be well received wherever he went'.[8] Such was the man sent to Ireland.

It may well have been Aherne who late in 1795 wrote to Director Lazare Carnot, informing him of the increasing levels of discontent in England, and urging that now was the time to act.[9] Aherne was still in Ireland as the start of 1796, and sent word to the Directory in a letter dated 1 January 1796 that Ireland was impatient for rebellion.[10]

Having travelled in Ireland and England gauging support for an invasion and opinion regarding a French invasion, Aherne was back in France by spring. The Irish Catholics it seemed would welcome the French with open arms as liberators. He sent a second dispatch to the French government dated 27 January in which he sought to activate the plan drafted by Paine in 1792 to send money and 20,000 men, adding that the news received from his agents indicated the Irish were willing to rise as long as the French landed.[11] On the strength of this intelligence, in France 'the organizer of Victory', General Lazare Carnot, and fellow Directors began thinking of an invasion of Ireland once more. Aherne was back in Paris by March.

The Return of Wolfe Tone

Being aware of the level of discontent in Ireland, Adet, the French Ambassador in America, forwarded to France a report from Wolfe Tone who was then living in Philadelphia. The report was clearly written with a view to stimulating French interest in Ireland. Wolfe Tone was naturally enough unaware of Director Carnot's own interest in Ireland and plans already being formulated, as will be demonstrated. The forthright young man was 'chancing his arm' to be part of the émigré community in Paris and to be at the heart of the decision-making operations for an invasion. This highlights the burgeoning of his egomania which demanded he was centre stage and hero of the hour. Wolfe Tone's memorandum arrived in France on 1 October 1795.[12] Archibald Hamilton Rowan sent his own thoughts on the chance of invasion of Ireland, received on 14 December.[13] Wolfe Tone and Rowan's dispatches largely confirmed what the Directory already knew thanks to the good services of Aherne. With support from Adet, Charles Delacroix, the French foreign minister, agreed to both men being granted leave to enter France.[14] Both men set sail for France, and with a French government already once again looking favourably on an invasion in Ireland, on 29 February 1796, Wolfe Tone presented in person his plan for an invasion of Ireland, which he confidently stated would trigger a nationwide uprising:

France, by establishing a free republic in Ireland, would make itself a faithful and grateful ally, a sincere friend and ready to come to its aid on all occasions, a neighbour who, by its situation and by the productions of its soil, would render it essential services.

By detaching Ireland from England, the latter is depriving it of its strongest support, the only one on which it can count for the recruitment of its armies, as well as for the equipment and supply of its fleets.

Not only France, but all the powers of Europe are interested in subduing the arrogance of England, and in circumscribing in just limits this enormous and ever-growing power that it arrogates to itself at sea. The emancipation of Ireland alone can produce this effect.

By adopting the measures proposed in these Memoirs, not only would the English fleets be deprived of their regular resources for their equipment and supply, but it would also be very possible that they would soon see a large part of it swell the Irish navy.

The Irish people are fully united; he is ready to rebel, and waits to act only to have the means.

Not to mention the sound politics and just spirit of revenge which command the French Republic to seek to humiliate a haughty and irreconcilable enemy, it would be a sublime act of generosity and humanity on its part to snatch a foreign nation from the slavery under which it has been groaning for six hundred years. After having emancipated Holland and admitted the Belgian people to the number of his children, his glory lacked only to create in Europe a new free Republic. It is in his interest to take advantage of the opportunity to take half of its resources away from England and make it almost impossible for it to employ those that would remain.

According to all these considerations, I come in the name of justice, of the freedom of my own homeland and of France itself, to beg the French Government to take into consideration the state of Ireland and, in return for the protection of the Republic, to put the country in a position to demonstrate its recognition, to claim its freedom, to humiliate its tyrant, and to resume among the nations of the earth the attitude of independence for which nature has destined it by the fertility of its soil, the nature of its productions, its position, its population and by the happy character of its inhabitants.[15]

For Wolfe Tone, Ireland was ready for revolution but needed help from France. Charles-François Delacroix, the minister for foreign affairs from 3 November 1795–15 July 1797, was already working with Nicholas Madgett senior and documents held in the Archives Nationales in Paris suggest – as will be demonstrated – that Delacroix was not so sure of the passionate young man. France had been planning its own initiative in Ireland, which Wolfe Tone haughtily disregarded. Wolfe Tone was a man who liked to be in charge and for 'things to be done his way'. Wolfe Tone, in his writings, says that he only became aware of French activity in Ireland through a chance meeting with William Duckett. He denounced Duckett as a scoundrel and was opposed to Carnot and inter alia the Directory's mode of subversive warfare and Carnot's plans for retaliatory attacks following the English raids in the Vendée.[16] If the United Irish were to achieve their ambitions, what was needed was co-operation with the French and not to cause rifts between the Irish and the Directory: Wolfe Tone quickly alienated Madgett, Carnot and others who had been 'running the show' since 1792 so he could be centre stage. This is not leadership. Wolfe Tone's narcissistic tendencies, and those of Napper Tandy and the megalomania of Arthur O'Connor, derailed the United Irish project before it began. Ultimately, the United Irish leadership's lack of unity was the cause of their downfall.

No doubt feeling that he was being deliberately sidelined – which was very likely – Wolfe Tone re-submitted his memorandum to the Directory during the middle of March.[17] Unwilling to remain on the sidelines, a week later, Wolfe Tone wrote to General Clarke censuring Carnot's plan regarding Ireland, emphasizing the disadvantages of

Carnot's idea of provoking an insurgent uprising by sending a small body of troops and agent provocateurs to 'Chouanize Ireland'. Wolfe Tone stated that only a full-scale invasion would liberate Ireland, and added that he did not relish the 'horrible mode of warfare'.[18] What Carnot and the Directory felt to this condemnation of their plan which had been in gestation since late 1795 is probably all too easy to imagine. Despite being at loggerheads with the Directory, Wolfe Tone demanded money for his lodgings in Paris.[19] By late spring an uneasy truce between the two Parisian factions seems to have developed. What was happening in Ireland at this time is impossible to untangle, so it cannot be determined what level of support there was for the two conflicting methods of liberating the island from British rule.

Scotland Forever

As well as Irish radicals, the French found willing allies in the United Scotsmen who were an extension of the Scottish constitutional radicalism of the early 1790s. If one stands on the Scottish west coast on a clear day, you can see northern Ireland, and therefore it is no surprise that the influence and involvement of United Irishmen in the development of the United Scotsmen was considerable. David Black, a Dunfermline weaver and United Scotsmen member, believed that 'persons from Ireland ... were the original founders of the Society of United Scotsmen'.[20] As well as electoral reform, the United Scotsmen advocated a republic. The 'Pike Plot' of June 1794 demonstrated to the British Crown the seriousness of the radicals, intentions in Scotland.[21] Poor harvests, grain shortages and price rises lead to sporadic outbursts of violence in Scotland and became 'the recruiting sergeant' for the United Scotsmen. By the end of 1795 it was estimated that there were more members of the United Scotsmen than the actual Scottish electorate – about 3,000. If France was to invade Ireland, a diversion in Scotland would prevent the British Army from counterattacking in Ireland with overwhelming strength. The Scots now became part of a 'game of chess' that was being played out in England, Ireland, Scotland and France to topple King George.

Despite Wolfe Tone's pleadings and desire to be 'in charge', at the end of March Delacroix dispatched Jean Mengaud with orders to travel to England to contact radical groups and report back on public opinion and the economic conditions in England. Furthermore, his mission brief was also to travel to Ireland and gather intelligence on the Defenders. Mengaud was in England by April 1796.[22] Presumably Delacroix wanted more recent information than Wolfe Tone could provide, as he had not been in Ireland for over a year, and if the

French were to support the United Irish, quite rightly, the French needed up-to-date information. As Aherne had noted, France needed to be kept informed of the changing situation in Ireland as the famine and disturbances in England were seemingly over. Concern that the revolutionary opportunity had passed was uppermost in Delacroix's mind.

A report arrived from agent Mengaud on 8 April. He said that he had obtained a passport and travelled to London and Ireland as well as Scotland to link up with radical groups. Overall, he noted, the outlook was positive; the revolutionary mood was still growing in all three countries, and in Ireland the Defenders were making progress in organizing themselves and obtaining arms as a militia. However, he noted the Defenders needed money and arms.[23]

The Aborted Mission of Eugene Aherne

Factionalisim among the differing political groups in Paris now reared its ugly head. Madgett senior, sitting behind his desk at the Ministère de la Marine, clearly felt sidelined by recent events and urged that one of his operatives be sent back to Ireland. Madgett, like Wolfe Tone, was a large personality, who had to be 'centre stage'. If Ireland was to be liberated it was to be via his actions and secret agents. For Madgett Aherne was to be sent back to Ireland with all possible speed and on 3 March he petitioned Minister Delacroix to this end. Aherne's mission brief was that he would visit Edinburgh to link up with the 'society there' and then travel on to Ireland.[24] On finding no support from Delacroix, Madgett petitioned Carnot directly to send Aherne back to Scotland.[25]

The grudge between Madgett and the French Foreign Ministry brought him into an alliance of necessity with Wolfe Tone. At Madgett's behest, Wolfe Tone petitioned Carnot that Aherne was to travel to Ireland, to link up with Oliver Bond, John Keogh, Thomas Russell, Samuel Neilson and Dr William James MacNeven among others. Aherne was 'to ascertain the aims and resources' of the Defenders, to identify if they were solely Catholic and if the Defenders had an alliance with the largely Presbyterian – Unitarian – United Irish as well as to establish regular communications with France.[26]

While this wrangling was taking place, William Duckett re-enters the story. His whereabouts over the previous year are not known. He was in Ireland during the Jackson fiasco, and may well have been in Ireland since 1794. He was certainly in Ireland at New Year 1796 as he reported in February that, having toured Ireland, he felt that 'the spirit of the [Irish] people is favourable to all republican undertakings'.[27] Duckett, also a 'big personality', brought yet another layer of complexity to Irish and Parisian politicking. The lack of unity and sense of purpose was the Achilles heel of the United Irishmen. No one man was leader, no single plan was agreed upon. Wolfe Tone, Madgett and Duckett barely tolerated one another.

Despite the deepening rift becoming evident in the Irish émigré leadership in Paris, Carnot continued developing his ideas. In an undated document – but clearly from early 1796 – Carnot reveals plans for an audacious guerrilla campaign in England and Ireland, namely 'Chouanization'. To 'Chouanize' Ireland would create a situation of immense internal conflict, the term referring to the Chouan counter-revolutionaries in the west of France where civil war raged from roughly 1793–1800 backed by British arms and gold. Unable to invade France, as noted earlier, the British Crown supported the insurgent forces in France, with both sides committing what would now be considered genocide and war crimes. The British Crown's hatred of the French Republic resulted in it supporting insurgent forces recruited from French Royalists and radicalized Catholics to cause chaos, murder and mayhem in France. Little wonder that Carnot's hatred of Britain grew with every dispatch from the Vendée of atrocities funded by British money. Carnot's 'Chouanization' therefore aimed to create reciprocal violence and bitter civil strife in England, Scotland and Ireland. The other benefit of the chaos would be to divert the military resources from defending England, if the Irish situation did not force them to sue for a more permanent peace.[28] The plan was similar to that outlined by Hoche in 1793. General Lazare Carnot reported: '… this plan is limited at present to worrying the government, to occupying part of its forces, to returning to it the evil done to us by the *Chouannerie* organized and fed by it in the midst of the Republic, and thus to forcing it to desire and provoke the cessation of a war …'.[29] Carnot hoped that random attacks in England by either home-grown sympathizers or a handful of French troops who would have landed unnoticed would cause disorder and insurrection, and 'tie down' thousands of troops, thus limiting the number of soldiers available to fight in Europe or defend Ireland. As part of the plans, agents were to: 'To announce to the people war against the castles and peace at the thatched cottages … To talk a lot about freedom, but to have positively only the project of destroying and not of edifying …'.[30] The irony of fighting militant Catholics and Royalists in the Vendée and then backing militant Catholics in Ireland seems to have been lost on Carnot. However, Carnot was perfectly correct, for the invasion to have any hope of success, 'hearts and minds' had to be won over. William Duckett concurred:

A few words about a descent in Ireland. Today there is talk of a descent into my country. Would you like to allow me to share with you some ideas on this subject. I will speak as a free man.

I repeat what I have already said to the current government. There is only one moral force that can destroy British influence in Ireland ... It cannot take place unless it is supported by the people of Ireland and their true friends ... Above all, it is necessary to enlighten the public mind on your views, and it is by means of some patriotic newspapers that you will achieve this goal.[31]

He repeated this view in a letter dated 30 May:

There is no people today more willing to a revolution than the Irish people ... Its independence must come from outside. Ireland does contain the force necessary for this great operation, but it is necessary that the lever that gives movement to this force finds a point of support outside its home. The French people, in saving Ireland, must base its independence on the main supporters of its own freedom ... can the oppressed love his oppressor?[32]

Duckett was concerned that the French, once they had helped liberate his homeland, would in essence come to dominate the country as much as the British Crown were doing: a very legitimate concern. But for Duckett to write as he did it seems likely that the Directory was well advanced with plans to land a force in Ireland.

The factionalisim discussed previously now reared its ugly head once more. The choice of Aherne to travel to Ireland was not accepted by the Directory, possibly because Aherne was already compromised by his closeness to Wolfe Tone, both men were lodging in the same house. At the same time, Henri Clarke – Irish by descent, who would be Napoléon's Minister for War and elevated to Marshal of France in later years – wanted to take more active participation in the liberation of his 'homeland'. Clarke, rather predictably, insisted that his cousin, Richard O'Shee, was to go to Ireland as a secret agent in Aherne's place. Clarke used his influence to ensure that Carnot backed his recommendation on 28 March.[33] Wolfe Tone was aghast at the change of plan. Madgett senior's thoughts on this matter, or those of Duckett, are not known. O'Shee had become attached to the 'Army of England' and seems initially to have been concerned with obtaining maps of England, Ireland and Scotland.[34]

On 7 May, Wolfe Tone demanded to know why Aherne had not left for Ireland in a terse letter to General Clarke. Wolfe Tone also curtly told the Directory of his importance in the United Irish movement, and the vital role he could play in any intervention in Ireland.[35] No recorded reply can be found in the French archives. Does this mean that Wolfe Tone was still very much 'sidelined' by the Directory? On 15 May he asked for a certificate of good conduct from General Clarke in the name of James Smith,[36] and sought a residency permit in Paris the following day.[37] Wolfe Tone's concerns over the lack of action were raised by the Directors on 27 May 1796. However, the Directory's reply was probably not what Wolfe Tone had anticipated. Most likely the squabbling and factionalism had not gone unnoticed: did the Directory want to be heavily involved in internal power struggles over who would lead the liberation of Ireland? Rather than applaud his efforts, Carnot and his fellow Directors questioned Wolfe Tone's information-gathering methodology:

> The Directory, informed, Citizen Minister, that Citizen Aherne has not yet left Paris to go to Ireland and that he is detained there by accounting details ... desirous of seeing the accomplishment of the mission with which citizen Aherne was charged and is of too great an interest to be deferred any longer, casts their eyes on citizen Richard O'Shée, retired battalion commander and who, by his living in Ireland and England, can be of great service. This officer will present himself to you without delay to receive your orders, and you will give him all the means he will need to fulfil the delicate mission which must be entrusted to him.
>
> You will give him the instructions which were to be given to citizen Aherne and you will attach to them those which the Directory has had drafted and which established requests for information absolutely opposed to those communicated by citizen Wolfe-Tone and which can be collected from English newspapers. The documents which he will provide can only lead to the knowledge of the true state of things in Ireland, and that is why the Directory had made outline some bases of instructions absolutely contrary to the accounts which were given by the citizen Wolfe-Tone. It is not useless to observe you, Citizen Minister, that this Irishman, who has a great deal of wit and whom the Directory intends to employ, has come to know some provisions which were to remain hidden until such time as the Directory deems it appropriate to entrust them to him. He even appears to have become somewhat intimate with Citizen Aherne, which might have been prejudicial, in view of the necessity which exists for the person to be sent to Ireland to be in some way on guard against Citizen Wolfe-Tone's reports, in order to better verify its certainty.
>
> Citizen Richard O'Shée should not be confused with Citizen Robert O'Shée, whose morality seems at least equivocal and who does not enjoy a good reputation in Paris.
>
> It will be necessary for Citizen Wolfe-Tone to tell Citizen O'Shée the names of the principal defenders.[38]

Clearly the rift between Wolfe Tone and the Directory was hardening. Wolfe Tone and Aherne, as mentioned earlier, shared lodgings and were now closely associated with one another, so much so that the Directory felt an independent agent was needed to produce impartial information. Yet, it also seems that Wolfe Tone was not going to be ignored forever by Carnot, clearly, he was a man who could be of use to the French. But it also seems that the Directory had not yet fully made its mind up about Wolfe Tone. The fear, it seems, was that Aherne would merely confirm the views of Wolfe Tone and not give reliable and accurate information. The Directory also felt that the mission was deeply flawed, and that Wolfe Tone through 'politicking' had obtained 'top-secret' information about the Directory's motivation in Ireland. The Directory and Wolfe Tone were working on the same project but pulling in different directions.

Factionalism was robbing the French plans of any sense of unity. Someone, somewhere had prevented the release of funds and a passport for Aherne and O'Shee to travel to Ireland – presumably Carnot and Delacroix. Was this to deliberately sideline Wolfe Tone – to ensure that O'Shee was dispatched or had Carnot simply thought better of sending any agent because of his concerns over impartiality? Despite misgivings, O'Shee finally travelled to Ireland on 4 June to report on the Defenders, to learn if they were 'Catholic fanatics' or a genuine revolutionary group uniting both Protestants and Catholics: this had been the concern of the French since 1793. O'Shee's mission was to build an alliance with the Irish radicals, promise 10,000 troops and 20,000 stands of arms to encourage an Irish insurrection.[39]

To Wolfe Tone's great relief, he was now employed by Carnot, but in a junior capacity as a propagandist. When O'Shee left for Ireland, he carried with him copies of proclamations written in French and English by Wolfe Tone:

At length the time is arrived when a friend to the Liberty and Independence of Ireland, may venture to speak the truth ... Six hundred years of oppression and slavery have passed in melancholy succession over our father's heads and our own, during which period we have been visited by every evil, which tyranny could devise and cruelty execute ... The pride and arrogance of England have at length called down upon her head the tardy and lingering justice, which her manifold crimes have so long provoked ... I see a new order of things commencing in Europe. The stupendous revolution, which has taken place in France; the unparalleled succession of events, which have, in defiance of the united efforts of all the despots of Europe, established that mighty republic on the broad and firm basis of equal rights, liberties and laws ... it is

England, who starves your manufacturers, to drive them into her fleets and armies; it is England, who keeps your wretched peasantry half-fed, half-clothed, miserable and despised, defrauded of their just rights, as human beings, and reduced, if the innate spirit of your country did not support them, as it were by a miracle, below the level of the beasts of the field; it is England who buys your legislators, to betray you, and pays them by money levied on yourselves; it is England, who foments and perpetuates, as far as in her lies, the spirit of religious dissention among you, and that labours to keep asunder Irishman from Irishman, because that in your cordial Union among yourselves, she sees clearly the downfall of her usurpation, and the establishment of your liberties ... we have now all we wanted: allies, arms, and ammunition, stores, artillery, disciplined troops, the best and bravest in Europe, besides the countless thousands of our brave and hardy peasantry, who will flock to the standard of their country. The sword is drawn, the Rubicon is passed, and we have no retreat; there remains now no alternative ... We must conquer England and her adherents ... my countrymen, you will embrace your liberty with transport, and for your chains you will break them on the beads of your oppressors; you will show for the honour of Ireland, that you have sensibility to feel, and courage to resent, and means to revenge your wrongs; one short, one glorious effort, and your liberty is established. NOW, OR NEVER; NOW, AND FOR EVER![40]

How effective the propaganda war was is unknown. O'Shee carried proclamations addressed to Irish sailors in the Royal Navy encouraging them to mutiny.[41] He also had printed proclamations and handbills which aimed to persuade Catholics in the Irish Militia to desert and join the Defenders and these were to be pasted on the walls of towns and villages.[42] O'Shee had a message from the 'Committee of the Independent Army' to the French émigrés in England urging support for the Irish invasion.[43] Finally, O'Shee carried an address to all émigrés urging them to support the French Republic and rise in revolt.[44]

He left Paris for Hamburg on 4 June, and seemingly nothing more was heard from him.

The day before O'Shee left, Wolfe Tone demanded an interview with Lazare Carnot.[45] The interview never materialized. As June progressed Wolfe Tone heard rumours that the Directory had committed itself to landing troops in Ireland. In a brusque letter to Carnot, Wolfe Tone demanded to know if there was any truth to the word on the streets that 15,000 men were to be sent to Ireland.[46] The rumour was indeed true: clearly the French plans did not include Wolfe Tone, which suggests he was still outside the decision-making loop, and he was making trouble to show himself as a leader or even going as far as getting written confirmation that he was not involved, so if the plan was unsuccessful, he would not be 'tainted' by the failure.

Enter Fitzgerald

At the same time as Wolfe Tone was becoming increasingly agitated, the situation facing the Directory became ever more complicated. Edward Fitzgerald and Arthur O'Connor had made their way to Hamburg, where O'Connor had arrived on 5 June. O'Connor was a key member of the United Irish executive and is a prominent figure in this story. The two men reported to the Directory via Barthélemy, the French minister in Basle, Switzerland, to outline their objectives for an invasion of Ireland. Barthélemy reported that:

> They have given me a great deal of information in order to prove to me that never has the time been more favourable to restore Ireland's full independence and to separate it from England, which would be a mortal blow to it. This truth is indisputable. But the party of the discontented, which is very numerous and very powerful, needs help and the help of the French Republic to bring about an outburst that would be very useful to us. Although I was struck by the correctness of their observations and data, of which, at my request, they have drawn very quickly before my eyes the attached overview, I cannot give them back to you. You can't write about projects like that. You have to talk to each other and explain yourself. Therefore, they extremely aspire to be within reach of opening up to the Executive Board or to the people it deems appropriate to establish to hear them, etc.[47]

Two days later Barthélemy wrote to Minister Delacroix that O'Connor and Fitzgerald were eager to make a personal representation to the Directory and enter France, adding that:

> They feel that the French government may, at first sight, desire and demand that before manifesting itself on the shores of Ireland, that insurrection first breaks out in Ireland. They cautioned that this was an impossibility as people have no weapons, especially in the south of this kingdom, the English government having taken all those of individuals in order to avert danger ... The time is fast approaching when the Executive Directory will be able to take revenge for all the atrocities committed by England against the Republic. Everything that happens in Europe tends to facilitate the separation of Ireland from the body of the British Empire. The establishment of Irish independence will crush England.[48]

Barthélemy's dispatches to Paris fortified Carnot's planning with the Directory, yet it is undeniable that Arthur O'Connor's egomania was to wreak havoc within the United Irishmen in Ireland, Paris and later Hamburg. A gifted speaker, he won support for the movement, which he sought to harness to bolster his own megalomania. Yet, for all his faults, it seems that Fitzgerald and O'Connor were key persons in the events of 1796, linking French plans to Ireland.

Chapter 11

ENGLAND AND SCOTLAND

Thoughts of a simultaneous landing in Ireland, England and Scotland came to figure large in French planning. General Lazare Hoche now enters the story. He was a gifted and charismatic soldier who had made his reputation in the vicious insurgency in the Vendée.

On 19 June the Directory confirmed the rumour that Wolfe Tone had heard days earlier: 16,000 men under the command of generals Humbert and Quantin would land in Ireland during September. The same day as the Directory confirmed its intentions regarding Ireland, the war minister received a report that the United Irishmen, who were ready to rise up and remove the 'odious English', had been secretly armed and were willing to give their support to any French troops who landed in Ireland. On the following day Hoche was named commander-in-chief.[1]

Jean Joseph Amable Humbert now appears and becomes a constant character throughout the story. Born in La Coâre Saint-Nabord, outside Remiremont Vosges, on 22 August 1767, he began making a living as a rabbit hunter. He was appointed a sergeant in the National Guard of Lyon at the start of the Revolution in July 1789. Three years later he joined the 13th Battalion of Volunteers of Vosges and that August was promoted to captain and then lieutenant colonel in the battalion. In April 1794 Humbert was made general of brigade and employed in the Army of the Coasts of Brest. The following year he fought under the command of Lazare Hoche in the Army of the Rhine and Moselle, hence his involvement with what was being planned for Ireland. Trusted and known by Hoche, his appointment was clearly facilitated by him. Hoche and Carnot planned an ambitious two-pronged assault: the French would land small detachments of troops at different points in England where they would link up with the United Englishmen. Hoche argued in favour of landing men on the coast of Wales to burn

Chester, Liverpool and Bristol to begin a 'Chouanization' operation as a diversion. A major invasion force would sail for Ireland and link up with the United Irishmen.[2] Navigating waters that had sunk the Armada in 1588 to Wales or Ireland passing Scotland or going around Cornwall posed a major risk. The presence of the Royal Navy close to Brittany and Norman coastal towns dictated this mode of attack despite its dangers. With the British Army tied down defending the coastline and containing the United Englishmen and French forces, the success of the Irish invasion was considered to be a foregone conclusion.[3]

Just days after the Directory had agreed to the invasion, on 23 June 1796 the Irish and United Scots emissaries in Paris proposed a two-pronged attack. It was impossible to attack the English south coast due to Royal Navy dockyards at Plymouth and Portsmouth, while Scotland was largely unguarded and ready for rebellion. The report suggested that a raid on the south coast would be profitable in drawing the British Army to the south leaving Scotland and Ireland exposed. Gunships were to target Dover and Brighton, armed with heavy calibre weapons and 'mortars to firebomb the towns and sink shipping whilst 200 ships sailed from Dunkirk, Texel and Rochefort'.[4] A British spy, French émigré Puisaye, reported that by the start of July an Irish Officer was with Hoche.[5] Who was this? Wolfe Tone had not arrived yet. Was this Lewines or perhaps Duckett?

On 12 July Hoche took command of 15,000 troops which he was given free range to select from the Armée des Côtes-de-l'Océan and ensure that a revolution took place in Ireland.[6] On Bastille Day 1796, Hoche asked 'for precise instructions on the conduct to be followed when the insurrection in Ireland breaks out'.[7] Based on later events, it is certain that he received these orders. Key to the revolution would be the United Irishmen.

To ensure that both the Scots and Irish were kept informed of planning in France, soon after two delegates from the Belfast United Irishmen, Joseph Cuthbert and Thomas Potts, were sent to Scotland. They carried with them a copy of the new constitution of the United Irishmen 'for the inspection and approbation of the Scots'.[8] The United Irish delegates reported that 'the Scotch were willing and ready to act with the Friends of Liberty in Ireland'. However, at much the same time, another delegate to Scotland, from Ulster, reported that 'the Scotch were not possessed of sufficient energy'. Despite the conflicting nature of these accounts, both provide evidence that the Scots would act with the Irish when the time came.[9]

Indeed, this is what a French agent told Carnot. The last that was heard of Eugene Aherne was that he was prohibited from travelling as a secret agent to Ireland and Scotland. Clearly, key archive documents are missing as remarkably Aherne reported to the Directory on 29 August that he had returned from a successful mission to Scotland, and told Carnot that the Scots were ready to rise once the French confirmed their intentions.[10]

Richard O'Shee now suddenly re-appears in the story, when, on 22 August, he was entrusted with a mission to deliver the equivalent of 10,000 francs to Ireland to fund the Defenders.[11] Where had he been since the start of June? Had he ever arrived in Ireland or simply remained in Hamburg? Or had he been to Ireland, reported back to Clarke in the War Ministry and been assigned a new mission? Three months would have been sufficient for such a journey. The lack of archive sources here leaves a question that cannot be answered. Be that as it may, O'Shee, once he was in Ireland, was to promise the Irish leadership that 10,000 French troops and 20,000 muskets would be sent as soon as the Irish rose in rebellion. Furthermore, he was instructed to study the Defenders, to discover if they were only Catholics or if they represented a broader religious base that encompassed Presbyterians. O'Shee was also tasked to discover what form of government would be welcomed in Ireland.[12] In a letter dated 29 August Hoche deplored the French government's decision to send O'Shee to link up with the United Irishmen.[13] O'Shee then 'drops out of history again' with his cousin Henri Clarke fearing that he had absconded with the money.[14]

Perhaps the unreliability of O'Shee explains why Lazare Carnot sent a young wine merchant from Bordeaux, Jean Berthonneau, ostensibly to report on émigré activities in Hamburg at the start of August. Was Berthonneau sent to Hamburg to find the absconded O'Shee? Perhaps. Carnot instructed Berthonneau that: 'the aim of your mission will be to assist in the establishment of a *chouanerie* in revenge for the atrocities committed daily by England on French Territory'.[15] Paid for by the French secret service, Berthonneau was to arrive in England and establish a network of agents across the country, using the radicals and 'disaffected' to organise sporadic revolts, promote popular unrest at the bread shortages, food prices, low wages and other grievances and turn the workers against their masters. His task was to cause chaos and recruit like-minded Englishmen to the cause.[16] If Berthonneau could attract the English radicals to his cause – which he seemingly did, he could draw on a network of 72 societies with almost total national coverage and a membership of perhaps 10,000 or more.[17] A formidable army in waiting.

Jean Berthonneau was dispatched to England travelling under the name Roger Fils: Berthoneau is a mystery wrapped in an enigma.

Fils reported to the Directory in a letter of 27 August that there was a spirit for revolution in London and England and if a force of 15,000 men landed in England the anarchy facing the British Crown could be complete. John Horne Tooke 'was a special man, who would lead the people in a united effort with the movements of the French Army,' reported Berthonneau to the Directory. He added:

> The Catholics in Ireland, and the Presbyterians in Scotland and in England are fanatics, jealous of the pre-eminence and the riches of the Anglicans. They are essentially revolutionaries: they are essentially enemies of the current mode of government ... if there is not a revolution it won't be for the lack of effort by the Presbyterians on their part or the Catholics. They are both same.[18]

In England at least, and perhaps Scotland, for Presbyterian, we must read Unitarian. By the 1770s, the liberal English Presbyterians had largely adopted Unitarian theology and Whig politics, as noted earlier. For good reason Fergus Whelan on the Unitarian element in the United Irishmen called his book *Dissent into Treason*. Berthonneau engaged with the London Corresponding Society and John Thewell, as well as other like-minded radicals in London. It was through this connection that Scottish national Dr Robert Watson, the society's president, enters the story. So too John Ashley, the secretary of the society, and the two Binns brothers. All four men were committed to French intervention in English, Irish and Scottish politics, and would help complete the transformation of reformist associations into radical republican organizations.

Watson was born in Elgin in 1746. He was a professional solider who had been wounded in the American War of independence, 'which gave him, on his retirement, the rank of a colonel, and some land, which he sold soon after'. Returning to Scotland from America, he graduated as MD, and then settled in London. He was secretary to Lord George Gordon at the time of the riots of 1780, and reports he was 'intimate with Washington'.[19] He was arrested for conspiracy in 1794 and languished in Newgate Gaol, held without trial.

The Invasion that Never was
By August 1796 plans were being formulated to make landings in England. Rather than send a large force, the Foreign Ministry planned to send a small force of 10 frigates carrying 5,000 men commanded by General Quantin. The first target was to be Jersey and Guernsey. However, Quantin was instructed that if the circumstances prevailed,

the fleet was to break out by sailing to the Netherlands, and then head into the North Sea. A landing was to be made at Yarmouth, the harbour burnt, warehouses destroyed and as much devastation inflicted as possible. A second force was to land at the mouth of the River Tyne, burn as much shipping as they could and cause havoc on their march to Newcastle, where the soldiers would link up with a party of republicans, who would have been inspired to rise in insurrection by the landing of the French, and burn and destroy as many warehouses and coal mines as they could. Machinery such as pumps and steam engines was to be smashed. A third force was to enter the River Humber and carry out a similar mission in Hull and Yorkshire.[20] Clearly, the French were confident of swelling their ranks from among the starving poor and disaffected: these men would be the United Englishmen.

Agent Berthonneau was still in London. From there, using the name Fils, he wrote to the French government at the beginning of September about the sentiment in England and Ireland for a French invasion from London and that the Irish in London would rise as soon as the French landed.[21] His activities are now obscure: who he met is lost to history until he arrived in Worcester in late September using the name 'John Brown'. In sleepy Worcester, ironically known as a centre of loyalism for its stance during the English Civil War, 'Brown' met a contact of the late Revd William Jackson as well as a party from the *'révolutionnaire anglais'*. Unfortunately, the names of who he met or what exactly this group was have not been recorded. It is possible this was a gathering of Irish and English radicals, like the group Talleyrand dealt with in 1792. From the letter it is certain that the Revd Jackson was not working alone and was networking with radical groups and no doubt other agents. It also seems clear that despite Jackson's mission being fatally compromised, the French never knew, otherwise they would not have linked up with the same network. It can only be assumed that the contact was an associate of John Hurford Stone, John Horn Tooke or John Thelwall based on later evidence. 'Brown' also met with leadership from Ireland, a 'Colonel' identified as Saint-Clair, and representatives of Simon Butler.[22] According to a British agent writing in April 1795, Butler was a member of the clandestine 'Strugglers' Club', which consisted of leading United Irishmen, and was reported as inciting Catholics to riot after the dismissal of Earl Fitzwilliam.[23] Butler frequently expressed his contempt for the timidity of the United Irishmen and had met with Revd Jackson in 1794, but had avoided any entanglement in his scheme by treating his invasion proposals as a joke. By this stage he seems to have been living in London. Whatever

Butler was planning, he does not seem to have been in contact with Fitzgerald and the Irish leadership. Yet, given the very nature of the United Irishmen, the lack of archive papers does not mean Butler was an integral part of event planning and had changed his mind over the French proposal to invade. Possibly he had come to the view that without French help Ireland would not be free. The identity of 'Saint-Clair' is not known.

It was clear from Berthonneau that by summer 1796 the London Corresponding Society had become revolutionized – it would seem largely down to Irishman John Binns – and that agitation against the Test and Corporation Acts by Unitarians and other Dissenters could be harnessed into a revolutionary army in England. It was from Berthonneau's meeting in London with Dr Robert Watson, secretary of the London Corresponding Society, and others that the first glimmers of the Naval Mutinies of 1797 are seen to emerge. It is beyond reasonable doubt that tens of thousands of British subjects – mostly it seems in the North of England in Manchester, Stockport, Halifax, Wakefield, Leeds, Bradford, Sheffield and other places – now crossed a line: they were prepared to take up arms to help a foreign power invade their country to ensure that their political ambitions were met. About such activities Terry Crowdy, a noted Napoléonic scholar, comments:

> Napoléon used radicals in Italy to cause all sorts of mayhem in 96/97. Sedition is a well-known technique of state craft. If the opportunity presented itself, I am sure he would have indulged it. There's no real desire to 'liberate' people, just to cause mayhem. Napoléon immediately sold out the Piedmontese Jacobins in 1796. The poor souls had no idea the French did not want a Jacobin style revolutionary government on their doorstep.[24]

In September, a secret agent named Moyen reported that British Ambassador Lord Malmsbury had denounced Lord Fitzgerald and O'Shee and other English subjects residing in France, and made it crystal clear to the Directory that the Royal Navy and the British Army were too strong 'for France to be able to attempt a landing'. Carnot and Berthonneau had reached the same conclusion, arguing Ireland offered the best hope of success and in order to keep the seaways clear of the Royal Navy, this would be achieved with a 'raid of destruction against Sheerness and Chatham, the ports and shipyards on the Medway'.[25] Moyen sketched out a full proposal for the Directory and this included a raid against Portsmouth dockyard.[26]

Chapter 12

PLANNING INVASION

After months of delay, infighting and the lack of any clear objectives about invading Ireland, on 16 September the Directory ordered:

> The Directory, wanting to put an end to the audacity and perfidy of the cruellest enemy of the Republic and use a legitimate reprisal … An army of fifteen thousand men, under the orders of the General Hoche, will be landed in Ireland as soon as possible. A corps of five thousand men, commanded by General Quantin, will also be landed on the east coast of England.[1]

The attack on England was to distract Crown forces and allow Hoche to land in Ireland and form an Irish Republic. Once Quantin had landed, the fleet would return to Brest to carry reinforcements to Ireland and England, which would include General Humbert at the head of 5,000 troops headed for England. Humbert was told specifically not to approach Scotland, but to threaten London. Colonel Tate was ordered to land in Bristol with a few thousand men taken from the prisons across France as well as 'and foreigners, refugees or deserters' to cause havoc. They were instructed to burn down warehouses, factories and inflict as much damage as possible. Quantin was to command the 21e and 139e demi-brigades.[2] Quantin demanded maps and charts of England from Clarke.[3] However, the commanding officer of the 21e demi-brigade refused to serve alongside the Corps Francs led by Tate, demanded their owed wages, refused to obey orders to embark and fostered mutiny in the troops assembled at Brest.[4] Thanks to the calm of the soldiers and the agreement of Quantin, General Liébert, commander of the Department of the North, and an emissary sent by Hoche, Lieutenant Muskein, the mutiny was suppressed.[5] British gold seems to have been behind the mutiny. The French naval base at Brest was under observation from secret agents working for the émigré spymaster Prince de Bouillon. These men were all Royalist Catholics and were armed by the British Crown to burn down factories and warehouses and to subvert soldiers and sailors. In the wake of the mutiny, Bouillon informed London that Hoche had taken action to prevent English agents gaining access to the base by increasing surveillance at the port.[6] General Hoche was perfectly correct in his suspicion that the mutiny was funded by the English.[7] The delay caused by agents working for the British Crown meant that the window of good weather for the attacking force to sail in was lost. In a war of subterfuge and secret agents, the British were winning. Despite these setbacks, Quantin planned to sail on 12 October 1796.

However, before the departure date arrived, Admiral Bruix, who was placed at the head of the invasion fleet, reported in October he was short of men and money and that the sailors were demoralized. For the admiral, now was the wrong time to sail.[8] He was correct. The North Sea in winter is treacherous, and any invasion force leaving the French coast would be at the mercy of Atlantic storms. However, attacking at the least opportune time gave the French the advantage of surprise to some degree.

On 1 November, it was formalized that the French were to sail to Bantry Bay, and a diversion attack on England was to follow.[9] Hoche reluctantly agreed, and insisted he would lead the 'Advance Guard'.[10] General Humbert was to command the troops sent to England.[11] Lewines reported in November that the Irish, if led by men such as Arthur O'Connor, Drennan and Archibald Hamilton Rowan, would rise up in support of the French and the United Irish.[12] Tellingly, there was no mention of Wolfe Tone as a candidate to lead Ireland.

The Mission of Bernard MacSheehy

In order to confirm Lewines' report, Hoche demanded an emissary be sent to join his forces with the Irish: he chose Bernard MacSheehy, who had been sent to link up with the United Irishmen from France two years earlier.

MacSheehy was born in Ireland on 2 December 1774, the son of Bernard MacSheehy and the fourth generation of his family – which had roots in County Kerry – to serve in the French Army. He was orphaned when young, and was brought up by his uncle, Jean Baptiste MacSheehy, a doctor to the king. Shortly after the September massacres, Bernard denounced to the Girondist faction perhaps to ingratiate himself with the Jacobins.[13] Bernard was a fee-paying student at the Irish College in Paris when the Revolution began, and, as mentioned before, associated

89

with Lord Edward Fitzgerald at White's Hotel. When he joined the French Army is unclear. He was appointed to the staff of General Félix Dumuy and was to have been an interpreter on his planned expedition to the East Indies in May 1794. His direct involvement with Madgett and the Jackson plot is difficult to confirm, but he presented a petition to the French government on behalf of the Irish on 17 May 1794.[14] For two years he was secretary to General Jacques Hatry, commander of Paris. In August he presented a report via Madgett to Clarke about Ireland, signed by Eugene Aherne and John Sullivan, 'ancient professor of mathematics at La Flèche and Fitzsimons a former capuchin monk', and noted that he was Hatry's secretary.[15] Fitzsimons was another secret agent in the employ of France and an Irish émigré, and, like William Duckett, fell foul of Wolfe Tone. Fitzsimons had been one of Lebrun's agents and had travelled to Ireland in 1793. In April 1796 he was tasked with travelling to Ireland, ostensibly to carry out the mission that had been given to Aherne and then O'Shee. In fact, Aherne had travelled to Scotland – on whose orders? – and O'Shee had disappeared with 10,000 francs, or so it seemed. Wolfe Tone, always scathing of others – and especially those who were not in his personal circle, described Fitzsimons as a 'damned Dunce … a blockhead'.[16] Wolfe Tone's bitterness was perhaps a result of not being involved in the decision-making process; he complained bitterly about 'the idiots from the ministry'.

MacSheehy served with the Army of the Moselle at the siege of Charleroi and also with the Army of the Sambre and Meuse in winter 1795–6. In March 1796, Hatry was named commander of the 17th military division and commander-in-chief of the Army of the Interior after General Bonaparte was reassigned to the Army of Italy. Six months later the Army of the Interior was disbanded. Perhaps this was why at this point, with his interest in espionage and Irish affairs, he was attached as an interpreter to the French force led by Jean Joseph Humbert and thus came to the attention of Lazare Hoche and Wolfe Tone. The latter regarded him as a 'blockhead' which seems rather unlikely given his later career as well as Hoche's glowing commendation of 28 January 1797. General Louis Chérin noted: 'I cannot praise enough in favourable terms his talents and Republican zeal of this officer who was charged by General Hoche with a very difficult and important mission'.[17] He was promoted to battalion commander in recompense for the valuable service he had rendered France. MacSheehy recorded:

General Hoche requested that I joined his staff in the quality of captain; this general as charged with the command of the expedition to Ireland, and I was to provide intelligence from the leaders of the partisans of

Independence on the Island ... I replied that this mission was delicate and difficult, and aged just 18 years with little experience and judgement in the matter I sailed from Brest and debarked at Portsmouth; I made my way to London where one of my companions on the journey, a messenger for the King, charged me to carry documents to the Vice Roy of Ireland.[18]

MacSheehy clearly entered the murky world of espionage, and in working for the British Crown had a robust cover story to get to Ireland. Unlike Duckett, MacSheehy's loyalty was never questioned, so it must be assumed it was never in doubt. From his letter to Hoche, MacSheehy tells us that he left Brest on 7 November on the American ship *Washington*, and first passed through the Isle of Wight and thence to London, where he stopped for four days, and then went to Dublin where he arrived on the 27th, having travelled via Holyhead. He met Oliver Bond, William James MacNeven and Richard McCormick from whom he obtained information on the state of the government's forces and of the pro-French party, as well as advice on the policy France should adopt towards Ireland. He informed the United Irish that the French would land at Lough Swilly in two waves: the first comprising 5,000 men with arms for 40,000 men and the second 12–16,000 men with 50,000 muskets. The garrison of Ireland he estimated as 45,000, and added that 20,000 Scottish fencibles and 25,000 militia made up the bulk of the forces, the majority of which he was told were Defenders. He reported to France that there were 10,000 fencibles in Dublin and 5,000 in Belfast.[19] He added that if the cavalry arrived dismounted, it would be easy enough to round up 6,0000 horses.[20] He wrote to General Hoche:

I have the greatest difficulty in gaining their trust and persuading them that I am Ireland's friend. However, I managed to do so by dint of steps and explanations. They told me that the tyranny exerted on Ireland was at its height, and that people of all ranks could no longer bear them; that the French would not fail to be well received there, and that we were only waiting for this moment to interfere and to destroy everything that held the English Government in Ireland; whereas the United Irishmen association was taking on new increases every day; that the north was filled with their supporters and that several of them were already widespread in the west and south; whereas most of the militias had already taken an oath to support the people and join the French; that nothing should be feared of the cavalry composed of the yeomen.[21]

Having done his duty, MacSheehy left Dublin on 29 November, and arrived back in London six days later. From London he headed to Weymouth and returned to France.[22] His reports, which give precise information on the preparedness of Dublin Castle to resist a French invasion and of the armed United Irish to support one, are of more interest to historians than they were useful to Hoche. Yet, it is undeniable that the United Irish leaders in Dublin benefited from his mission – they learned of the activities of Wolfe Tone in France and perhaps something, at least, of the preparations being made at Brest for a French invasion of Ireland. Despite Wolfe Tone's still poor opinion of him, which was likely grounded in jealousy rather than any objectivity, MacSheehy served on the Rhine – for the second time – and in Normandy (April 1797–May 1798) with the position of battalion commander carrying out the functions of a staff officer. He joined Bonaparte's expedition to Egypt. After leaving Toulon he organized the Maltese legion which was later incorporated in the main French force. Bonaparte made use of his undoubted talents and aged just 23 he led a forward reconnaissance unit. From his own account, his mission objectives sound very much like British Army operations in Iraq and Afghanistan during the first two decades of the twenty-first century and certainly nothing like the conventional warfare of the time. He was at the siege of Cairo and the recapture of Suez, for which action he won promotion to adjutant commandant on 21 February 1800 and received glowing recommendations from General Jean Baptiste Kléber. MacSheehy returned to Europe in 1801 with General Menou, and was regarded by the French government as an expert on Irish affairs and may even have visited Ireland in the period 1802–3. For his services to France he was awarded a sabre of honour and then the *Légion d'honneur*. When Bonaparte, as first consul, issued a decree for the formation of an Irish legion on 31 August 1803, it was MacSheehy who was charged with its organization.[23] Disagreement within the officers of the unit meant he was forced to leave, and MacSheehy met his death on the battlefield at Eylau on 8 February 1807, killed by a cannonball while serving as a *chef d'état-major*, 1er Division, 7ème Corps de la Grande Armée.[24] MacSheehy was far from the blockhead that Wolfe Tone paints him as: he was probably one of the most talented of the United Irishmen.

Royalist Agents

Unsurprisingly, planning for the invasion of England and Ireland in France had not gone unnoticed. When he landed in England, Berthonneau was accompanied by Jean Colleville – an émigré called John Colville. Colleville was a double agent working for French émigré Royalists.[25] In London Colleville informed Royalist agent Duthiel of

Berthonneau's mission and reported back to the British Crown about his activities.[26] The British Crown now knew in detail what was being planned and redoubled their efforts to sabotage the French. Duthiel was part of a wider network of French Royalist Catholics in France and London who were working for the Prince de Bouillon. His network had sabotaged the French fleet in Brest and now expanded their operations. Their leader was Philippe d'Auvergne, who was a British naval officer and the adopted son of Godefroy de La Tour d'Auvergne, the sovereign Duke of Bouillon. He had joined the navy in 1770 and was demobilized in 1784. In 1793, at the beginning of the French Revolution, d'Auvergne was based in London. The Governor of Jersey, Alexander Lindsay, had opened communications between England and the Royalists in that year, and was transferred to Jamaica in 1794. He was replaced by d'Auvergne who was provided with a budget of £30,000 a month by the secret service of the British government to use to cause unrest in France, primarily through smuggling arms, ammunition and other supplies to the French Royalist Army. For example, in September 1795, Bouillon, aided by Huskisson, shipped two consignments of muskets to France to arm the Royalist army and Chouan insurgents.[27] This comprised '2000 stand of arms, 200 barrels of gunpowder, 30 millions in assignats'.[28] Bouillon noted to William Windham, Secretary of State for War, that he had 5,000 trained and armed men at his disposal for operations in the Vendée.[29] Bouillon's opponent in the Vendée was none other than General Lazare Hoche who on 20 July 1795 annihilated the émigré expedition Bouillon had established. Undeterred, Bouillon sent arms, equipment and men to France in March 1796 to counter the French offensive.[30] He was still engaged in arming insurgency operations in France in 1799, when he sent muskets, ammunition and equipment.[31] The 'festering sore' that was the Vendée uprising was backed, paid for and armed by the British Crown.

Bouillon's network of spies managed to enter the very heart of the French government.[32] One of his agents had infiltrated the headquarters of General Lazare Hoche and passed to the British Crown via Boullion minute details of what Hoche was planning. The agent told Bouillon that in order to aid the Irish, Hoche was initially planning a raid on Ireland with no more than a few thousand men, but on the strength of the representations from the Irish he had rapidly changed his plans to encompass a full-blown invasion.[33] On 14 July, Bouillon reported to the Home Office 'some extended project' by Hoche, and informed his handlers about a new spy organization that Hoche had established.[34] It is assumed this was network which included MacSheehy.

Bouillon's network now went into 'over drive' to keep the British Crown informed of what was being planned in France. Lazare Hoche, the commander of the invasion forces, was followed, and intelligence reported back to London.[35] Bouillon recruited more agents to widen his information-gathering network.[36] A British spy was safely concealed in Hoche's organization in September and a spy reported that Colonel Tate's 'Légion Noire misbehaves en route to Brest', that at 'Brest preparations seem genuinely destined for Ireland, where clandestine arms landings may have occurred' and warning that '25–30000 troops are gathered around Brest but the administration is confused'.[37] By early October the British knew what the French plans were: agent Prigent had 'been secretly communicating with Hoche and his agents'.[38] So compromised was Hoche's headquarters by the Royalists that one of Hoche's agents, a woman, was arrested and interrogated.[39] From this abduction, Bouillon reported Hoche's invasion plans to the British Crown at the end of November, complete with date of sailing from France.[40] Bouillon was able to provide the British Crown with a detailed list of the ships in the invasion fleet, as well as the names of the officers.[41] Hoche never realized his headquarters and planning had been fatally compromised. In the game of 'cat and mouse' between secret agents, the British agents were consistently one step ahead of their French counterparts.

The French invasion force, drawn from the Légion Francs and the 21e and 139e demi-brigades de la Ligne, were ready to board their transports on 27 October 1796. All was set: revolution was coming to Yorkshire and the North East. Yet, thanks to a tip-off by a Royalist agent, the Royal Navy appeared outside Dunkirk. This caused panic and consternation. The invasion was off.[42] The Royalist spy reported that thousands of troops had assembled in Holland to invade England, and that he had overheard an American captain, whom he identified as an Irishman, say that there was a camp of 85,000 men near Dunkirk destined for England and Ireland. The spy noted that small fishing boats and other craft had been assembled at Dunkirk to act as landing barges, and that British officers on parole in Dunkirk had been confined in case they should see what was happening and inform the British government.[43] On the strength of this report, the British Crown ordered the immediate blockade of Dunkirk by the Royal Navy. The invasion of England was 'off', at least for now. Did the French suspect the presence of secret agents? If so, nothing is recorded in extant archive papers.

With Humbert neutralized by the Royal Navy blockade the British Crown now planned to stop Ira Allen – who remember was heading to North America to foment revolution and found United

Columbia. Allen set sail on or about 1 November.[44] Thanks once again to the Royalist spy network, the Royal Navy knew where Allen was heading and his approximate route, and his ship the *Olive Branch* was intercepted by HMS *Audacious*, commanded by Davidge Gould, on 19 November 1796 and brought into Portsmouth. The *Olive Branch* was discovered to be loaded with 15,000 muskets with bayonets, 21 bronze 4-pounder field guns and 3 gun carriages. Allen was accused of shipping arms to aid the United Irishmen.[45] This was an obvious, if incorrect, assumption to make. In Canada, Governor Prescot ordered one of Allen's accomplices, David McLane, to be hanged outside the walls of Quebec, then decapitated and disembowelled in July 1797 for conspiring for a French-backed revolution in Canada.

Two revolutions had been 'nipped in the bud'. Fate intervened with the third.

Chapter 13

BANTRY BAY

Colonel Tate and 'Chouanization'

Irish American Colonel Tate now enters the story. Having been involved in a projected invasion of Florida, he fled to France in 1795. In July 1796 he proposed an invasion of Bermuda to Minister Delacroix,[1] and put the same plan to General Clarke.[2]

The plan never materialized, but Tate somehow managed to get himself involved in the invasion of Ireland. He had proposed using 'undesirables' to form a raiding party to emulate the 'Vendée Terrorists', and this force came to be known as the Légion Noire.[3] The men, like those in the Légion Francs, were 'the sum of the earth' and mostly prisoners with little or no prior service other than burglary, arson and thuggery. The plan was based on that developed by Carnot earlier.

By November, after liaising with Wolfe Tone, to provide a diversion for the invasion of Ireland, Tate was ordered to take 1,050 men from the Légion Noire into Lancashire to create chaos by conducting a 'Chouanization' raid, and rally the United Englishmen. Wolfe Tone noted that: 'If Tate is a dashing fellow, with military talents, he may play the devil in England till he is caught. His Object is Liverpool ... a thousand of these desperadoes, in their black jackets, will edify John Bull exceedingly, if they get safe into Lancashire.' By the end of the month the new target was Bristol:

> If he arrives safe, it will be very possible to carry it by a *coup de main*, in which case he is to burn it to the ground. I cannot but observe here, that I transcribed with the greatest sangfroid, the orders to reduce to ashes the third city in the British dominions, in which there is, perhaps, property to the amount of 5,000,000l. But such a thing is war! The British burned

without mercy in America; they endeavored to starve 25,000,000 souls in France; and, above all, they are keeping, at this moment, my country in slavery, my friends in prison, and myself in exile. It is these considerations which steel me against horrors which I should otherwise shudder to think of.[4]

The attack on Bristol was to be a diversion for the landing in Ireland. Bristol had replaced the raid on Newcastle and Yorkshire. For the French Directory, Ireland was now the objective with a diversionary attack on the west coast. The Dunkirk force was stood down on 27 November.[5] Forces beyond the control of the French and United Irishmen now intervened.

In November, a spy called de La Boessière confirmed that Hoche was heading to Ireland.[6] At the close of the month the network reported that '9000 men already embarked on warships and signs that, in all, 20–2500 are so destined' to land in Ireland.[7] Exactly as had been feared by Admiral Bruix, October and November storms held Hoche's force in port and caused the fleet to suffer severe damage as soon as it tried to get out. The need for troops elsewhere as well as the storms in the North Sea meant that the Dunkirk force destined for England was stood down on 27 November.[8]

Hoche eventually sailed in December. His departure had been witnessed by the crew of the French sloop *Les bons Amies*, which was captured by the Royal Navy.[9] The sloop's master, a man called Legardes, and a passenger known as Mr Brian under interrogation revealed that they had seen Hoche's fleet of fifty-three ships set sail from Brest on 16 December. Furthermore, Mr Brian gave the course which the invasion fleet had taken and noted Hoche carried with him three months of provisions.[10] The British Crown knew the French were at sea and heading to Ireland, but did not know where in Ireland the fleet was to anchor. Just like 1588 and the fate of the Spanish Armada, adverse weather conditions scattered the French fleet. Hoche's ship and the main body of the fleet were delayed in arriving at Bantry, and General Grouchy found himself isolated on 24 December with a few thousand men, rather than over 20,000. Undeterred, he told the United Irishmen:

Republicans, The hazards of the sea separate us momentarily from General Hoche. As the custodian of his plans, instructed in the plans he would have followed to lead you to victory, I see myself called by circumstances to fulfil the glorious task imposed on him ... The English alone are your enemies. Gathered with the Irish, many of whom are waiting for you to break their shackles, you will triumph, do not doubt it ... For too long the proud English have laid down their despotic yoke on its neighbours and on its own children. For too long they have regarded Ireland as a conquered province from which it was allowed to export sailors and soldiers, whose trade it was convenient for it to hinder in order to make its own flourish, whose resources and treasures it was wise to exhaust in order to render it powerless to claim its rights.

How many times have you not been outraged by England's misuse of the taxes it takes away from you? How many times have you not called against the British Parliament's attacks on the rights and freedoms of the Parliament of Ireland? ... the hour rings when you can break this tirannic scepter [sic].[11]

Grouchy demanded that the troops he had with him, the 24e and 94e demi-brigades totalling 6,450 men, were to disembark and carry out the written orders of Hoche on 25 December. Holding a council of war, Grouchy's subordinates refused to act until Hoche arrived to give the order to disembark and land. They further argued it was impossible to put ashore without reinforcements. Yet, history shows us what Humbert achieved with less than a quarter of the forces available to Grouchy, but that was in the future. All that mattered now was that the moment for the French to land was slipping away. The fleet commander, Admiral Bouvet, took matters into his own hands and ordered the anchor cables cut, and the fleet sailed back to France in direct contradiction of his orders. Grouchy regretted he had not seized 'Bouvet by the collar and thrown him overboard the moment he attempted to raise a difficulty to the landing'.[12]

The presence of the French fleet at Bantry was a great 'what if moment' in history. But the reality was that due to the cowardice of Admiral Bouvet, and bad weather, Bantry Bay was an undeniable failure. From this date on, Dublin Castle stepped up its war against the United Irishmen, infiltrating their ranks with spies and informers, invoking draconian legislation against subversives, turning a blind eye to military excesses, and to those of the resolutely loyalist Orange Order, and built up its defence forces lest the French should return in strength.

General Grouchy landed his battered, tired and seasick men back in France in January 1797. Grouchy laid the blame for the failure of the expedition on the cowardice of the French Navy.[13] He immediately requested permission to attempt a second invasion of Ireland before local support dwindled and the British could move reinforcements there. Grouchy planned to land a small force of three demi-brigades of infantry in Ulster, to link with the United Irishmen to create chaos in Ireland to 'buy time' until a new force could be assembled and transported to Ireland using the Batavian fleet at Texel.[14] As soon as the plan was drawn up, it was quickly reported back to the Home Office in London by the ever-efficient Royalist spy network.[15]

Grouchy, after much haggling with the government, was named commander of the new invasion force on 10 January 1797. He was given command of the 94e demi-brigade de la Ligne, and the 24e demi-brigade Légère.[16] The Ministère de la Marine gave him control of ten ships of the line.[17] A day later, Minister Petiet added the 21e demi-brigade de la Ligne, an additional 5,000 men to the force. The minister further confirmed that Colonel Tate would take with him the Légion Noire on three frigates commanded by Captain Castagnier.[18] Grouchy was to land in Ireland and Tate was to head for Bristol to create a diversionary attack. As might be suspected, a Royalist spy in the French Ministère de la Marine sent word to London.[19]

Meantime, on 28 January 1797, Hoche had written to MacSheehy thanking him for sending his report and telling him that the government could not think of resuming the Irish expedition.[20] In a scathing letter to the Directory William Duckett – no doubt smarting from Hoche's censuring of his involvement – pithily commented:

> I need not mention the motives that made the plan fail ... which promised, until the moment of its execution, the most unexpected and happy effects. Envy, jealousy, and perhaps bad faith are encountered in the bold but unfortunate expedition of Ireland ... The appearance of the French fleet in Bantry Bay finally reassured the Irish patriot, promising him a relief that he had hitherto regarded as illusory, and conceived only in political views by the French government. The current events in Ireland leave no doubt about the good it has produced.[21]

Duckett was correct: the Bantry Bay debacle was the best 'recruiting sergeant' the United Irishmen ever had. It had shown the French were prepared to come to their aid. Men flocked to the cause in their thousands.

Invasion

Out of Grouchy's event planning came the invasion of Fishguard in February, to be a diversion for Grouchy landing in Ireland with three regiments. Tate's objective was to land near Bristol, then England's second largest city, and destroy it, then to cross over into Wales and march north on to Chester and Liverpool. He set sail on 21 February, and on the 22nd entered the Bristol Channel: three of his frigates were observed off Ilfracombe. Local fencibles and Volunteer units were called out to guard against a potential invasion.[22] Wind conditions made it impossible for the four French warships to land anywhere near Bristol, so instead they headed to Cardigan Bay, where they arrived on the 22nd.

Tate landed his force the following day, and Captain Castagnier spent two days waiting for Grouchy to join him. With Grouchy's forces missing, Castagnier sent the squadron up the coat to reconnoitre Liverpool and observe the passage to Dublin. In theory Tate was to head to Chester and then Liverpool where they would re-embark after burning everything in their path. Tate's ad hoc force surrendered on 24 February and Castagnier sailed back to France.[23]

Where was Grouchy? Had he failed to support Tate as some would say he did at Waterloo all those years later? From the archive records, it seems Grouchy had put to sea with a force which it is assumed comprised the 21e and 94e demi-brigade and 24e légère, roughly 13,000 men, and had sailed for Dublin. A captain of one of Grouchy's ships tells us a strong storm, described as a tempest, blew up and scattered the squadron.[24] This implies that Grouchy's force had indeed set sail, but had been forced back to port due to adverse weather: the midst of winter was not a good time to try and invade Ireland with heavy seas and frequent storms. Arguably, bad weather had 'saved the day' twice for the British Crown, just as it had done in 1588.

Fishguard must be seen as an abortive attempt at 'Chouanization'. Carnot identified that: 'Wales and the County of Cornwall must be regarded as a useful diversion capable of greatly contributing to the success of the Great Irish Expedition.'[25] The lack of regular troops and militia in Wales led to the Revd Edward Edwards, Rector of Llanrwst near Conway, North Wales, writing to the Home Office seeking troop reinforcements, and expressing his fears that the French were about to land at Llandudno and Llandrillo Bay.[26]

In retrospect the expedition may appear to have been foolhardy, even suicidal, within the terms of reference set out, but the objectives were clear. It was to cause as much damage as possible to a variety of installations, and thus draw valuable resources away from other areas where they were needed. Indeed, this process had begun with military units from other parts of the country being sent to Pembrokeshire when the news of the invasion broke. The threat from 'Chouanization' is constantly downplayed: the invasion at Fishguard is seen as 'a joke' and even a 'non-event'. It was never planned to be an invasion. It was a terror raid, to burn houses and barns and wreak havoc in retaliation for British raids in France, to provide a diversion for Grouchy. The French, led by Tate, were to conduct the raid and then hastily re-embark and sail home. British history, however, presents a very different story to the facts of the matter; the perils of studying history solely from British-held documents rather than looking for broader context in European Archives. Tate's force has been seen as a definitive attempt at invasion, which it never was. The fact that Tate failed to land in Bristol was due to bad weather, and his failure was perhaps a forgone conclusion. The Légion Noire was not an effective combat force for anything other than causing havoc. As could be reasonably expected, former convicts made bad soldiers and terrorists, especially when tasting freedom and finding stocks of alcohol. If Tate's men had been regular soldiers, the outcome would have been markedly different. Regular soldiers could have made Bristol, or headed to Chester and Liverpool and caused chaos. It is a 'what if' moment in British History. Had Tate with regulars made it to Liverpool, would the United Englishmen have risen? Perhaps. Yet, the French realized that they had a potent weapon in 'Chouanization', which would be deployed with spectacular success a year later.

Chapter 14

FAILURE

The Bantry Bay episode terrified the British Crown and Dublin Castle. It was now clear that the French were prepared to commit substantial resources to invasion, and that radical groups at home were a potent threat that needed suppressing. Ireland now became centre stage of British politics. An eyewitness to the events writes:

> We have been very much alarmed by the French Fleet seen from Bantry Bay. It is impossible to express the [illegible] that were [illegible] on the occasion, the truth was bad enough & and we can never be thankful sufficiently to the almighty for the great deliverance we had. We may indeed say the Lord fought our battle for had it not been for the storm (which dispersed the fleet) there is no doubt they would have landed and in all probability the consequences would have been terrible. However, it has distressed the credit of the Kingdom by so much, no money to be got and trade of course openly hurt, if the French should attempt coming again (Which some seem to think) we are now better prepared for their reception as all ranks of people are soldiers now all the counties have formed corps and say they will never let our enemies land.

The writer, Eliza Paine, continued that 'there are a number of disaffected people in the north of Ireland, who publickly declared they would assist the French'. Due to censorship, the letter from sister to brother was opened and read at Dublin Castle before being dispatched on the 29th.[1] Paine was an English Anglican émigré living and working in Dublin, and for her, God was clearly Anglican and it must be assumed that her views were representative of society in Dublin. Eliza placed her faith in the Irish Militia and Volunteer regiments to defend the Anglican ascendancy.

Others felts differently. Concessions to the Catholics it was hoped would calm the situation. In March 1797, in the light of events in Ireland Earl Fitzwilliam pressed once more for Catholic emancipation.

Fitzwilliam wrote a *Memorial on the State of Ireland* in which he called for emancipation and the sacking of anti-Catholic members of the Irish government, which would reconcile Catholics to British rule and halt the spread of Jacobinism. He spoke in the Lords to put forward these proposals, which went to the vote where it was rejected by seventy-two votes to twenty.[2] Any hopes that change could be obtained through legitimate lines of grievance were again dashed. Moderates now joined the ranks of the radicals: armed insurrection was seen as the only way of 'redressing grievances'.

The United Irishmen and their allies in France, particularly William Duckett and Nicholas Madgett, began to mobilize an underground army.

Hoche Returns

Anxious to make contact with the French, during the first days of March the United Irish leadership in Dublin dispatched Edward Lewines to liaise with Paris. Before he left Dublin to travel to Hamburg to re-open communications with France, Lewines had met with Marcus Edward Despard and Lord Edward Fitzgerald in Dublin. A spy reported back saying that Despard 'was an agent for the Directory in France' who 'had obtained for Lewines a French passport'.[3] Despard was an Anglo-Irish officer in the British Army and an exceedingly skilled colonial administrator. He had entered the army in 1766 and attained the rank of colonel. After serving in Jamaica, in 1781 he was sent to Central America; there he was made governor of Roatán Island, off the Honduras coast, and soon afterwards of the British Mosquito Coast and Gulf of Honduras. In 1784 he took over the administration of Belize. There he supported the land claims of recent immigrants from the Mosquito Coast against those of earlier settlers, whose complaints resulted in his recall in 1790. Charges against him were dismissed in 1792, but the British government refused to employ him further. He entered radical Irish politics. Lewines arrived in Hamburg at the end of March. Based on information received from spies for the British Crown, William Wickham reported to the Home Office that:

> ... a man of the name of Lewins was sent to Paris under the name of Thompson by a number of persons calling themselves the Executive Committee of United Irishmen sitting at Dublin, as their accredited minister or agent – that this Lewins [*sic* Lewines] was, among other things, expressly charged to solicit an immediate invasion of Ireland, and to concert with the Directory and its Generals the means of carrying this project into execution – that he proceeded first to Hamburg, where, among other papers that were intended to have the effect of credentials, he delivered to Mr. Reinhardt, the Resident of the French Republic ...

in consequence of instructions to that effect, received from the Minister for Foreign Affairs at Paris, he was permitted to proceed to that place, taking Frankfort on his way, near which General Hoche then resided that he had a letter of introduction from Mr. Reinhardt to that General, with whom he was particularly directed to communicate confidentially on the subject of his mission – that he left Hamburg late in the month of May; was admitted to a conference by General Hoche, and received by him in a confidential manner; and that, on his arrival at Paris, the French Government gave him strong assurances of support and co-operation, the nature and extent of which were immediately transmitted by him to Dublin –that he has ever since (with some short intervals) resided at Paris as the avowed Agent of the United Irishmen.[4]

The report is perfectly accurate. Lewines met Reinhardt on 31 March, and explained that the Irish had not risen when the French had landed off Bantry because the time and place of the French landing was unexpected. Lewines is being disingenuous here as MacSheehy had been present to liaise between the Irish and French.[5] Adding to this untruth, Lewines boldly declared to Reinhardt that 100,000 Irish were ready to rise against which the British Crown could only bring 18,000 regulars and 25,000 militia and yeomanry. Lewines' estimate for the Crown forces was true enough, and he further noted that the Catholic members of the yeomanry and militia were aligned to the Irish cause and would defect upon the French landing, giving the United Irish a pool of trained and armed men. Lewines was naïve in his thinking, but he did supply the French with accurate details on the strength and location of British garrisons.[6] The naïve thinking about the number of United Irish who would rise in support of the French fatally undermined the cause. On paper 100,000 may have joined but translating that to active participants prepared to be killed or gaoled was another matter altogether, as will be seen when the French landed.

April came and went and still no firm plans were put in place: however, it was not until 19 May that Minister Reinhard informed Citizen Delacroix that he had spoken to an Irish émigré called James Thompson:

> Now here's the news that travellers from Ireland have brought. The unrest in Ireland is on the rise; the Midi is organized like the North … The number of Irish associates is doubled. The discontented of all classes rally as oppression weighs on everything. The same spirit wins over the troops, etc. He repeated that his instructions instructed him to offer Ireland's formal commitment not to make peace until France and Spain had fully achieved the goal, they could propose to themselves, even the cession of Gibraltar and Jamaica.[7]

Thompson was none other than Edward Lewines, who had been correctly identified by the spy.

Events in England changed everything.

Mutiny!

At the beginning of March, Nicholas Madgett informed the Directory that reports from agents in England suggested that the British government was making progress in stopping the spread of 'the French epidemic', i.e., Jacobinism and political reform. Madgett added that a committee composed of French émigrés had been formed in London to put under surveillance fellow countrymen who they suspected of being republicans, and that the British government had established a secret committee of espionage to report on foreign affairs and suspected British Jacobins.[8] Furthermore, Madgett noted that the Royal Navy had over 15,000 Irish serving on board: it was hoped that the liberation of Ireland would result in a mass mutiny in the Royal Navy and the Irish sailors taking their ships to ports in Ireland.[9] However, if the invasion was to succeed, the Royal Navy had to be overcome. Outclassed by the Royal Navy, other means of crippling the navy had to formulated. If the Irish sailors in the Royal Navy could be persuaded to mutiny, then the seaways were clear.

British gold had sabotaged the French Navy and thoughts in France turned to trying to cause the Royal Navy to mutiny. If somehow the Royal Navy could be 'gotten out of the way' then a major force could land unopposed. Could the Royal Navy be radicalized and induced to mutiny thus freeing the Texel fleet to sail to invade Ireland? Well, yes and no.

The British Crown knew some of this. It was reported to John King at the Home Office that the French agent Berthonneau had been instructed to arrange arson attacks on ports, and to invite Irish sailors to help in the liberation of their homeland, asking them to rise in concert and sail their ships to Irish ports.[10] Right on cue, England's 'Revolutionary' moment came with the naval mutinies of 1797, which seemed to open the door to French armies and announce the fall of another *ancien régime*. Contemporaries regarded the prospect with horror or delight, but nobody could ignore what was going on. For two months the British Crown was paralysed first with the mutiny at Spithead from 16 April–15 May 1797 and then at the Nore on 12 May 1797. There can have been few events in modern British history on which so much turned. How involved the United Irishmen were in the mutinies is almost impossible to say but the Crown, terrified of further mutinies, gave in to the mutineers' demands. The historical record tells us that our old friend William Duckett and unreformed old Jacobin Léonard Bourdon were behind this, visiting Portsmouth and Plymouth to stir up trouble. Leading mutineers Bartholomew Duff, Valentine Joyce and Charles McCarthy were Irish.[11] One of the ship's company of HMS *Repulse* was, Robert Powell described, 'a United Irishman and would die in the cause'. Powell was arrested for saying: 'Bugger the King, Vive le Republic and success to the French.'[12] An unknown spy reported that the United Englishmen upon learning of the mutiny of the fleet at Portsmouth sent Dr Robert Watson and John Bone to confer with the mutineers and when mutiny broke out at the Nore the United Englishmen also made contact with the mutineers there.[13] From the scarce information available, it seems that the United Irishmen had infiltrated the Royal Navy but the extent to which the United Irish leadership or the French influenced the mutiny cannot be determined. Yet, the French quickly learned of the events as they unfolded.

The French Response
On 6 May, the Directory was presented with a dossier about the mutinies by Madgett.[14] Two days after the Spithead mutiny ended, a plan was quickly hatched to invade England, dated 14 May.[15] A few days later on the 17th, Jean François Noël wrote from La Havre about the mutinies, expressing the hope that the events could be exploited.[16] Dr Robert Watson who seems to have taken an active part in the mutinies contacted Léonard Bourdon in Hamburg and told him that if the French landed, 50,000 would rise in Scotland and 200,000 in England.[17]

If the situation was to exploited and the revolutionary moment seized, bold and dynamic action had to be taken: this was something the French were deplorably bad at. In Paris an ambitious plan was sent to the War Ministry proposing that 40,000 men were to assemble at Flushing and 15,000 at Ostend and Dunkirk, and a further 15,000 at Cherbourg, with 12,000 men from Rochefort destined to land in Ireland. The expedition from Dunkirk was to burn Chatham docks and surrounding coastal communities and link with the Batavian fleet from Texel. The plan envisioned that the Texel fleet would head into the North Sea and land troops on the Scottish and Northumbrian coasts to attack Newcastle, Glasgow and Edinburgh, burning and destroying warehouses, factories, mines, workshops and generally causing terror, while the fleet from Dunkirk and Ostend would land in Chatham and Harwich, and the troops from Cherbourg attack Portsmouth and Plymouth and burn the dockyards. Troops were to land on Jersey in a diversionary attack.[18]

Another plan – which bears all the hallmarks of Humbert – recommended the 'Chouanization' of Yorkshire. The Yorkshire coast was judged to be extremely vulnerable, and the raiding party was to 'bring extreme terror' upon landing, with factories, warehouses, mines, pumping engines all on the list of key targets to be destroyed. The port of Kingston upon Hull was identified as a priority to 'burn to the ground' in an action which was to be co-ordinated with a 'Chouanization' raid along the Thames and in Ireland.[19]

In the midst of the planning being undertaken in Paris, Lewines met Lazare Hoche on his own account on 29 May in Hesse Cassel and requested that the French send 20–25,000 men as well as 100,000 muskets. He added that France could render Ireland independent with the minimum of assistance, and that the Spanish minister in Hamburg would advance the Irish money to pay for the expedition.[20] Hoche wished to exploit the Royal Navy's mutiny and, in dialogue with Lewines, hoped to land 13,544 men.[21] Hoche presented his case carefully, as he was not fully aware of the intentions of the Directors toward Ireland: he seems to have been ignorant of the planning being carried out in Paris to make the most of the mutiny in the Royal Navy.

Hoche sent his adjutant Simon to Paris to press the Directory and the Minister of the Navy on the Irish cause. His timing was perfect. Simon reported to Hoche on 7 June 1797 that the Directory was still willing to send support to the Irish. He said that he met Lazare Carnot who reported that there was an agreement with the Batavian Republic to make available as many troops and arms as they could spare, and Hoche would be in charge of arranging this. Simon noted that no plans were being considered for a major invasion attempt in Ireland.[22] However, the peace preliminaries between the British Crown and France derailed any invasion attempt. Simon concluded that the Directory: 'would very much like to do something, but it dare not. It has little confidence in its own resources and is afraid of the possible outcome at a time when it is negotiating peace with England.'[23] The Directory wrote to Hoche on 9 June:

We were already informed by the correspondence of citizen Reinhard that Mr. Luynes [sic] has been sent to you ... the state of disaffection in Ireland is such that it offers the most favourable opportunity to reduce England. But we cannot immediately operate the planned expedition. The fate of the continent must be determined before attempting it, and the preparations of the three powers that must contribute to it still require a long space of time, in order to give it all the development it must have. But if a few months is still needed for this decisive operation, we can prepare for its success and perhaps even obtain the main results by partial and successive shipments of arms and ammunition of war to Ireland.

The London cabinet, in fomenting in this way the insurrection in the Vendée, has itself taught us how powerful such a measure must be to strengthen the energy of the United Irish, and bring them to an open split with England. Our interest is to see them proclaim the independence of their island and to support them in this generous undertaking, but without guarantees on our part. The Minister of the Navy is in charge of immediately preparing the transport of arms and ammunition to Ireland, and he will invite the Batavian government, which has 30,000 muskets on board, to pass part of it in a row. But before sailing, it is essential to know the precautions that the United Irish have taken to receive this aid and put it in safety. Thus, we urge you to ask Mr. Luynes and to send us all the necessary information on the landing points where these weapons can be deposited and on the leaders of the insurgents to whom they must be handed over. You will communicate directly, for greater speed, to the Batavian Committee on External Relations the concepts that will be useful to it to direct the shipment of arms and ammunition that the Minister of the Navy undertakes to carry out on his side. It would be advantageous to bring at the same time to Ireland some brave, intelligent, and jealous officers to stand out in this new career, and we allow you to do so, if you have any near you that are specific to this destination.[24]

Agents provocateurs were to be sent to Ireland to keep the French in contact with Hoche at Texel and also the Directory. However, reading between the lines the Directory had in essence withdrawn from Irish affairs. Sending arms and sponsoring insurrection was very much all that the Directory would commit to as they explained to Hoche: 'It is our interest to see them declare independence of their island ... but without guarantee on our part ... we have made no agreement to sustain their new political status for fear of damaging the re-establishment of peace'.[25] Peace preliminaries with England were more important than Ireland.[26] A French émigré reported to the Home Office that plans for an invasion were abandoned at the end of August.[27]

After his visit to Hamburg, Lewines headed to Paris where he met Wolfe Tone. In an undated note to General Clarke, he offered to travel clandestinely to England to gather information on the number of British troops available to defend the country, and the places where they were stationed.[28] Lewines seems to have been the author of a letter to the Directory that stated it was necessary for the French to found a 'French party' in London.[29] Was it Lewines that was behind the 'London Directory'? It is a reasonable suggestion.

Dr William James MacNeven

United Irish strength was now arguably greater than it had been a year earlier in readiness for Bantry Bay, and the Batavian fleet had superior ships, materiel, supplies and morale than the French Navy. Acting on his own initiative, James Napper Tandy arrived in Paris in early June via Hamburg.[30] The United Irish leadership was impatient for the French to land. Despite the French government's reservations concerning Ireland, the Dublin headquarters of the United Irish wanted to bolster Lewines' endeavours in France, a British spy reporting:

> It further appears that, about the time that Lewines was sent from Ireland, a confidential person was sent by the Directory to treat immediately with the Executive Committee at Dublin ... It further appears that the Executive Committee, towards the end of June in the same year, directed Dr. M'Nevin, one of their members, to proceed to Paris, by the way of Hamburg – that the principal objects of his journey were to give additional weight and credit to the mission of Lewines; to confirm the information that had been already transmitted on the state of Ireland.[31]

Dr William James MacNeven arrived in Hamburg on 23 June under the pseudonym of Williams. He headed to Paris and carried with him a report about the state of Ireland which he gave to the Directory on 13 July:

> The appearance of the French in Bantry Bay has encouraged the least energetic Irishmen, and caused them to conceive hopes of shaking off the yoke of England. The event has proved how false was the idea that Ireland could not be invaded but by means of a superior fleet ... there are not fewer than 100,000 United Irishmen, and ready to march ... we should think that we want at this moment 5,000 French troops, if we were not of opinion that the number ought to be 10,000, with a considerable train of flying artillery. We shall need a numerous staff, engineers, and general officers. We wish that the expedition should be commanded by General Hoche, and that such Irish officers may be appointed to serve under him as the Government deems deserving of its confidence by their fidelity and their talents.[32]

This document outlined troop strengths and garrisons in Ireland and made its way to the British Crown via the effective spy network. The British Crown knew what was being planned all along. In a separate letter, MacNeven reported that the French: 'count on the cooperation of the poor and adjoining classes. Their hatred for English despotism and the vexations they endured from their lords caused the most ignorant of them to act in the same direction as the most enlightened minds'.[33] Williams – Dr MacNeven – informed Paris in August that 150,000 men had joined the United Irishmen, of which 100,000 were in Louth, Armagh, West Meath, Longford, Kildare and Dublin. Killbeg was identified as a suitable landing point for the French, and MacNeven noted 'that 10,000 United Irish would attack Enniskillen Castle', which was a key objective if the invasion was to succeed. Worryingly, he reported that the Crown had sent 6,000 reinforcements to Ireland, mostly cavalry.[34]

Simultaneously another United agent arrived from Ireland: Samuel Turner was sent off to Hamburg. Turner's mission was prompted by what would become terminal disagreements about communication, command and control of the movement. The rupture between Turner and MacNeven resulted in the former turning spy for the British Crown.[35] Neither the French or Irish ever realized that Turner was a spy, which was a huge mistake, as will be shown.

Coup and Plot

The fleet from Texel was due to sail on 16 July: it never left. Hoche, realizing that the Dutch, in order to regain national pride, wanted the expedition to Ireland to be purely a Dutch affair, withdrew his French troops and renounced his command. Simultaneously, the French Directory began to reshuffle the government: in particular, Lazare Hoche was named Minister of War. Under the guise of amassing a force to land in England, the new minister brought his troops to Paris. The councils immediately and vehemently condemned the Directory. The failed coup was prompted by the result of elections held earlier in the year, which had given the majority of the seats in the Corps Legislatif to Royalists: it was feared they would initiate a restoration of the Monarchy. In this case, the law was on their side: Hoche did not meet the legal conditions for his position as he was too young to be a minister and his soldiers had violated the constitution when they arrived within 60km of the capital. The Directory was forced into an embarrassing 'U-turn'. The plot to establish a direct dictatorship had been uncovered, but this did not stop Barras in wanting to rid himself of Royalists in the country's governance. Hoche was dismissed and his men were ordered to leave the Paris area. If Paul Barras had been planning a coup, it had totally failed. Carnot severely reprimanded Hoche and sent him back to his command on the Rhine in disgrace. Carnot was now in the ascendancy over Paul Barras, who was also now in disgrace. Hoche told Lewines, who was now in Paris, at the end of July that they had been betrayed and urged him not to speak with anyone.[36] Panicked, Lewines wrote to Hoche asking if the invasion was still likely to happen. Simon, Hoche's capable adjutant, replied on 8 August, assuring Lewines 'that the expedition will soon be ready in spite of the personal enemies of General Hoche, who seek to harm him'.[37]

Paul Barras had not given up hope of cementing his position, and began planning a second coup. Without Hoche, the Directory turned to the young general Napoléon Bonaparte. In order to avoid compromising himself directly or inciting a rivalry, Napoléon dispatched Charles Augereau to France. Augereau was an ardent republican but a mediocre politician. Learning from recent experience, Augereau's soldiers were suddenly given leave and were now able to approach Paris without contravening the law. A month later the Jacobin faction struck back against the Royalists. At dawn on 4 September 1797, martial law was declared in Paris, while a decree was issued asserting that anyone supporting Royalism or the restoration of the Constitution of 1793 was to be shot without trial. On Barras' orders, Lazare Carnot and Barthélemy were expelled from government. Furthermore, 214 deputies were arrested and 65 were subsequently exiled to Cayenne in French Guiana including Pichegru, Ramel and Barthélemy. The election results in 49 departments were annulled. In the aftermath 160 recently returned émigrés were sentenced to death, and about 1,320 priests accused of 'conspiring against the Republic' were deported. Barras had effectively neutralized the threat from the Royalists and the army. However, Barras' coup had fatally undermined any attempt to exploit the situation in England or Ireland following the mutiny in the Royal Navy. The moment for action had been irredeemably lost to further Paul Barras' grip on power, an event that cemented the young General Bonaparte as 'the man of the hour' and hero of France.

Further tragedy was to befall the United Irish: General Hoche died from tuberculosis on 19 September 1797. The paranoia around Hoche reached fever pitch. For months Lewines had been aware of a plan to undermine the invasion: had Hoche been murdered? An anxious Lewines wrote to Paul Barras demanding to know the cause of death. For Lewines, the independence of Ireland would cement the French Republic's position as it would neutralize the threat from England and the 'liberty of the continent'. He noted that MacNeven had returned to Ireland via Wetzlar and had given him two letters from Hoche, and asked if Barras would still honour Hoche's pledge. Hoche had committed 'to do the impossible to be ready to leave Brest on 20 October with 10,000 men and all necessary muskets, artillery and munitions etc', adding 'he would not wait for the Dutch Fleet'.[38] Barras responded to Lewines – who considered himself the official ambassador of the United Irish – that 'the project is not abandoned but cannot be completed before spring'.[39]

In October, Lewines again wrote to Barras, enquiring if the wintering of the fleet at Brest signified the abandonment of the French government's plans for Ireland. Barras scribbled on the reverse of Lewines' letter that he would not respond before he had spoken to the minister at the Ministère de la Marine about this.[40]

Chapter 15

SCOTLAND

Despite the political turbulence in Paris, invading Ireland was still a high priority for the Irish émigrés in France to achieve their ambition of liberating their homeland. Towards the end of October Wolfe Tone arrived in Paris, carrying with him letters from General Daendels which he communicated verbally to Barras on the 21st. A new plan of operations was sketched out, whereby a force of 5,000 French soldiers would land in Ireland, not later than February 1798, having taken a northerly passage in a 'Chouanization' raid contiguous to a landing in Scotland. Eugen Aherne was ordered to The Hague to meet with General Daendels to discuss the invasion.[1]

General Daendels' scheme, which had been passed to Hoche before his death – and presumably had been discussed with either Dr Robert Watson – of more later – or an unknown delegate from the United Scotsmen, set out that 15,000 Dutch troops were to land in Scotland, supported by a second wave of 15,000 French troops from Brest.[2] Daendels reported that spies had told him that war was crippling Scotland's economy and added that the Scots were forming themselves along the same lines as the United Irish. Daendels was clearly well informed about Scottish politics and it seems likely that Robert Watson and others were directly involved as well as Wolfe Tone. Although a year earlier he had been opposed to 'Chouanziation', so as to keep abreast of any planning for a landing in Ireland, through Lewines, Wolfe Tone inveigled himself into Daendels' circle. Daendels added that the actions of the British Crown in Ireland, notably in Ulster, had horrified public mood in Scotland and concluded that a French and Dutch army would be welcomed by the people of Scotland when set against recents events. Indeed, it was hoped by Daendels that the anti-militia riots then taking place in Scotland would help foment revolution, and it was essential that the invasion happened as soon as possible to

112

exploit the uprising. The landing in Scotland was, at Lewines' request, to be a diversion for a landing in Ireland.[3]

Daendels was perfectly correct about the rioting taking place in Scotland at this time. Aware that radical groups in sympathy with the French existed, the Crown embarked on a programme of repression to stave off rebellion. In the wake of the food riots of 1795, to bolster the troops available at home to put down rebellion and revolution, the 1796 Militia Act sought to double the strength of the militia; the supplementary militia was to levy 59,441 men.[4] When the supplementary militia scheme was announced, the Act was seen as an 'upper class plot' to force the poor to fight in defence of the rich. In Penrith protestors banged on the door of the public house where the ballot was being drawn and shouted 'No new militia', broke open the doors and seized the militia lists, tearing some and burning the remaining papers.[5] The magistrates at Ulverstone were met with shouts of: 'No militia! Why should we fight … if the French come they will not hurt us – they will only plunder those who have too much.'[6] Anti-militia rioting broke out in the West Riding, Nottinghamshire, Derbyshire, Norfolk and Lincolnshire.[7] When the Act was applied in Scotland, the *Edinburgh Evening Courant*, following the government line, reported that: 'The present opposition to the militia act was altogether unforeseen and unexpected. It was always understood that England was averse to granting a militia to Scotland; but it never was known till now that Scotland was unwilling to receive it.'[8]

On 24 August 1797, the same paper reported demonstrations against the Militia Act in Eccles and Berwick, where property was set on fire.[9] On 28 August a proclamation was drawn up by some of the inhabitants of Tranent in East Lothian to object to the enforced recruitment of Scots into the military for the purpose of controlling their own people or deployment overseas. The following day a group of protesters from the local mining communities in Tranent came face to face with the Cinque Port Dragoons. Tensions were high and the troops opened fire, killing the leaders. The fleeing crowd was then cut down indiscriminately as they tried to escape into the surrounding countryside: twenty were killed and a similar number wounded. James Kennedy of Paisley and Angus Cameron of Blair Atholl were key participants in the rioting. Barras seemed encouraged by the events and in a memorandum noted that Scotland 'for the last three or four years has exhibited very strong revolutionary sentiment', adding that the sentiment was strongest in Glasgow and other manufacturing districts, with leaders of the United Scotsmen being in frequent contact with their United Irish counterparts. It was hoped that if 1,200 agents provocateurs could act in the manner of those at the Fishguard landings in Scotland, it would trigger perhaps 15,000–30,000 discontented to rise up. It was essential, the report highlighted, that the landing of troops in Scotland took place as soon as possible as Scotland was almost devoid of regular troops and lacked a militia. Of key importance was the fact that the Royal Navy had withdrawn from blockading Texel until the spring. The invasion plan had the merit 'of being easily effected in the present circumstances' and would not prevent a successful landing in Ireland. Hoche felt that the plan was 'very feasible'.[10] In response, rather than being sent to England, Eugene Aherne and a second agent were dispatched to The Hague to discuss the Dutch operations.[11]

Lewines sent information to Barras sometime later the same month, with news from Edward Fitzgerald that gave an indication of the strength of the United Irishmen and public sentiment in Ireland.[12] Barras replied: 'the expedition is preparing with great means, the Government has only one goal: the independence of Ireland'.[13]

Thomas Muir

In the midst of planning, exiled Scottish radical Thomas Muir arrived in France. Tried for treason in 1794 and sent to the convict colony of Botany Bay in Australia, Muir had escaped and made his way to France via the Americas, in the process of which he lost his left eye after his cheek bone was shattered by a cannonball. Muir landed exhausted in Bordeaux in November 1797 where he was publicly proclaimed a Hero and Martyr for Liberty. Muir no longer accepted that the United Scotsmen would 'play second fiddle' to the United Irish. Weak, half-blind and with a perpetual grimace, he made his way north to Paris. Muir stepped into the factionalism between Napper Tandy and Wolfe Tone, which was ultimately to prove fatal to the United Irish movement. Muir backed Napper Tandy in wanting a major invasion of Ireland and told the Directory that the Scots were anxious to break the chains of English rule and establish an independent republic, adding reassuringly that the Scots would welcome the arrival of French troops.[14]

As 1797 drew to a close, Thomas Muir came to the fore in Irish and Scottish affairs to the chagrin of Wolfe Tone. In a later letter dated 29 December 1797, written roughly a month after he arrived in Paris, Muir asked the Directory for money on which to live, promising optimistically that it would be repaid 'by Scotland with interest and with enthusiasm', and declared that: 'Other nations offered me asylum. Frigates were sent out to rescue me, as the Minister of Foreign Relations well knows. But my heart is entirely French. I have sacrificed everything for the sacred cause of the Republic. I have very little blood left in my veins, but the little which remains will be spilled once again.'[15] A new plan of operations against Scotland was prepared and 'signed off' by the Directory, at least in theory, dated 15 January 1798. Written by Daendels, he explained to the French War Ministry that 13 ships of the line were to leave Texel and sail into the North Sea and land 25,000 Dutch troops in Scotland. Winter storms and the cold meant that the troops would not be able to embark till April. The delay would allow munitions and supplies to be assembled in 'good time' to ensure the fleet set sail on or about 1 April. To deceive spies, troops were to land in 'small boats used for cabotage'[16] and embark from Helder and other small ports. The Texel fleet would pick up the army in Denmark and then head to the Firth of Forth. Daendels noted that despite the British government boasting that the people would rise up and vigorously oppose invasion, he had been told that this was a mistaken belief when it came to the Scots, who would welcome the French. Edinburgh would be taken on the first day, Daendels promised, once his force had landed at Leith: Edinburgh was garrisoned by a single battalion which was no match for his 25,000 men. From Edinburgh, the army would travel along the Caledonian canal to the Clyde. The canal would also act as the French line of defence between Falkirk and Dunbarton. Once 'dug in' and provided with food and horses from the Scots, it would take the British Army months to gather an army strong enough to lay siege to Scotland. Once masters of the Clyde estuary, communication would be made with Ireland and a two-pronged assault would then be made on the north of England in conjunction with a French landing in the south. Daendels added that the fleet would be commanded by Admiral de Winter.[17] It is now that the 'the man of the hour' became involved in the bold and ambitious enterprise to invade Scotland. Charles Delacroix wrote to General Bonaparte the same day, informing him of Daendels' plan, noting that it was based 'on attachment to the French republic, devotion to the mother country, and shared common interests', i.e., the defeat of England. Delacroix told Bonaparte to be ready to sail in conjunction with the Batavian fleet.[18]

When Muir arrived in Paris he rapidly discovered that the United Irishmen in Paris were experiencing considerable internal turmoil caused by personality clashes and political differences between Napper Tandy and Wolfe Tone. Muir directly intervened in the dispute. One of the problems that the revolutionary underground – in Ireland, England and Scotland – was facing was one of communication and information gathering. No emissary had been sent to Ireland since Bernard MacSheehy had returned in December 1796: eighteen months is long enough for public mood to change. The underground movement could usually only communicate with the French government through agents who actually made the trip to Paris, or through émigrés in Hamburg and France, many of whom had not been in their homeland for a year or more and therefore were not that reliable when it came to understanding the 'public mood back home'. On 3 March 1798, Muir submitted a 'picture of the situation of the three nations of England, Scotland, and Ireland' to the Directory. He dismissed the claims of British expatriates, which he had first heard when he was in Paris in 1793, that the English were only waiting for a French invasion to rise up and overthrow their government. Instead, most English people did not support the French Republic because:

> ... there is not a more ignorant or barbaric people in all Europe. They do not educate themselves, they do not read (it is in the government's interest to perpetuate their ignorance: give that populace meat and beer, and they would slit the throats of their fathers). They are a people without character: today they will cry 'Long live the King', tomorrow they will shout 'Long live the Republic'.[19]

In an audacious letter published in the *Le Moniteur Universel*, Muir declared: 'I am a United Irishman, I am a Scot, I can speak in the name of both Nations', and in a final flourish: 'I reply to you, in the name of the Irish and the Scots, that we will break our chains over the heads of our tyrants.'[20] The newspaper was read in England, and it is clear he was hopeful of 'getting his message out' in France, Hamburg and London, no doubt to garner support in England and also it is assumed Scotland. Wolfe Tone was enraged by Muir's arrogance:

> ... of all the vain, obstinate blockheads that ever I met, I never saw his equal. I could scarcely conceive such a degree of self-sufficiency to exist. He told us roundly that he knew as much of our country as we did, and would venture to say he had as much the confidence of the United Irishmen as we had; that he had no doubt we were very respectable individuals, but could only know us as such, having shown him no powers or written authority to prove that we had any mission.[21]

The endless bickering between Wolfe Tone, Lewines, Madgett and Duckett had created a power vacuum that Muir filled. It is hardly surprising, therefore, that Muir had sidelined Wolfe Tone and Lewines, and got the agreement of the Batavian and French governments to back an invasion of Scotland.[22]

The Revd Dr Joseph Priestley, Unitarian divine and radical politician.

Major John Cartwright, political radical who inspired countless thousands of working-class people across the United Kingdom to agitate for the right to vote.

Henry Redhead Yorke, for a time an English Jacobin and Unitarian who agitated for an end to the slave trade and political reform in the manner of the French Revolution in England.

The Revd Thomas Johnstone, Unitarian minister and firebrand Jacobin and politician in the West Riding of Yorkshire.

Benjamin Vaughan, a Unitarian from London who was involved in a plot to invade England and establish a French-backed republic.

Arthur O'Connor, the Irish radical orator and leader who became a general in the French Army.

Lord Edward Fitzgerald, Irish republican and leader of the United Irishmen.

James Napper Tapper, abolitionist Irish republican and ultimately a serving officer in the French Army.

Robert Emmet, a leader of a
United Irishmen insurrection
in Ireland that failed.

William James MacNeven, a United
Irishmen who acted as delegate
between France and Ireland in
coercing the French to invade Ireland.

Theobald Wolfe Tone, Irish republican and hero of the United Irish movement.

Thomas Addis Emmet, who, along with his brother, organized a coup to bring down British rule in Ireland.

General Humbert, who led the French Army that invaded Ireland and sought to win Ireland freedom from Westminster.

Lazare Hoche, the French general who was central to the United Irishmen's hopes for a French invasion and liberation of Ireland from British rule.

Charles Maurice de Talleyrand, French foreign minister who did much to aid the United Irishmen in endeavouring to liberate their homeland.

Lazare Carnot, the French government minister who envisioned the 'Chouanization' of Ireland and England in retaliation for the British support of the French Royalist Army in France.

Chapter 16

THE MISSION OF FATHER O'COIGLY

As noted earlier, no direct contact had been made with Ireland or England since late 1796. It was at Muir's suggestion that contact was made, not with Ireland, but England. Daendels was still preparing the fleet at Texel. In order to provide a diversion to the French landing in Scotland the United Irish planned an English rebellion, backed up by a French invasion. A key person linking the Irish and English factions was Father James O'Coigly.

O'Coigly was the second son of James O'Coigly and Louisa Donnelly, born in the parish of Kilmore in County Armagh in August 1761. Little is known of O'Coigly's life prior to his ordination at Dungannon in January 1785. It is believed that he attended the Free School at Dundalk, where he received a classical education, and after this apparently lived for a few years with his parish priest. In June 1785, he arrived in Paris, where he remained until 12 October 1789, studying at the Collège des Lombard. On his return to Ireland, he became involved in Irish nationalism and is seems likely he was a member of the Defenders organized around James Napper Tandy.[1]

O'Coigly's presence in Manchester was largely due to the factionalism that beset the United Irishmen after the 1796 debacle. While the dominant moderate faction was determined to await French assistance before staging an Irish rebellion, frustrated by the inactivity of the moderates and in fear of arrest, O'Coigly, the Revd Arthur MacMahon, a Presbyterian minister, Samuel Turner and others left Ireland for England in June 1797. This exodus strengthened existing links between the United Irishmen and British radical societies and these groups were to play a significant part in attempts to attract French military assistance. O'Coigly was ideally placed to promote this alliance. His charismatic personality made him an effective missionary; he was no stranger to the English radicals, nor was this his first attempt to elicit French assistance. He had been to Paris in 1796 and on that occasion had carried with him an address from the 'Secret Committee of England' to the French Directory.[2] This may be the same group that Berthonneau encountered. In addition, O'Coigly had a radical social philosophy close to the egalitarianism of Thomas Paine which made him a powerful emissary among the disaffected textile workers of Lancashire. It was here too that he first met Robert Gray, who became an informer in March 1798 and organized a United cell at the White Hart in Sugar Lane. Other cells met at the Buck and Hawthorn in St Anne's Square and the Engine, with Isaac Perrins, in Lees Street.[3] Perrins was a prize-winning bare-knuckle fighter and one-time employee of James Watt and Matthew Boulton and encouraged the assassination of 'the petty tyrants of Manchester'.[4] After spending the summer in Manchester, O'Coigly appears to have travelled to Ireland and then headed to France. O'Coigly and MacMahon seemingly met with the United Irish in Paris. O'Coigly reported in October 1797 to the Directory:

> ... a Delegate from the United Scotch, sent expressly to London to know how far the English Patriots were willing to assist their Brethren in Scotland and Ireland in the great work of overthrowing Tyranny – he gave to understand, that the Scotch Patriots were very powerful and ready to act in concert with those of England & Ireland at any moment – the subscribers are ready to attend when & where it may be judg'd necessary to answer any question that may arise from the foregoing or to perform any thing that may be in their Power. For their conduct [and] veracity they appeal to their countrymen now in Paris engaged in the same cause of Liberty.[5]

It was pledged that: '1. The British Isles will form distinct republics, 2. That the republics shall choose their own form of government ... that those who join the invaders shall have arms provided'.[6] Everything rested on the Batavian fleet leaving harbour and the French and Dutch getting 'boots on the ground' in Scotland and England. Were troops heading to Ireland? The plan for a 'Chouanization' raid of 5,000 men that Wolfe Tone had supported seems to have been 'quietly dropped'.

On the way back to Manchester, O'Coigly was arrested and gaoled in Liège for spying along with John Tennant, Alexander Lowry and the Revd Arthur MacMahon.[7] Talleyrand, who was last mentioned leaving for exile from England in March 1794, had returned to France in September 1796 and been fully rehabilitated by the Directory. He was appointed foreign minister in July 1797, and it was on his orders that the prisoners were released on 20 October, noting that they were 'devoted to liberty' and had been forced to flee 'the odious English Government'.[8]

Bonaparte

As noted earlier, the hero of Italy, Bonaparte, was to spearhead an invasion of England. The signing of peace preliminaries with Austria by General Bonaparte of Compo Formio on 17 October meant that Paul Barras was now committed to aiding the Irish cause. The treaty freed up men, horses, cannon and money which could be directed elsewhere. Furthermore, Barras prudently realized that the young Bonaparte had to be kept away from Paris and given a project to manage to keep him gainfully employed now the fighting in Italy was over. Bonaparte was already considered a threat to Barras. The French, Barras promised Lewines, would land in spring 1798.[9]

To this end, General Desaix was named military commander of the 'Army of England' on 26 October. Bonaparte was made nominal head of the expedition. In December ships and men were assembled at Brest and Toulon. Wolfe Tone and Lewines now seemed to have 'buried the hatchet' and busied themselves 'courting' the young general Bonaparte and Colonel Bessières. The pair met Bonaparte for the first time at Rue Chanterine on 21 December, when Lewines and the general discussed the situation in Ireland.[10] On 23 December, Wolfe Tone gave Bonaparte a copy of his report on Ireland from 1796.[11] Yet, England was of more interest to Bonaparte than Ireland.

Part of this event planning included a report dated 2 January 1798 authored by Robert Pelleve. Pelleve was a French agent who had travelled to England and Ireland the previous November and sent a report to the directory concerning the defences of Portsmouth and providing a description of the south coast from Essex to Plymouth as well as reporting on Brighton and Lewes. He was working to identify landing points for the French forces. His reconnaissance also included Norfolk and Suffolk, as well as the North East, pinpointing Holderness as a suitable landing place and Hull and Scarborough as key targets.[12] In a separate report, Pelleve tells us that he interrogated British prisoners of war about England and the prevailing mood in the country and recommended that a key objective of any invasion was releasing and rallying the 23,000 French prisoners of war in England.[13]

On 8 February, Bonaparte conducted a whirlwind tour of the Channel ports. At Dunkirk orders were made to prepare ships to transport 50,000 men, 4,000 cavalry, and artillery and provisions to land in England.[14] The preparations at Dunkirk did not go unnoticed: a spy for the British Crown reported that Bonaparte would not be ready to sail until 19 May.[15]

However, things were not running as smoothly as Bonaparte and the British spy imagined. Daendels reported that the inaction 'of the French government is paralysing everything' in a letter to Wolfe Tone dated 12 March.[16] Perhaps realizing the unease and hesitation of the French government about the expedition to Scotland and England, on 21 March, Lewines handed over a dossier to the War Ministry about Ireland. The dossier reported that the population of Ireland was 450,000 Protestants, 900,000 Presbyterians and 3,150,000 Catholics. The Protestants formed the government and aristocracy, the Presbyterians the middle and merchant class and the Catholics the landless poor. Lewines and Wolfe Tone reported that the Presbyterians and Catholics were united in their republican sentiments and the independence of Ireland. Unlike in 1792, when independence was seen as a Catholic struggle, which concerned minister Lebrun greatly, it was now a clear-cut case of the majority against the minority for independence across religious lines. The United Irishmen were, after all, ecumenical in outlook. Wolfe Tone and Lewines informed Napoléon that a force of 30,000 men would be needed to take Ireland and that irregulars would be forthcoming from the United Irish. The Irish garrison was estimated at 25,000 with 18,000 militia, fencibles and yeomanry, many of whom it was hoped would defect to the Defenders, i.e., the Catholic insurrectionary movement. Wolfe Tone and Lewines envisioned that the invasion force would sail from Texel and Dunkirk and that 12,000 men would land in Galway Bay and the remainder in Carrickfergus and head to Belfast. Both columns would then converge on Dublin. Lewines believed that a successful landing would trigger a nationwide rebellion and, bolstered by the French regulars, seize Ireland. Certainly, Wolfe Tone and Lewines banked on 5–6,000 Defenders rallying to the cause and that 9 in 10 of the Catholic population were in favour of invasion, as were the Catholic and Whig clubs of Dublin and the north of Ireland. The new Irish government would be allies of France and once the English yoke had been removed the economy of Ireland would flourish. It was further hoped that the Irish sailors in the Royal Navy, on hearing the news of the invasion, would mutiny and sail their ships to Ireland and these would be at the service of the French and neutralize the Royal Navy.[17] It was a convincing but hopelessly naïve narrative. Daendels did not change his event planning, and nor for that matter did Bonaparte. Ireland, despite Wolfe Tone's pleading and Lewines' persuasion, seemed to be 'off the cards' at least for the moment.

William Duckett

Concurrent with planning in Paris, Duckett's next assignment was as personal secretary to Léonard Bourdon, who had been appointed the French agent in Hamburg (October 1797–February 1798), and then to Parandier, the French Consul at Altona, a suburb of Hamburg but in Danish territory (February–May 1798). Duckett and Bourdon's primary objective was to watch émigrés who threatened the French Republic;[18] however, the pair were in contact with English and Irish radicals Marcus Edward Despard and James MacNeven. Indeed, Bourdon emphasized the creation of a new intelligence network in England, Ireland and Scotland with the Dublin Defender turned United Irishman Christopher Carey, who moved in radical circles in England – who had been travelling with Berthonneau in the South West of England during 1796 – left to 'run the show' in Ireland, and Marcus Edward Despard was to head the English movement.[19]

During November 1797 Duckett recommended Despard to Talleyrand, the French foreign minister: 'He has a great deal of talent and is a friend of mankind . . . He is Irish with the full force of his heart.' After speaking with Despard, Duckett informed Talleyrand on 20 December 1797 that the 'friends of England' were desirous of the independence of Ireland, and that the government in London considered Ireland as already lost: it was with utmost speed that preparations needed to be made for a revolution and invasion in Ireland.[20]

In February 1798, Léonard Bourdon, *chargé d'affaires*, in Hamburg wrote to Paris informing the Directory that 'great discontent reigns in the Royal Navy, especially in the flotilla at Cork'. In order to build on this discontent, Bourdon sought permission to send agents to Ireland, as well as to England and Scotland. Bourdon informed the directory that Duckett had recruited:

... two Irishmen, one is now in Dublin the other in London, their patriotism makes them recommendable. One is called Lescure, the other Despard. The first has been in Ireland since July 1796. He is known in the French Revolution as a collaborator of Loustalot [*sic*] and a friend of Santhonax [*sic*]. You can consult someone who will recognize him in this double capacity. The other who has filled the highest positions in the West Indian establishments; he is known as the most energetic Republican in London. His principles have already exposed him to several ministerial arrests. Both his character and virtues allowed him to avoid further trouble.

Both are working to the same end: their goal is the independence of their homeland. Despard commanded an English regiment, and passes as for the first engineer of Great Britain, in vain the government had offered him the second command of the continental army. His sword, he answered, Will never be used except to help friends and against the enemies of freedom! No one knows better than him the military state of the three kingdoms.[21]

Until now it seems Despard had not come greatly to the attention of the French authorities. Léger Félicité Sonthonax was a French abolitionist and Jacobin before joining the Girondist Party, which emerged in 1791. During the French Revolution, he controlled 7,000 French troops in Saint-Domingue during the Haitian Revolution. Elysée Loustallot was a French lawyer, journalist and editor of the *Revolutions of Paris* newspaper during the French Revolution. He died in September 1790, mourned by Robespierre. Judging by the company he kept, Lescure was clearly a Jacobin radical, perhaps related to the general of the same name.

On the strength of Duckett's recommendation and his own experience of working with agents associated with Duckett and Irish matters, Bourdon recommended that O'Leary, Tremblett, Lescure, Despard, Hastings, Carey, Perks and Shugroe as well as agents Edward Ferris and Jeremy Curtayne were to be sent *en mission*.[22] Both Ferris and Curtayne were mentioned earlier.

On 28 April, Duckett reported that: 'the persecution of the patriots by the English ministers increases who are impatient for our support ... horrible excesses are carried out in Ireland'. He added that the Irish had sent agents via Hamburg and America to France seeking help 'for the independence of their father land'.[23] This placed Marcus Edward Despard centre stage in what happened next. The agents that Bourdon and Duckett mention are likely to be McCabe and Dowdall, but who they talked to and what was agreed upon is not known. Events now turned to fomenting revolution in England.

Yet, if preparations were being made to land in Ireland, nothing about this can now be found recorded in archive sources. Indeed, William Huskisson informed the Crown that his spy within the French Ministère de la Marine had reported to him the absence of any visible preparation for an invasion, but invasion was talked of among the Irish leaders in France. Rather than anything official by the French government concerning Ireland being discussed, the spy noted that 'clandestine projects against Ireland' were being planned.[24] Trouble was brewing in Ireland, yet no firm plans against Ireland had been at least officially made in France.

Chapter 17

ENGLISH REVOLUTION IS PLANNED

Despite lack of evidence from French archives, trouble was brewing in the north of England. O'Coigly's direction from Manchester, radicals in Yorkshire and Ireland were ready to rise in rebellion. On 30 January 1798, in London, the London Corresponding Society, then its death throes, issued an Address to the United Irishmen, declaring that: 'If to Unite in the Cause of Reform upon the Broadest Basis be Treason ... We, with you, are Traitors'.[1]

In one Manchester meeting O'Coigly produced a paper from the National Committee of Ireland reporting that there were 300,000 United Irishmen and 19,500 soldiers in readiness, and that before the rebellion was to begin, fear should be spread by assassinating some magistrates in Manchester. O'Coigly furthermore stressed the importance of procuring arms for the uprising and, when Gray said that people in Manchester were too poor and that trade was bad, he observed that there were plenty of arms in Ireland. Michael Quigley stated that the French belief was that the creation of a republic in Ireland would lead to spontaneous revolution in Scotland and England. He closed the meeting by saying that he and Arthur O'Connor were shortly to leave to talk with the United Englishmen in London and then travel on to France.[2] Quigley was a United Irishman, born at Rathcoffey, County Kildare, the eldest son of John Quigley, in 1768. Both he and his father worked for Archibald Hamilton Rowan as bricklayers making improvements to Rathcoffey House. Rowan's democratic ideas may have influenced Quigley junior in joining the United Irish rebellion in 1798.

In Ireland the United Irishmen were still anxiously waiting for the French to 'put boots on the ground'. Despite the factionalism that beset the Irish leadership Lewines was still *chargé d'affaires* at the close of the year, as Barras informed him that although English defeat was the priority for the Directory, they would give the United Irishmen 'the greatest means' to take action themselves.[3]

Having briefed the Manchester leaders, O'Coigly returned to Paris, where he met Talleyrand during December, and also Napper Tandy as well as those gathered round him, such as the veteran radical John Hurford Stone. He does not seem at any point to have met Wolfe Tone or Lewines to discuss planning, and indeed was party to a 'court martial' of Wolfe Tone and Lewines undertaken by Napper Tandy.[4] O'Coigly was clearly working for the Napper Tandy and O'Connor faction, so it is questionable how much he actually knew of the French plans. A British spy reported:

M'Mahon, Member of the Executive Committee, a Presbyterian parson from the County of Down, forced to emigrate in June last, came over to London, where he met with Quigley – O'Coigly, who was likewise obliged to leave Ireland. They stayed together in London, imitating the Patriots in the mode of forming Societies after the plan of United Irish. They had heard of the expedition at the Texel being intended for Ireland, and it was agreed on that an insurrection should be attempted in London, as soon as the landing was effected in Ireland. Colonel Despard was to be the leading person, and the King and Council were to be put to death, &c. Their force was estimated at 40,000, ready to turn out. M'Mahon, hearing he was traced to London, resolved on going for France, and took Quigley as his interpreter: he got a subscription made to pay Quigley's expenses, and collected twenty-five guineas, fifteen of which were given by a Mr. Bell, of the city (summoned on the trial of O'Connor), and ten guineas by Chambers, of Abbey Street, Dublin, who has been this long time in London, keeping up a correspondence (as I believe) between Lewines, &c.

M'Mahon and Quigley went over to Cuxhaven, thence directly for Holland, were on board the fleet, and, when the expedition went off, proceeded to Paris. They there found Lewines, but could get no satisfactory answers from him relative to his communications with the French Government. A quarrel was the consequence; and Quigley was dispatched privately by M'Mahon to London, to get some one sent over to represent the Patriots of both nations, and to replace Lewines. A paper drawn up by Benjamin Binns, and which they had brought over to sketch out something from, was made no use of; but Tom Paine told Quigley he might assure the English that France only made war against their government.[5]

The British Crown clearly knew a great deal: the letter also shows that the Crown took the threat of invasion and the United Irishmen seriously. It also suggests that both men had met Lewines. The disagreement reported by the spy appears to have largely triggered the 'court-martial' fiasco of Napper Tandy. Despairing at Napper Tandy's behaviour and arrogance, Wolfe Tone had attempted to court-martial Napper Tandy. Lewines had been invited to participate but refused. Napper Tandy's reputation was undiminished, but the United Irish leadership's lack of unity was starting to tear apart any hope of success.

How much he, or Napper Tandy, knew about French plans in detail cannot be determined, but at the end of his second trip to Paris, O'Coigly returned from France to London with news. On 3 January 1798, he met the national committee of the United Englishmen in London with advice that: 'France is watching for an opportunity to be given from hence by some popular commotion as anxiously as their friends here wait for some direct assurance of force to warrant their showing their faces.'[6] Within days O'Coigly and Benjamin Binns were travelling to Dublin with an address from the United Britons to the United Irishmen.[7] O'Coigly arrived in Dublin on 9 January and established contact with Lord Edward Fitzgerald. He carried with him an address to the United Irishmen from the United Englishmen.[8]

The Dublin committee agreed to send agents to Hamburg to liaise with Duckett and Bourdon. According to an informer this was to have been agent John Murphy.[9]

However for reasons unknown, Murphy did not travel and in his place went Edmund O'Finn, who left London on 18 January 1798 and landed at Rotterdam five days later, having sailed from Yarmouth to Cuxhaven. He travelled as 'Spencer' with his wife and a brother, identified as Francis. On arrival in Rotterdam, he was arrested as a British subject but soon released and permitted to go on to The Hague to meet Charles Delacroix. On meeting Delacroix, O'Finn handed him maps and detailed reports on the strength of the underground revolutionary movement in Ireland and England.[10] His journey had not gone unnoticed by the British Crown.[11] In Paris, the chaotic nature of the United Irishmen, who had broken into rival camps headed by Napper Tandy and Wolfe Tone, meant that any representative from England had to make a choice about which side to back. O'Finn chose Napper Tandy, becoming his aide-de-camp. Despite this, O'Finn met with Bonaparte and laid out plans for the invasion, which minimized the need for French military aid.[12] In later life O'Finn became an officer in the Garde Imperiale and was killed in action in September 1811 leading a reconnaissance patrol from the Lanciers de Berg.[13] Returning to O'Coigly, he came back to London in the first week of February. He met with the north of England radicals en route, informing them that this would be his last visit; if he returned it would be to see 'the Tree of Liberty planted in Manchester'. He brought with him a copy of an address from the United Irishmen to the radicals of Manchester, which encouraged the assassination of 'the petty tyrants of Manchester … and the rest would fear as they did in Ireland'.[14]

In London he met with O'Connor at the home of Valentine Lawless where they planned their mission to France. A spy reported that 90,000 United Irishmen were in London.[15] Napper Tandy himself estimated 30,000.[16] Marianne Elliott and others have often criticized Napper Tandy for over-estimating the strength of support in Ireland and England.[17] Yet, here is a report independent of Napper Tandy that suggests the United Irish and United Englishmen had attracted a huge groundswell of support. Napper Tandy's bragging, it seems, was based on what he – and the British Crown – considered to be hard facts. Events in 1798 would prove the reality of the situation, however.

The United Englishmen

As in 1796, the United Irishmen's plan required a simultaneous rising in Ireland and England, and the leadership had worked hard to keep the spirit of rebellion alive. They were so successful at keeping their organization 'off the radar' after the aborted rebellion of 1796, nothing is known of the activities of the United Englishmen until New Year 1798 when the Revd Thomas Bancroft informed the Home Office that in Bolton the active Jacobin club was 'almost exclusively composed of Dissenters [illegible] two meeting houses, Unitarian and Presbyterian'. His spy, he informed the Home Office, 'had infiltrated the club and been told that the French would invade on the Yorkshire coast as a diversionary attack for the main attack which would be on Ireland'.[18] Richard Ford at the Home Officer reported in April 1798 that over the past eighteen months emissaries from the Irish rebels had been recruiting in London, Birmingham, Manchester and Sheffield preparatory to an insurrection.[19]

French émigré Prince Boullion reported to the Crown at the end of 1797 that 'clandestine projects against Ireland' were being planned.[20] This was not merely wishful thinking: General Daendels proposed to the French Directory an attack on Scotland and Yorkshire in January 1798. It was hoped to separate Scotland from England, from where the French hoped to link with thousands of partisans as a feint for another attempt at landing in Ireland.[21] It was planned that United Englishmen in major towns and manufacturing centres would rise up on the same day, and that disturbances in England would provide a diversion from the landing in Ireland. John Ashley, the former secretary to the London

Corresponding Society, travelled to France in January 1798 and reported to Talleyrand in April 1798 that 30,000 'active and decided men … ready to co-operate against the government when opportunity shall present itself' were in London, and nationwide 100,000 were willing to rise.[22] All was seemingly prepared: everything rested on the French landing.

Clearly, this plan was communicated to the underground radical movement: spies for the British Crown reported that United Irish emissaries toured England and Scotland agitating for the formation of societies to make common cause with them, the 'three kingdoms being all united for the same Purposes to rise at the same time', to secure an equal representation of all the people by expunging the pocket boroughs, equal electoral districts, annual parliaments, universal 'manhood suffrage' and an end to the Test and Corporation Acts.[23]

However, the plans laid by Lewines and Wolfe Tone were not secret, and the British Crown was kept fully informed of what was being planned via Samuel Turner, a former United Irishmen now turned informer, who was assisted by George Orr. Without its network of spies, the British Crown would have been almost completely 'in the dark' about French invasion plans. Ironically, it was the French Royalists who saved the British Isles from invasion by their own countrymen.

Arrests are Made

Planning for the rebellion now 'moved up a gear'. The French Minister of War reported that 'the Irish Patriots are preparing to attack Dublin in three Corps, one from the south, one from the north, and from the west … The patriots … have been training in the mountains'.[24] Indeed, one informant for the British Crown, a former member of the Society for Constitutional Information, reported that the United Irishmen in London had plans to undertake 'some great design', and to that end had ordered that 'pikes were to be manufactured by Cook and Shirley at a forge at No 20 Pancras Place, London'.[25] Another spy informed the alarmed Home Office that pikes were being made in Liverpool and taken to Irish rebels and toasts were drunk wishing 'success to the rebels in Ireland'.[26]

A spy reported to the Home Office that the United Englishmen were starting to arm themselves, and were readying themselves to act with the United Irishmen led by Wolfe Tone as soon as the French invaded. The spy noted furthermore that a well-known Jacobin, John Astley, and others were in France as delegates from the United movement.[27] An informer, Catholic priest John Waring, in a letter dated 15 February 1798, stated that Bernard Kerr had passed him information about the United Englishmen:

> There are here said at [illegible] twenty thousand of this society in Manchester ready to join the French in case of an invasion – their plan is to overturn the Constitution of England and to have an equal representation of the people in Parliament ... they have delegates at Paris whom they change from time to time as circumstances may allow.[28]

When asked by Waring how Kerr dared show him the rules of the United Englishmen, Kerr replied that he trusted a priest to keep a confidence and did not want his name publicized in case of attack by 'those infernal assassins'. Kerr also reported that printers in Birmingham, Manchester and Sheffield had printed the rules of the United Englishmen and distributed them in those towns.[29]

Informants for the Manchester bench reported to the Home Office that for the past eighteen months emissaries from the Irish rebels had been recruiting in London, Birmingham, Manchester and Sheffield preparatory to an insurrection.[30] From Nottingham came reports that two shopkeepers had stated that if there was an invasion by the French, they would support them.[31]

Thanks to the efforts of the informer Samuel Turner, on 28 February 1798, O'Coigly, John Binns, Arthur O'Connor, his servant O'Leary and John Gale Jones were arrested in Margate with a letter from the 'Secret Committee of England' to the French Directory inviting Napoléon Bonaparte to invade Britain. The address, written by Dr Crossfield, read: 'With the Tyranny of England, that of all Europe must fall. Haste then, Great Nation! Pour forth thy gigantic force! We now only wait with Impatience to see the Hero of Italy [General Bonaparte], and the brave veterans of the Great Nation. Myriads will hail their arrival with shouts of joy!' In Paris Wolfe Tone expressed amazement; he had little sympathy for O'Coigly but dreaded to think of a man of O'Connor's talents being caught in such extraordinary circumstances. In Dublin, however, McNally reported that the moderates were not sorry to have the 'impetuous' O'Connor out of the way. The newspapers were filled with accounts of their arrest and the five were reported to be in possession of 'a traitorous correspondence' between Ireland, France and England. Fortunately for them, O'Leary with great foresight disposed of the most significant documents in the privy of the King's Head. The primary target of the prosecution was Arthur O'Connor, yet, when placed on trial a parade of progressive Whigs mounted the stand to vouch for him: Charles James Fox, Richard Sheridan and the Duke of Norfolk. William Dowdall travelled from Ireland to defend O'Connor but was later arrested and sent to Newgate Prison in Dublin a few weeks after. William Pitt was engaged when O'Connor and the

Binns brothers were acquitted, along with John Allen and Jeremiah Leary. The Crown wanted to make an example and Father O'Coigly became the victim.[32]

Further arrests of leading members took place. On 19 April 1798, the 'Central Committee of Delegates' was raided at a pub in Drury Lane, London. Together with parallel raids on corresponding societies in Birmingham and Manchester, a total of twenty-eight people were arrested, among them Thomas Evans, Marcus Edward Despard, John Bone, Benjamin Binns, Paul Le Maitre, Richard Hodgson and Alexander Galloway. The next day, Pitt renewed the suspension of habeas corpus absolving the government of the need to present evidence prior to imprisonment. The prisoners were held without charge until hostilities with France were (temporarily) halted with the Treaty of Amiens in 1801. Despite some rallying among the United Englishmen in the immediate aftermath, there were further arrests of leading members across the country in April 1798. A former member of the Society for Constitutional Information turned government agent reported that the United Irishmen in London were undertaking 'some great design' and that pikes had been manufactured by Cook and Shirley at a forge at 20 Pancras Place, London. He added that the two Binns brothers were the principal members of the United Irishmen, and Galloway and Evans were key members of the United Englishmen. He added that Evans and Galloway had corresponded over whether to assassinate witnesses in the approaching trials.[33]

In London, Thomas Evans, Alexander Galloway and Thomas Spence were arrested.[34] In the north of England James Dixon was arrested in Manchester.[35] Under interrogation, Dixon confessed that he had been told that membership of the United Irish in County Cork was 65,000 and was armed with 28,000 weapons, of which 12,000 were muskets and the rest pikes, and that these had been landed from a French vessel. When asked about the state of the United Englishmen in Manchester Dixon revealed that he had informed delegates from Ireland that it was declining.[36] William Moores and three others in Manchester were arrested following receipt of secret intelligence that they were to 'debauch the minds' of employees of a large factory and the Little Lever Volunteers.[37] Well-known Mancunian radicals Joseph Hanson and Thomas Walker were implicated in giving funds to the United Englishmen. James Hughes was arrested and charged with sedition.[38] On 16 February, General Daendels informed Wolfe Tone that he had received maps of Scotland and requested Eugene Aherne to return to The Hague. In his letter to Wolfe Tone Daendels made no mention at all of Ireland.[39]

A member of the London Corresponding Society informed the Crown that members now planned and hoped for a French invasion to establish a republic in England, and that despite arrests arrangements were still being made to rise in rebellion and gather arms to support the French when they landed. The informer reported that seven sections of United Englishmen existed in London and that they had made a 'union' with the United Irishmen. A British agent reported that Alexander Galloway and Thomas Evans were the principal members of the United Englishmen, and the Binns brothers were the foremost leaders of the United Irishmen. He added that both groups were associating with Archibald Hamilton Rowan 'who lately fled to France with Baily of Canterbury'.[40]

The trials climaxed with the execution of O'Coigly: caught with the address to the French Directory in his pocket, he was found guilty of treason. Despite considerable inducements to turn 'King's Evidence', O'Coigly went to his death on 7 July keeping his secrets: he was hanged and then suffered the ignobility of being decapitated.[41]

It was clear that the United Irishmen, which had begun as a legal reforming society, was now an underground army which was at least 100,000-men strong. Across the Irish Sea, the United Englishman had followed the same trajectory, perhaps counting an underground movement of the same strength. Arms raids took place in Ireland and Yorkshire. Blacksmiths and carpenters were singled out, as in 1794, for producing pikes. Ireland wanted her independence, and émigré Irishmen were at the heart of the United Englishmen movement. Forced to flee their homes and families after the French invasion of 1796, the Irish diaspora fuelled radical politics across England, and found willing accomplices in Yorkshire, Lancashire and London. The French via its secret agents were building a secret underground army from the ranks of the radicals, reformists and disaffected poor in England.

Chapter 18

REBELLION AND INVASION

In Ireland, despite the arrest of O'Connor, revolution was still being planned. Fitzgerald had met with Minister Reinhardt, a representative of the French government, in Hamburg to promote a French invasion.[1] Clearly, whatever was being planned in Paris was in conjunction with Duckett in Hamburg, as well as the group around O'Connor and O'Coigly. An informant for the Crown reported that the: 'People was all armed with pikes or guns and I was informed that the lower class gave a shilling a piece for their pikes', adding:

> ... that a delegate from the county went to Scotland in December and staid [sic] there upwards of three months ... [who at a] ... baronial meeting of the town land of Ballybun ... brought some very good news ... the French intended ... that they should be able to land their men in the beginning of May. The people to keep still such times as the standing army was drawn off to face the enemy and they were then to attack the yeomanry and cut off the provisions to the army.

Whatever was being planned was clearly in conjunction with the United Scotsman. The timing of the middle of May accords directly with the date set with Bonaparte for his departure for Ireland, as mentioned previously. At long last a unified plan of action between radical groups in England, Scotland and Ireland had been created and agreed to. Tellingly, the informant noted: 'the people of the South would not wait till such times as the French came as they said that they had been let down by the French before'.[2] This is perfectly true. The Emmet brothers and their supporters in Ireland did not want to wait for the French. Fitzgerald urged caution and the lack of unity between the Fitzgerald supporters and those of the Emmets undermined the events as they unfolded.

Fear that the Texel fleet and ships gathered at Ostend would head to Scotland as planned resulted in the British Crown taking pre-emptive action. Aware that a large number of small craft was fitting at Flushing for the transport of troops, and were about to be conveyed by way of the Bruges canal to Ostend and thence to Dunkirk, the Royal Navy struck on 18 May. The lock gates and sluices at Ostend were destroyed so rendering the canal useless and several gunboats were burned out. The raiding party was captured by the French 46e and 94e demi-brigades.[3] Despite this small French victory, the raiding party had achieved its objectives. Dunkirk and Ostend were blockaded and any hope of a break-out was over. The British Crown's spy network's work leading to the arrests in England and Ireland, as well as the pre-emptive strike, had destroyed the United Irish network in England, and the threat of invasion was over. In Ireland, however, sectarian violence erupted in Protestant loyalists against the United Irishmen, backed by the Crown. Fitzgerald's social position made him the most important United Irish leader still at liberty. On 9 May, a reward of £1,000 was offered by Dublin Castle for Fitzgerald's apprehension. Since the arrests at Bond's, Fitzgerald had been in hiding, but had twice visited his wife in disguise and was himself visited by his stepfather Ogilvie and his friend William Lawless. He was caught on 19 May, shot in the shoulder by Major Sirr and conveyed to Newgate Prison, Dublin, where he was denied proper medical treatment and died there on 4 June 1798.

Bonaparte arrived at Toulon on 9 May and embarked on the 19th. When he did set sail, rather than travelling north the general headed to Egypt. Bonaparte's destination ended any pretence of the French landing.

On 26 May came stunning news of the summary execution of some thirty-four suspected United Irishmen at Dunlavin, in south Wicklow, who had been killed a week or more earlier; this was quickly followed by a report that at Carnew, across the border in Wexford, thirty-five prisoners had been summarily executed. Fevered rumours of extirpation now appeared to have substance. In terror, the peasantry – United Irishmen or not – prepared to resist. The initial outbreak of the rebellion was confined to a ring of counties surrounding Dublin. Only in County Wexford did the United Irishmen meet with success. The fighting in the rebellion was marked by an extreme ideological and increasingly sectarian bitterness. Prisoners on both sides were commonly killed after battle. The fall of Wexford was the high point of the rebellion in the south-east. While rebellion had been raging in the south-east, the north had generally been quiet.

In the north, the mainly Presbyterian United Irishmen launched their own uprising in support of Wexford in early June, but again, after some initial success were defeated by government troops and militia. Their leaders, Henry Joy McCracken and Henry Munro, were captured and hanged, Munro outside the front door of his home. At Ballynahinch, some 12 miles from Belfast, the United Irish were routed on 12–13 June, suffering several hundred casualties. Military losses were three dead and some thirty wounded. The rebellion in the North East was over.[4]

Knowing that without French help the revolution would end in certain defeat, the United Irish leadership sprang into action. Edward Lewines wrote to the Directory under his own name requesting 5,000 muskets and an invasion force of 30,000 men. He noted that the French would be received as friends and liberators, and that on their arrival Ireland would rise in support.[5] Almost simultaneously, on 16 June, Lowry, Hall, William Henry Hamilton and Teeling presented a petition. The leaders noted that in the space of three days, 2–26 May, 1,500 Defenders and United Irishmen had been killed and that if the rebellion was to succeed, they desperately needed reinforcements. The United Irish demanded 1,000 men and 5,000 muskets.[6] At Brest a few days later, on the 19th, Admiral Bruix ordered four frigates to be dispatched immediately to Ireland carrying troops, 1,000 muskets and 40,000 cartridges.[7]

Two days later, on 21 June, General Gerard Lake attempted to surround Vinegar Hill with some 20,000 men in 4 columns of soldiers, in order to prevent a rebel break-out. Battle was joined. It lasted about 2 hours: the United Irish were routed. The rebellion in the south-east was over.[8] Reprisals followed immediately. One informant told Crown forces to search for arms and ammunition in 'the barn floor of Hugh Thompson of Killinchy for pikes; the outhouses of James Orr of Granshaw for ammunition; and cottages in Granshaw and Ballybun for pikes as people living there had not given up any arms'.[9] The British Crown dispatched 10,000 men as reinforcements to Ireland.[10] One observer, the Revd Handcock, reckoned the rebellion in Ireland was to set up the 'popish religion' and that the Irish Catholics were going to assassinate anyone who obstructed them. Furthermore, Handcock reckoned a French invasion of Ireland was no longer expected, but as soon as English troops were sent to counter the rebellion an invasion of England would take place.[11]

The rebellion in Ireland caught the French Directory off guard. An address of the legislative council of the Directory on the Irish cause, on 14 July, stated: 'All free men and men who want to become free are our brothers: but they are more so when their efforts concentrate on an arrogant and treacherous country … Ireland does not only set a great and virtuous example for other nations: she fights for the whole of Europe, for the human cause.'[12]

Seemingly, the Directory was goaded into action by events and planned a full-scale invasion. Four fleets were assembled at Brest, Dunkirk, La Rochelle and Texel. General Hardy was appointed to command a force of 10,000 men, with 4,000 under his orders and a similar number commanded by General Rey at Dunkirk.[13] A spy for the British Crown reported in July:

> At Flushing there are a great many French soldiers, to the amount of twenty-five hundred: there are, I understand, as many Dutch.
> General Creevey, a young man who goes with the great expedition, called on me one day at Paris, and stayed for dinner. Muir and Madget [sic] were of the party. It was for the purpose of inquiring into Wolfe Tone's character, which we gave him. Madget [sic] and Muir swore me into the Secret Committee for managing the affairs of Ireland and Scotland in Napper Tandy's place: there are only we three of the Committee. A young man, of the name of Thomas Graham, same place as Muir and Smith, arrived at Paris the day before I left: he sailed from Scotland for Embden, was taken by a French privateer, and brought into Holland. He was coming to France at the time: he was obliged to stay five or six weeks at the Hague with O'Herne before he could get a passport; for his letter to Muir had been suppressed through the contrivance of Lewins [sic] who strives to prevent any person doing anything with Government but himself. The French gave orders for 20,000 muskets at Hamburg … They had a map of Ireland, as old as King William, on which they were trying to find out the safest places for debarkations. The west coast seemed to be the most eligible, from Derry up to Galway. They told me they supposed France had sent off some corsairs with muskets and ammunition.
> Left Paris 30th. One Keith, a Scotchman, got leave to go over to England by Muir's means. He is a banker at Paris, I believe; he had his passport the day before I came away … three expeditions are to go from France, viz.: Rochefort, consisting of frigates; the grand expedition from Brest, and privateers from Dunkirk and that coast. There is to be one from Holland, but that, I think, will be for Scotland, where Graham says there are 200,000 now arming themselves.[14]

In the midst of the panic over Ireland, Muir and Madgett senior were clearly working on Daendels' scheme. It is also known via a British agent that Aherne – O'Herne – was at The Hague. The spy also notes, where French archives are lacking, that thousands of muskets were loaded onto three frigates on the orders of Admiral Bruix and dispatched to Ireland.[15] The spy adds that stores had been sent from Morlaix in June to be used for the expedition in Ireland.[16] Where and when the arms landed is not known.

By the start of July, a firm plan of action beyond sending arms had been made. A squadron would sail from Texel, led by Major Michel, General Rey would sail from Dunkirk with at most 4,000 men and the main force of 5,000 men, complete with field artillery, under General Hardy would sail from Brest. Napper Tandy was sent to Dunkirk. He along with General Rey intended to sail first and provide a rallying point, such was the belief in France of the level of support he would receive and he honestly believed would be forthcoming. Hardy was to land afterwards simultaneously with Humbert. The French were to land at three different points in Ulster. Wolfe Tone and his brother Mathew and Bartholomew Teeling joined Hardy at Brest, while other Irish émigrés flocked to Dunkirk to rally to Napper Tandy.[17]

Humbert's Invasion

Assembling a large force would take time, and thoughts turned once more to Carnot's ideas for 'Chouanization' and its leading exponent, the former rabbit catcher turned general Jean-Joseph Humbert. On 18 July, Humbert was ordered to prepare a small invasion force of a battalion of infantry, a half company of foot artillery, armed with 3 4-pounder field guns, and to carry with him 3,000 muskets with bayonets, 3,000 gibernes, 400 sabres, 200,000 musket cartridges and 1,000 French uniforms. Later Humbert had an additional battalion of infantry and two squadrons of cavalry, from the 3e Chasseurs and 12e Hussard, attached to this force. If the landing was to achieve success, it was vital that Humbert rallied the United Irishmen to his colours and Humbert was authorized to use a spy network to gather as much information as he could about events in Ireland and also in England, the Directory stressing the importance of aiding the United Irishmen in the cause of liberty.[18] Preparations for the invasion had not gone unnoticed: the British Crown's spy network reported: 'Levying of Norman and Breton seamen (for Brest) and of Flemish seamen (for the Texel and Dunkirk) all intended for Ireland.'[19] Humbert replied to the Ministère de la Marine at the end of the month: 'The enthusiasm is such that I have no doubts about the success of our expedition. I only have one prayer left is that you give us orders to set sail. Time is precious and each soldier burns to know his destination and to deserve the esteem of the government.'[20] Humbert was now to lead the advance guard, with Hardy and Rey landing once he had secured a beachhead.[21]

The long-nurtured hopes and dreams of the United Irishmen for a French invasion were finally realized when, on 22 August, three frigates, *Franchise*, *Médée* and *Concorde*, landed at Kilcummin flying the English colours. Edwin and Arthur Stock, sons of the Protestant Bishop of Killala, who had sailed out to meet them, greeted the ships. The English colours were struck and the tricolour was run up. The French force of some 1,100 men, under the command of General Humbert, waded ashore at Kilcummin Strand, near Killala, County Mayo at about 2pm: a picket of cavalry had watched the French land and a group of 10 United Irish met the French on the beachhead. The Irish delegates told the French that Ireland was ready to rise up in revolution to aid the French. 'Citizen Savary', who would later go on to run the secret police under Napoléon, was placed in command of 200 men from the 70e Demi-Brigade to garrison Killala.

By the evening 3,000 Irish had joined the French Army. One of those marching to join Humbert was Francis Moffatt, a young man from Wicklow with a commission as a lieutenant. He and his troop of fifty yeomen deserted to join the United Irish cause and fight with General Humbert. He tells us that he personally orchestrated the defection of his troop of yeomanry – who it is presumed enlisted to learn to be soldiers – and led them to join the United Irish Army, and served alongside the French cavalry. He later served in the Guides of the Army of England.

By about 7pm the landing was complete. General Sarrazin and Catholic priest Father O'Kane set out for Killala to survey the town. On approaching, O'Kane was challenged by a yeoman from a side street: in the ensuing short struggle he shot the yeoman dead. Sarrazin and his men arrived moments later, where they were met by a volley from Crown forces. Instead of opening fire, the French and United Irish surged forward with an audacious bayonet charge, swept away the dismounted yeomanry and captured the town. Bishop Stocks' palace was taken over as Humbert's headquarters. Several of the yeomen were taken prisoner while others fled towards Ballina. A French soldier climbed to the top of the palace and removed the British flag, which was replaced by a green and gold flag bearing the inscription '*Éirinn go Brách*' ('Ireland forever').[22] In total, the French transport landed 1,025 men, along with 3,000 muskets, 400 pistols, 400 sabres, 3 4-pounder field guns with caissons, 30,000kg of powder, 66,000 cartridges and 1,000 uniforms for the Irish which were lodged in the palace. A further 1,000 students from Dublin flocked to the

French and 'wore the uniform of the French solider'. The French forces were swelled by 13,500 United Irish Infantry and 600 United Irish Cavalry.[23] One of those joining the French was Wicklow man Francis Morfet, who described himself as a yeoman who along with '50 men passed into the service of the United Irish under the orders of General Humbert'.[24] However, these irregulars could never replace over 1,000 sabres from the 3e Chasseurs and 12e Hussard, which together with the 1,400 infantry from the 1e Demi-Brigade failed to land due to bad weather.[25] Despite these setbacks, Humbert knew that a further 3,000 men under General Hardy with Wolfe Tone at their head were due to sail from Brest and 4,000 from Dunkirk.[26]

General Humbert began operations to march on Dublin, to seize the capital and proclaim the republic.[27] Humbert declared:

> Liberty, Equality, Fraternity, Unity! Irishman, You have not forgotten Bantry-Bay; you know what efforts France has made to help you. Their affection for you, their desire to ensure your independence have never failed you. After some unsuccessful efforts, here the French are in your midst. We come to help your courage, to share your dangers, to join their arms with yours, and to mix their blood with your blood for the sacred cause of freedom.
>
> Brave Irishmen, our cause is common. Like you, we hate a greedy, bloodthirsty and oppressive government: like you, we regard as imprescriptible the right of nations to freedom; like you, we are convinced that the peace of the world will always be disturbed, as long as there is still an English ministry to deal with industry, labour and the blood of the people with impunity. ... We guarantee you the most solemn respect for your properties, your laws and your religion. Be free; be the masters of your country. We seek no other conquest than that of your freedom, no other triumph than yours ... The time to break your chains has arrived. Our victorious troops are now flying to the ends of the world to destroy to the roots the power and tyranny of our enemies. The frightening colossus falls into dust on all sides. Would there be an Irishman vile enough to lose interest in the happiness of his country? ... Unity, Liberty, Irish Republic! This is our cry, and let us advance![28]

Acting on Carnot's 1796 plan for 'Chouanization', having captured Killala, Humbert sent two groups under generals Sarrazin and Fontaine to capture Ballina. That night a fight took place between Sarrazin's troops and the British at Rosserk. The English eventually retreated in confusion. The next morning the French/Irish troops captured Ballina under cover of darkness. Humbert scored a striking victory at Castlebar:

I arrived on the 10th Fructidor, at six o'clock in the morning, on the heights behind Castlebar. I recognized the position of the enemy which was very strong. I ordered General Sarrazin to start the attack. The enemy's riflemen were pushed back sharply. Battalion Chief Dufour drove them to the foot of the enemy army position. The grenadiers moved to the charge pace on the line of battle; the line infantry followed them.

The deployment of the columns took place under the fire of twelve pieces of cannon. Then, General Sarrazin had the left attacked by a battalion of the line which was forced to retreat, coming under fire from more than 2,000 men. General Sarrazin flies to his rescue at the head of the grenadiers and repels the enemy. The English made, for half an hour, a terrible fire of musketry. General Sarrazin forbids to retaliate. Our proud capacity baffles the English general. As soon as the army has arrived, I order the general attack. General Sarrazin, at the head of the grenadiers, tumbled back to the enemy's right and seized three pieces of cannon, Battalion Chief Ardouin forced the left to retreat into Castlebar.

The enemy, concentrated in the city and supported by his artillery, fired terrible fire. The 3rd Chasseur Regiment made a charge on Castlebar's main street and forced the enemy to cross the bridge. After several very deadly charges of cavalry and infantry, led by General Sarrazin and Deputy Adjutant General Fontaine, the enemy was driven out of all his positions and pursued for two leagues.

The enemy lost 1,300 men, including 600 killed or wounded and 1,200 prisoners, 10 pieces of cannon, 5 flags, 1,200 musket and almost all their baggage. The standard of the enemy cavalry was captured in a charge by General Sarrazin, whom I appointed major general on the battlefield. I also appointed, during the action, General Fontaine to Brigadier General; Battalion Chiefs Azemard, Ardouin and Dufour, Brigade Chiefs; Captain Durival to squadron leader, and Captains Toussaint, Zimmermann, Ranon, Huette, Babin and Ruty, to battalion chiefs. I ask you, Citizen Directors, to confirm these appointments and to have the patents shipped as soon as possible; it will produce a very good effect.[29]

Humbert established his headquarters at Castlebar from 27 August–4 September. On 31 August, the United Irishmen proclaimed a 'Republic of Connaught', which lasted a mere twelve days. On 5 September, the British forces were again defeated at Collooney. The string of French victories drew more United Irishmen to the colours, and by 8 September, their strength was over 15,000.[30] However, it soon became apparent that Collooney was an empty triumph. On 8 September, at County Longford the French force came face to face with Crown forces led by General Cornwallis. Vastly outnumbered, the French Army and Irish allies laid down their arms after a short battle lasting about 30 minutes.

The French were treated as honoured prisoners of war, but the United Irishmen were not so lucky: they were summarily executed.[31] Killala was retaken on 12 September. The captured French soldiers were transferred to England and eventually repatriated. The French officers of Irish origin were hanged in Dublin with the Irish rebels.[32]

Napper Tandy

This was not the end of Irish émigré hopes for an invasion. On his arrival in France, Napper Tandy, as befitting his megalomaniac tendencies, had exaggerated his military experience, his influence in Ireland and the willingness of the Irish to support a French invasion. In the same way, from France he exaggerated to the United Irish leaders in Ireland the preparedness of the French to invade; to the British authorities he signalled his presence in France by declaring through the press his attendance at a grand St Patrick's day dinner (17 March 1798). The Directory had little choice to recognize the existence of the two camps by appointing Napper Tandy a *général de brigade*, despite his lack of military experience other than as a colonel of the Dublin Independent Volunteers. He now outranked Wolfe Tone and understood that HE was in charge of operations. He organized an expedition to Ireland with a staff consisting of his own followers. A spy reported from Hamburg that:

> August 16. Napper Tandy having quarrelled with Lewines and Tone called a meeting of United Irishmen in conjunction with Muir, Madget, and Stone. At the meeting a division took place; the numbers pretty equal. Muir waited on Talleyrand with a petition, which Talleyrand took instantly to the Directory. In consequence, Napper Tandy was appointed General: those that sided with him compose his staff, viz.: M'Mahon, Coigley's companion, to be a Colonel and Aide-de-camp; O'Finn, Carey, brother to the priest, Waldron, and Pharis, with one Lyster, and two or three others, Irish-Americans. A Captain Blackwell is appointed his Adjutant-General. They all left Paris on Tuesday, 11th July, to go (as I believe) to Dunkirk. Mrs. Blackwell told me they were to go in a small corsaire, with only 40 or 50 men. Madget said they were to have 1500. O'Finn's wife left Paris the day before, to go to England. Government gave them money, &c. Teeling, with a brother of Tone's, and one Sullivan, nephew to Madget, set out for Rochfort on Saturday, 21st.[33]

Clearly, the old radical John Hurford Stone was still engaged in planning revolution. Napper Tandy accepted the offer of a corvette from the French government and sailed from Dunkirk accompanied by a few United Irishmen, a small force of about 340 grenadiers and a considerable quantity of arms and ammunition for distribution in Ireland. A spy reported:

He promised to raise for them in Ireland a legion of 10,000 men, but they suspected his means of doing this, as well as the weakness and vanity of his disposition. Being importunate, the Directory made him a General provisionally (provisoirement) he pledged his head for the success of his proposition, but, to his woeful experience, could not raise a single man, and had scarcely set his foot on Irish ground until obliged to make a precipitate retreat ... sailed about the 3rd or 4th of September, 1798, at four o'clock in the afternoon; had on board a crew of about 50 seamen and marines, 30 cannoneers, 3 curricle guns, 1000 muskets, 800 pair of horse pistols, 1000 sabres, and plenty of ammunition – destination, the north-west coast of Ireland. There were on board, besides Tandy, holding the rank of general, provisionally, from the French Directory, Blackwell, educated under the Jesuits; but, at the commencement of the French Revolution, being able to proceed no further in that line, entered the army; and, on the 14th July last, got the command of a company of hussars, was, shortly after, made a colonel; and, during the passage, compelled Tandy to give him first the rank of adjutant-general, and next that of general of brigade ... My opinion of Tandy is, that he is too weak to conduct any extensive plan, too wicked not to be abhorred by all who know him – and too insignificant for the British Government to take any other notice of him than to despise him.

His weakness appears very prominent in the following circumstance: he has got a few laced coats, which he is eternally overhauling and gazing on. The day he landed, for a few hours, on the Isle of Arran, at Rutland, he intoxicated himself to such a degree as to be incapable of getting to the boat, and p-d on the shoulders of those who carried him to it; and one of the French officers says he paid him the like compliment in his boots; and, during the action with 'The Tom', armed merchantman, he squatted on the deck, with a pint bottle of brandy, which he emptied twice.[34]

Napper Tandy arrived on Arranmore Island, off the coast of County Donegal, on 16 September 1798, seeking to raise the county in rebellion to aid Humbert: he had not heard of Humbert's capitulation. The locality, however, was sparsely populated and showed little enthusiasm for joining with the expedition. He carried with him the following declaration:

First Year of Irish Liberty. GENERAL JAMES NAPPER TANDY TO HIS COUNTRYMEN. What do I hear? The British Government have dared to speak of concessions. Would you accept of them? Can you think of entering into a treaty with a British Minister – a Minister, too, who has left you at the mercy of an English soldiery, who laid your cities waste, and massacred inhumanly their best citizens; a Minister the bane of society and the scourge of mankind? ... Horrid crimes have been perpetrated in your country: your friends have fallen a sacrifice to their devotion to your cause – their shadows are around you, and call aloud for vengeance; it is your duty to avenge their death – it is your duty to strike from their blood cemented thrones the murderers of your friends. Listen to no proposals, Irishmen! Wage a war of extermination against your oppressors, the war of liberty against tyranny, and liberty shall triumph.[35]

Napper Tandy took possession of the Island of Rutland, where he hoisted an Irish flag and issued a proclamation., However, learning of the defeat of Humbert's expedition and that Connaught was now subdued, the futility of the enterprise was soon apparent. Napper Tandy sailed his vessel round the north of Scotland to avoid the British fleet. He reached Bergen in safety having brought with him a British ship captured along the way. Napper Tandy then made his way with three or four companions to the free port of Hamburg, where he met a British officer and warned him to go into hiding.[36] Napper Tandy will reappear later in the story.

Chapter 19

THE FATE OF WOLFE TONE

On 30 June, Hardy made a plan to sail in conjunction with Humbert at the beginning of August. The significant delay was due to bad weather, bad luck and bad man management. By August, Hardy was ready to set sail, but a mutiny over pay – which it was suspected had been organized by agents for the British Crown – meant Hardy could do nothing until this had been supressed. When he eventually set sail, Hardy encountered a strong storm that forced him back to harbour and he was ordered to postpone his operation on the 26th. Hardy eventually set sail on 20 September with reinforcements to aid Humbert.[1] He carried with him 6 field guns, 6,000 muskets, 1,000,0000 cartridges, 6,000 gibernes, 2,000 uniforms and 150 sets of saddle, harness and sabres for 150 dragoons, along with 4,000 men.[2] On 23 September, the force at Dunkirk under General Rey was stood down.[3]

General Hardy reached the shores of Ireland on 11 October; by then the revolution was over. Undeterred, he attempted to land but was decisively defeated by the Royal Navy at Lough Swilly.[4] An eyewitness recorded: 'Admiral Warren fought off Lough Swilly, we have taken an 84 gun ship several frigates and there was seven thousand men taken to have landed all which are prisoners ... a Brig made off as soon as Warren appeared. We have much damaged the French ships that have escaped.'[5]

The most notable casualty of the entire fiasco was Wolfe Tone, who was captured in the fighting at Lough Swilly. His loss was a major blow to the United Irish cause, which now effectively lacked a single determined leader. At his trial by court martial in Dublin on 8 November 1798, Wolfe Tone made a speech avowing his resolute hostility to England and his intention 'by frank and open war to procure the separation of the countries'. Recognizing that the court was certain to convict him, he asked that 'the court should adjudge me to die the death of a soldier, and that I may be shot'. Reading from a prepared speech, he defended his view of an Irish state:

> I entered into the service of the French Republic with the sole view of being useful to my country. To contend against British Tyranny, I have braved the fatigues and terrors of the field of battle; I have sacrificed my comfort, have courted poverty, have left my wife unprotected, and my children without a father. After all I have done for a sacred cause, death is no sacrifice. In such enterprises, everything depends on success: Washington succeeded – Kosciusko failed. I know my fate, but I neither ask for pardon nor do I complain. I admit openly all I have said, written, and done, and am prepared to meet the consequences. As, however, I occupy a high grade in the French army, I would request that the court, if they can, grant me the favour that I may die the death of a soldier.[6]

On 10 November 1798, Wolfe Tone was found guilty and sentenced to be hanged on 12 November. The day he was found guilty he wrote to the French Directory. In his letter he decried the fact he had not been permitted the death of a soldier of France, declaring: 'I have served the Republic with fidelity, I go to my death as your brother.' He requested that his three children should be cared for by the state and not left destitute and to grow up in a land of liberty and freedom, and again stated that he had done everything he could for his 'fatherland' in sacrificing his life for the Republic.[7] Denied his 'soldier's death', Wolfe Tone attempted suicide by slitting his throat. The story goes that he was initially saved when the wound was sealed with a bandage, and he was told if he tried to talk the wound would open and he would bleed to death. He responded by saying: 'I can yet find words to thank you sir; it is the most welcome news you could give me. What should I wish to live for?' Theobald Wolfe Tone died on 19 November 1798 at the age of 35 in Provost's Prison, Dublin, not far from where he was born. He is buried in Bodenstown, County Kildare, near his birthplace at Sallins.[8] One eyewitness in Dublin was loyalist Eliza Paine who wrote to her brother in England on 26 October:

> I cannot give you an idea of what I have felt since the rebellion broke out – not a day that I did not hear of the murder or burning of a house of someone I knew, many of my friends and acquaintances have fallen victims to the barbarians of the savages in the Country. In the County of Wexford they are still committing horrid murders and burning houses.[9]

Eliza continued that she had 'for some time been expecting a rising of the rebels in Dublin', noting further that 'there is one [illegible] a rebel general that is committing great depredations in the county of Wicklow & large parts of the army are in pursuit of him'. Concluding her letter, she hoped:

> ... that we may have peace once more restored to this now unhappy country, God of Mercy grant that their hearts may be turned and that they accept of the mercy now offered. But the almighty knows best what is fit for us, and to his wisdom we must submit and hope in his own good time he will be graciously pleased to put a stop to the profusion of human blood.[10]

In an addendum, Eliza thanked 'God for so wondrously saving us from the hands of the wicked', but acknowledged that 'there is a great murmurings at the taxes, which by all accounts are small to yours in short there is a general dissatisfaction among the people'. She noted that the authorities at Dublin Castle had uncovered a plot to place barrels of gunpowder in the cellars of a number of houses in the city, and to explode them to signal a general uprising. Eliza concluded: 'I hope the French will not attempt paying us any more visits as all their schemes have been frustrated.'[11] She was wrong.

The Secret Expedition
Humbert's failure, and that of Hardy and Napper Tandy, was, however remarkable it may seem, not the end of the French endeavouring to send aid to Ireland.

Long before Humbert set sail, thoughts in Paris turned to the Batavian fleet at Texel which had been assembled to invade Scotland, but was as yet uncommitted to that enterprise. Despite Muir's hopes that the Texel fleet would sail and liberate his home country of Scotland in conjunction with whatever was being planned concerning Ireland, Admiral Bruix informed General Joubert, commander of French forces in the Netherlands, on 26 June 1798 that the fleet that was due to head to Scotland was to be re-directed to Ireland.[12] Bruix ordered that invasion fleet to sail north from Texel into the North Sea, head to the north of Scotland before turning into the Atlantic at the Orkney Islands and from there head south to Ireland.[13]

Political events in the Batavian Republic now took the lead, much as they had done in France a year earlier. Daendels and Charles Delacroix had been instrumental in a coup on 22 January 1798, which put a radical government into power in the Republic. At the behest of Delacroix, the new government moved against 'counter revolutionaries' which alienated Daendels from the regime he had helped into power.

On 12 June 1798, Daendels arrested Delacroix at a dinner party by putting a pistol to his chest. A new government was in place by the end of July. This new regime now started to implement the policies that their radical predecessors had written into the constitution. The coup of June, therefore, was not a reactionary revolution, but simply brought about a change in personnel. It was not until late summer that the government was secure enough in its position to be able to contemplate aiding the French concerning Ireland.

The Dutch National Archives hold documents that reveal that on 4 October over 5,000 men embarked on their transport ships at Texel: 6 battalions of infantry some 198 officers and 3,000 men, 1 battalion of Jaegers, 30 officers and 600 men, 8 squadrons of cavalry mustering 64 officers and 800 men, 32 artillery officers and 600 men, 30 engineer officers and 30 men. In addition, 3 tonnes of powder and 10,000 muskets were assembled to arm the Irish.[14]

Duckett's Mission

Independent of a main invasion force for Ireland, in order to send aid directly and quickly to Ireland, on the first day of July, the Ministère de la Marine ordered two ships to be prepared at Texel carrying just 280 men, 20 officers and stores.[15] These were to be sent with all haste to aid the Irish and show the United Irish leadership that the French would honour their pledge.[16] It is now that the William Duckett returns to the story: he was to advise the Franco-Batavian forces on the best place to land in Ireland.[17] This mission became part of a wider operation run from Hamburg.

Ensconced in his office in Hamburg, Bourdon was planning to promote mutiny in the Royal Navy and wrote to the Directory about what he had learned from Duckett 'on the means of maintaining secret intelligences in England and Ireland and on the discontent which reigns in the English navy and in particular in the fleet of Cork'.[18] Duckett endeavoured, backed by new agents such as O'Finn, to provoke mutiny among the Irish in the Royal Navy, and this was integral to French naval planning. Thousands of printed addresses to Irish sailors in neutral ports across the Atlantic Seaboard and North Sea ports were distributed, urging them to mutiny against the Royal Navy.[19]

William Duckett was to advise the Franco-Batavian forces on the best place to land in Ireland. In addition, he was given a budget of some 24,000 francs in hard cash to fund the Irish rebellion; he was also allocated funds in an attempt to neutralize the Royal Navy by sponsoring another mutiny.[20] Both Duckett and Léonard Bourdon had been formulating such a move since February.[21] Duckett left

146

Hamburg for Paris in the first week of June with orders from General Joubert to do everything in his power to aid the Irish, and to cause mutiny among the Irish in the British Army and Royal Navy. He arrived in Hanover on 17 July: being well known to the British Crown thanks to the spy Turner, he was arrested. The British minister in Hamburg, Sir James Crauford, was well aware of Duckett's activities. Hanover was technically a neutral city state despite its elector being King of England, George III. The legalities of what happened next set the scene for what was to come in 1803. The British Crown had no right to seize Duckett, and France objected to the arrest of a man they regarded as a citizen, and Duckett was ultimately set free in September and sent back to Hamburg.[22] In Paris, the arrest confirmed to John Hurford Stone, who was still involved with the Irish émigré community in Paris, that Duckett was a spy who had once more 'sold out'. The factionalism between Wolfe Tone and Napper Tandy now erupted in a division over the rights and wrongs of Duckett's innocence. The spy Turner wrote to London that 'there never was a set of people more perplexed and embarrassed than the French government'.[23]

Yet, what of his mission objectives? It is known that the crews of HMS *Captain*, HMS *Caesar*, HMS *Defiance* and HMS *Glory* included United Irishmen, and that these men planned to seize their ships and sail them to France or Ireland. The affair was uncovered by loyalist informers who reported to the Crown what was in the offing. In the resulting court martial seventy men were tried and seventeen executed.[24] Was this the work of Duckett's agents? Possibly, although it cannot say for certain, but it does seem that the French secret service did indeed 'step up' its endeavours to infiltrate the Royal Navy.[25]

Duckett's arrest coupled with political instability meant that the frigates under the orders of Major Michel, the *Waakzaamheid* and the *Furie*, which had been ordered to sail at the end of July, now set sail in the middle weeks of October, carrying 300 troops, 6 field guns with 500 rounds per gun, 2 howitzers with 40 shells and 200 rounds of canister, 6,000 muskets and 480,000 cartridges.[26] Just as the spy reported, they were heading to Scotland as ordered in July.[27]

As with all French attempts to land in Ireland and Scotland, the French suffered more than their 'fair share' of bad luck. The *Waakzaamheid* and *Furie* ran into HMS *Sirius* on 24 October. The *Waakzaamheid* was under the command of Senior Captain Neirrop. She was armed with 24 9-pounder guns on her main deck and 2 6-pounders on her forecastle. She had 100 Dutch seamen aboard her, as well as 122 French troops. The *Furie* was armed with

26 12-pounders on her main deck and 10 6-pounders on her quarter-deck and forecastle. She had a crew of 153 Dutch seamen, augmented with 165 French soldiers.[28]

The capture of the two Dutch ships ended any hope of a major breakout by the fleet at Texel. The 13 ships of the line destined for Ireland had the 5,000 men onboard disembarked on 9 November 1798.[29] While it is not helpful to dwell on speculation, one can easily imagine how history may have been different if Hardy's force had been supported by the Texel fleet along with General Rey. Ireland surely would have been liberated by the French: but for how long it cannot be said as it seems reasonable that the British Crown would not have tolerated a Jacobin republic 'on its doorstep'. Civil war would likely have been the outcome and total re-conquest the end result. The news of the Texel fleet putting its troops ashore and not sailing arrived in London on 16 November.[30]

Reflection

It is now worth pausing to reflect on these momentous events. The invasion was never going to be easy and the unpredictability of the Atlantic and North Sea weather as well as the Royal Navy made the situation very uncertain. Being out of contact with the main force made Humbert vulnerable. Yet, despite this he conducted his campaign with aggression, and acted like the main force in attacking Castlebar and venturing off towards Donegal in the hope that the north-west would rise in rebellion. The insistence of the Irish leadership, including Wolfe Tone, that landing in the west or north-west would motivate a major insurgency was founded on wishful thinking and poor intelligence. Those who did 'rise' turned out to be more of an impediment and provided Humbert with men who could not march, manoeuvre or handle weapons to any useful degree. Perhaps understandably, Humbert did not wait for Hardy to arrive, but this seems to have made matters worse. Humbert had been ordered to act as an *avant-garde*, to operate as diversionary force and hold on as long as possible without a decisive engagement until Hardy arrived: if he had done so, he would have kept Cornwallis west of the Shannon long enough to have made Dublin and the south-east vulnerable.[31] Yet, not knowing where Hardy was, Humbert took the only sensible option, and that was to attack and hope that the United Irish would flock to his colours. Communication failure and Hardy's inability to land changed everything.

Unknown to Humbert, the Ministère de la Marine had been infiltrated by Royalist émigrés working as spies for the British Crown. Prince de Boullion on Jersey had been keeping the British Crown informed since June about when the French would sail, what their destination would be and where to intercept them.[32] These 'strategists' knew what they were doing in order to impede the whole project, and it is incredible that their activities were not discovered. The French put British interception down to bad luck and not the more obvious fact that British had known exactly where to find the French. Hardy had sailed on time but had been intercepted by the Royal Navy and forced to make a large detour to shake them off which meant he arrived behind schedule. A spy in the French Ministère de la Marine reported on 17 October that 3 frigates from Rochefort were off the coast of Ireland and 6 ships of the line carrying 12,000 troops were being readied to sail.[33] The authorities were being given timely details of all key events. Had Hardy aimed for the east or south-east coast instead of the north-west, he would have divided the Royal Navy and land forces in Ireland. As it was, Marquis Cornwallis was able to 'sail' down to the midlands by canal, and General Sir John Moore was able to garrison Athlone, which meant that his force was in position to strike in any direction, should the need arise. Moore had already abandoned the war against the mountain rebels in Wicklow, which would have enabled an attack on Dublin, now poorly defended, or anywhere along the east coast.

The failed revolution of 1798 showed how vulnerable Ireland was to French invasion. The British government considered Ireland not only a 'rightful' colonial possession, but also a lucrative recruiting base. The loss of Ireland would be a serious blow to the British war effort and would provide a 'springboard' for French troops to land in England. British Crown forces unleashed a wave of terror against Catholics in a heinous foreshadowing of the brutality of the 'Black and Tans' over a century later. The country remained under military law, overseen by Lord Lieutenant Cornwallis. For the eighteen months following the rebellion British Crown forces held courts martial across Ireland, which were reported by the French press as extending into December 1799, if not later.[34] These reprisals generated hatred against the British Crown and Protestants, and made the United Irishmen redouble their efforts to expel the hated English. A loyalist in Dublin wrote in March 1799: 'I am sorry I cannot give a better account of our country but it is still in a dreadful state, and tho the rebels not come to a regular battle, there is scarce a night that we do not hear of a murder and robberies.'[35] It is estimated that the Crown forces killed over 30,000 Catholics, often for no other reason than they were Catholic, and they were treated little better than rebellious colonials in India. Sectarian madness was destroying Ireland, fuelled by the British Crown desperately wanting to keep Ireland part of the Empire.[36] Indeed, in November 1798 news was sent to the Home Office that pikes were being made in Liverpool and taken to Irish rebels and toasts were being drunk to 'success to the rebels in Ireland'.[37]

The British Crown sought to strengthen its control over Ireland through the Act of Union. It was not enough for England to secure itself against any threat from Ireland: Ireland had to submit to British political hegemony. The parliament of Ireland, which was already subordinate to England's and could only approve legislation that British Parliament had first passed, was to be formally disbanded, stripping away the charade of self-governance after the 'golden age' of Grattan's parliament: Westminster would rule unopposed.[38] The danger of the Union was all too clear to those on the Whig benches. Fitzwilliam declared that he would support a Union but only if it would actually unite the two kingdoms noting 'the measure cannot be carried but by the length of the sword. It cannot be a Union of consent on the part of Ireland.' He added that the removal of the Penal Laws which were 'framed against a particular description of persons which now ceased to exist: they were directed against superstition, bigotry and disloyalty; and therefore, should not affect the liberal, the well-meaning, and the loyal Catholics of the present day' would be more beneficial. Emancipation, he believed, should be enacted without Union, lest it drove the Catholics back into the arms of the French and radicals.[39] He was quite correct. In response, Irish revolutionaries redoubled their efforts to secure French sympathy and support for future collaboration. *Le Moniteur Universel* published articles expressing derision about how much of a 'union' this really was.[40]

Chapter 20

COPING WITH DEFEAT

The events of 1798 had scared those in Ireland and England. The British Crown feared both an invasion from France, but also revolution at home. Harsh draconian reprisals in Ireland meant that hatred of the English intensified. The direct response to the failed revolution was the Act of Union. The Crown redoubled its efforts to crush dreams of Irish Home Rule, and also any hint of political reform. The actions of Pitt, coupled by famine in Ireland – snow fell in April 1799 – kept the flame of revolution burning. Despite Humbert's failure, hopes remained high that the French would come back, and soon.

The British Crown's hatred of anyone involved in the 1798 rebellion was not limited by national boundaries. James Napper Tandy was one of the most prominent United Irish radicals to escape Ireland after the failure of 1798, making his way to the free imperial city of Hamburg along with his companions James Blackwell, Henry Morres – he is discussed later – and William Corbet. They arrived there on 2 November 1798. The British Crown desperately wanted these 'renegades' and in the early hours of 22 November, English officials in the city, having discovered the true identity of the incognito Irishmen, succeeded in getting permission from the chief magistrate to arrest them as British subjects. Two days later, on 24 November, the Hamburg Senate approved their transfer to British authority, despite Napper Tandy and Blackwell being commissioned as French officers, the former a brigadier general and the latter a colonel.

The arrests caused outrage in France, where public sympathy was mostly in favour of the Irish captives, who were expected to be hanged on their return to Britain. In consequence Hamburg became the scene of an international incident: Holland joined France in petitioning for the prisoners' release. The Austrian foreign minister urged England towards moderation in the matter.[1] It was not until 1 October 1799, almost a year later, that the English ship *Xenophon* sailed from Hamburg with the prisoners.

In Paris, Thomas Muir, Watson and Lewines now led what remained of the United Irish in exile. In Ireland the leadership was either dead, gaoled or had been forced to flee. Yet, coping with defeat was far from the minds of Muir and the Irish. Lewines was able to report to the surviving United Irish leadership in Dublin an assurance of another attempt to invade Ireland (February 1799); but he could not speak authoritatively to the French.[2]

Planning Invasion

Despite Humbert's failure, that winter the French had begun to prepare a new invasion force for Ireland, 12,000 men and ships of the line.[3] In theory, any chance of invading Ireland in the course of 1799 was 'off the cards'. The influx of Crown forces meant that any uprising would be crushed, but harsh reprisals by the Crown drove republicanism onwards. A fresh wave of Irish émigrés arrived in England and also France. A spy reported that remnants of the United Irish leadership were in contact with France, noting that: 'the communications by small smuggling vessels from the Western peninsular of Britanny is still maintained with Ireland, and there is a French agent at or near a place called Wicklow on the coast of Ireland who also communicates with Roscoff. The pretext is smuggling but the real purpose is the transmission of correspondence'.[4] Another spy for the British Crown noted that in Dublin two United Irish leaders outlined a plan that sought to exploit the disaffection that remained from the abortive 1798 rebellion. The plan centred on London and an English rebellion. At some stage a delegate from London arrived in Dublin to co-ordinate activities. This plan was identical to that which would be forever associated with Marcus Edward Despard, and perhaps this was the genesis of that plot. The insurrection was only to take place once the French had landed.[5] Another informant told the Crown on 8 December 1798: 'The French are fitting out four sail-of-the-line and two large transports to carry troops to Ireland'.[6]

It is now that the French émigré spy network became involved. An émigré reported that the French were in secret communication with the United Irishmen in January 1799.[7] Alarmingly, the Crown's spy network reported on 19 January 1799 a scheme to ship arms and ammunition and about 250 Irish rebels from Brest to Youghal (County Cork) under the leadership of Thomas Harnett and Thomas Mannen. These men may have been transported on ships being readied to sail at the end of 1798. In London, the Home Office reported on 28 February

1799 that the United Irishmen in Dublin and Belfast were in contact with the French government. Some sort of plan was in place by March.[8]

With paranoia levels reaching fever pitch, another agent for the British Crown told the Privy Council that an invasion force was to leave Brest and land in Ireland in the course of April 1799. From the recovered documents, it was hoped that risings by the United Englishmen and their allies amongst the Black Lamp in Bristol, Manchester, London and other northern towns would provide a sufficient distraction for Crown forces that the French invasion would go unopposed.[9] The plan for such a rising had been brought from France by William Putnam McCabe, who stressed that the lack of action in England during Humbert's invasion would be overcome by a contingent of United Irishmen taking charge.[10] By March, for the disaffected in England and London, revolution could not come soon enough: John Heron a private in the 1st Regiment of Foot Guards was denounced to the Home Office for reporting that the English would rise to demand their rights when the French invaded Ireland and most troops had been sent to Ireland to confront the French, and for this purpose the French were assembling their fleet in Brest.[11]

Concurrently, an Irishman named O'Reilley was dispatched from Ireland and met Duckett in Hamburg having travelled via Copenhagen in February 1799. He was on his way to Paris by the end of the month and was reported in Amsterdam on 12 March. It is not known if he arrived in Paris to speak to Lewines, but by April he had reached London. He is reported by the British Crown's spy network as 'being in France on business from the London Corresponding Society', which places Robert Watson centre stage, and hoped that 'the expedition which is preparing at the Texel for Ireland' would soon set out. The Crown lost track of him towards the first week of May.[12] Departing from Hamburg was French agent Sidderson – he was last encountered travelling with Duckett in 1794. He was on his way to Ireland in mid-March, where he was to re-connect the new Irish leadership with his office in Hamburg.[13] Aware of planning going on in London, the British Crown struck.

On 10 March, the British Crown carried out a series of raids against known United Irish leaders in London. The first raid failed to apprehend any leaders: Lawless, Doyle, Binns and Bonham were still at large in the city. British Crown secret agents had reported in March that 8,000 United Irish were ready to rise in Manchester, and perhaps as many as 40,000 in London in case of a French invasion.[14] William Graham, a serving solider in the 1st Regiment of Foot Guards, opined that the English 'would rise to demand their rights when most troops had been sent to Ireland to deal with the invasion for which purpose the French', he asserted, 'were assembling their fleet in Brest'.[15]

153

On 16 March, John Binns was arrested and imprisoned in Clerkenwell until May 1799, when he was moved to Gloucester. For the Crown, it was 'one down, three to go' of the men on the 'most-wanted list'. Lawless and Farrell were apprehended on 4 April 1799 on suspicion of treasonable practices.[16]

On 9 April, the Nags Head public house in London was raided: papers were recovered which presented a plan to foment mutiny in the Royal Navy. Papers seized later revealed that six resolutions were put forward and agreed by the seventy-five seamen present, who swore:

> ... to do everything ... to unite English, Irish and Scotchmen in brotherhood for the purpose of having the entire grievances of the Fleet redressed and to give liberty to the People ... our fathers, mothers, brothers, sisters, sweethearts and dearest friends are suffering at home the most dreadful oppression. ... in England have we not the most arbitrary laws to prevent petitioning their grievances.

From papers recovered later it is learned that the Nags Head meeting further agreed that the British Crown was deaf to the cries of the people and that legitimate lines of protest, nothing short of revolution, were needed, concluding, 'Liberty or Death!!!'[17] One of the men arrested at the Nags Head, John Poppleton, admitted to writing letters to France.[18] William Putnam McCabe and John Farrell were reported to be travelling from Ireland via London to France.[19]

On 20 April, a French spy from Hamburg arrived in Liverpool headed for Ireland.[20] The Home Office papers reveal that such a threat of invasion was taken seriously, with English and Irish ports put on full alert for more agents arriving from France or leaving the country.[21] The Secret Committee of the Home Office reported that: 'a very dangerous conspiracy ... had manifested itself in some parts of the Country ... from all its forms and habits affords the strongest presumption of mutual intercourse between those conspirators and the United Britons'.[22] In direct contradiction to the evidence uncovered, former United Irishman George Orr, who had travelled with John Murphy in April 1798 to The Hague and now had turned his coat, reported to the Home Office that: 'I do not find any attempts are making in this country at a reorganisation of the United Irish or of the disaffected'.[23]

By the end of April, a young Hanoverian named Lischam had arrived in Hamburg, ostensibly reporting that he was employed to visit England to discuss with the Wedgwood pottery family about opening a manufactory in Paris. Once under the influence of 'drink', Lischam spoke carelessly about French plans to invade Ireland, and a spy for the British Crown in Paris noted that young Lischam had been a frequent visitor to the home of Thomas Muir in Paris before departing for Hamburg. Fully aware of his mission to link Paris, Hamburg and Dublin, Lischam was arrested in London in early May carrying letters from Edward Lewines and other United Irish leaders.[24] Lischam confirmed the Crown's worst fears: the French were planning to invade.

General Humbert Returns

So what was going on? Documents preserved in the French Army Archives reveal that, undeterred by his failure in Ireland, General Humbert was planning a new wave of 'Chouanization' based on lessons learned in Ireland.

Humbert, in a report dated 12 January 1799, informed the French Directory that if an invasion of Ireland was attempted, it would be difficult, if not impossible, unless a diversionary attack was to take place which would prevent reinforcements flooding Ireland. Realizing that a major French fleet could never hope to evade the Royal Navy, Humbert calculated he needed no more than 15,000 men, and that reinforcements would quickly come from the English radicals. He requested 32 ships and 14,786 men.[25]

Whatever Humbert had hoped to do, he found that rather than sailing to invade Ireland, he was packed off to Switzerland in April 1799. At the head of a division, in May he was driven out of Luzisteig. Following this defeat, he was transferred to serve under Soult and was lightly wounded by a shot during the defence of the camp near Zurich on 4 June. He was given command of the reserve of grenadiers at the Battle of Zurich, 25–26 September 1799. He was in action at Andelfingen in October before being transferred to the Army of the West. Bearing this in mind, it may be why Citizen Charles Théveneau de Morande now enters the story. He was one of the most notorious men of the eighteenth century: blackmailer, pornographer and spy.[26] At some point in 1799 he compiled a comprehensive eight-part dossier on political discontent, political radicalism, the collapse of the British economy and the best way to invade. He reported that 'the indignation of a great number' against Pitt made 'the majority cry for Revolution'. If the French were to provide aid, however, the threat from the Royal Navy was considerable.[27] Théveneau recommended that the Medway was to be the target of any invasion force, particularly Sheerness and Chatham, and recommended sending raiding parties of 400 to 500 men to burn the docks, adding that if a frigate left Dunkirk at 4pm, the raiding party could be ashore by midnight the same day.[28] Ireland and Scotland seemed a better prospect, if the Batavian fleet could sail undetected, reported Thévenau, then a landing could be possible and a new government formed around Fox, Sheridan, Grey and Erskine.[29] France, now allied to Spain, could also draw on the Spanish fleet to transport troops to Ireland and England and also disrupt English trade to Portugal. Théveneau postulated that an economic war could bring about a peace compromise. English trade relied on exporting broadcloth to Russia and Lisbon, 'where many British houses have established their presence'. Economic collapse would precipitate internal disturbances and make an invasion easier or lead to a change of government and therefore peace formulated.[30]

A person identifying himself as Colonel Hanger – unlikely to be Colonel George Hanger, Lord Coleraine, political ally of Charles James Fox and Sir Francis Burdett – reported that if the French were to land, Chatham and Sheerness were ideal targets. More daringly, Hanger outlined a plan to kill the king and described in detail the personal escort to the king in London, Windsor and Kew. It was simple enough to shoot the king, plant a bomb or corrupt the soldiers to do so, Hanger argued. He added that in 1780 during the Gordon Riots 400 brigands had held London captive for 3 days, and over 100 houses had been destroyed, and that this could easily be repeated. The Gordon Riots showed how vulnerable London was to 'mob violence'.[31] Clearly, Ireland and England were still places of interest for the French information-gathering network, and a more formal plan appeared in the spring.

Émigré Robert Constant DuPont d'Erval now enters the story. Born in the Elbeuf region of France in 1758, by trade he manufactured broadcloth for the army. With the outbreak of the Revolution, he abandoned his factory and his fortune and emigrated to England, where he enlisted as a volunteer in the York Rangers and received a temporary commission of major. At the dismissal of the York Rangers on 24 August 1797, the brevet of major was granted to him by Louis XVIII on 31 December 1797. Yet, within two years he was back in France, informing the Directory in considerable detail about England and her armed forces. On 16 March 1799, he argued in favour of a renewed attempt at 'Chouanization' in Ireland, with men landed at Youghal, where the French would link with the United Irish. This seems very similar to the plan the British Crown uncovered in January and gives credence to the reports. DuPont d'Erval noted that Humbert's raid in 1798 had failed because of the strength of the Royal Navy and the fact that the attack had been launched at only one point, therefore, the Crown forces could overwhelm the small invading force. The best course of action was to land in

156

Ireland at multiple points with a diversionary attack. DuPont d'Erval furthermore recommended Youghal Bay and Kinsale as key landing places, which would enable Cork to be seized. Bantry Bay was identified as a landing ground, and from here the main road to Ross and Kinsale would be taken and used to great advantage. Macroon was also selected as an important objective. A simultaneous landing in Galway Bay and the River Shannon would allow troops to head to Clare. In the north, Donegal and Londonderry were strategic objectives. Remarkably, Dublin is missing from this list, perhaps due to its garrison, and DuPont believed that the French would receive considerable support from the people of Ireland. The invasion fleet was to depart from Brest, Spanish ports and at other places along the Brittany coast with the goal of the force remaining undetected by the Royal Navy. DuPont, as far as it is known, had never travelled to Ireland and was clearly working on information received from a secret agent.

DuPont d'Erval's plan was presented to Paul Barras – nominal dictator of France – on 9 March 1799, and was then passed to the Ministry of War on the 16th. In his plan he argued that in order to draw the Royal Navy away from Ireland, a series of lightning raids would be launched along the south coast of England, the landing places having being identified by a spy as follows:[32]

1. Harwich with landing on the Orwell and Stour to burn the harbour and Colchester.
2. Sheerness to allow an attack on Rochester.
3. Thanet to burn Sandwich and Margate and to control the mouth of the Thames.
4. 'The environs of Sandwich' to raid Canterbury.
5. Deal.
6. Rye to burn Maidstone.
7. Winchelsea to burn Brighton.
8. Brighton.

At the same time as the landings occurred in Ireland, DuPont's raiding parties would land and fire ships would be launched into Plymouth and Portsmouth to cause havoc. The British Crown was aware of a rise in United Irish activities and increased confidence regarding a new invasion by the end of March.

For the French, timing would be essential, as the War Office in London was in the final stages of an Anglo-Russian invasion of the Netherlands. The French had to strike and cause sufficient chaos for the British Army not to cross the Channel. If towns in the north of England could rise in revolution, the troops destined for the Netherlands would be sent north, and any reinforcements needed for Ireland would be pinned down to defend London. A plan was formulated to land 2,000 men in Newcastle to act as a diversion to a French landing in Ireland and on the Clyde.[33] The plan rapidly developed into sending 'Chouanization' raids to Bristol, Exmouth and Wales to strike at Chester and Liverpool as well as Newcastle.[34] In order to gather fresh intelligence and report on the plans being developed in France, a spy was sent to England.

The Mission of Charles Cavan

A French spy landed at Lowestoft on 6 March, having travelled from Flushing.[35] This individual seems to have been Charles Cavan.

Cavan was Irish and was employed by the French as a spy. Documents gathered by the Secret Committee of the Home Office in London note that Cavan had been arrested previously for spying along the English south coast, sailing from Dunkirk or Flushing in 1797. In 1798 Cavan was released from custody; he had been travelling under an American passport when he was apprehended at the request of the American minister. Rather than being exiled to America, Cavan was released and exiled to France.[36] Presumably, it was Cavan's reports that allowed the development of French plans. The French Army Archives hold detailed information, unfortunately not dated, about the south coast, with a sketch plan of Rye. It is presumed that these extensive notes were prepared by Cavan as part of the preparation for the invasion.[37]

In his report, the spy – very likely Cavan but this cannot be proved beyond reasonable doubt – states that he sailed from Flushing to Lowestoft, where he landed on 6 March. From Lowestoft he travelled to Yarmouth, where he watched a Royal Navy squadron being readied to sail to observe the Dutch-Batavian fleet at Texel, as well as the embarkation of Crown forces to sail to Ireland. On 10 March, the spy was in London where he visited several secret societies and gauged public opinion about the government as well as the level of 'malcontent' in the capital. The spy visited '3 or 4 cafes a night', which probably refers to public houses across London, until the 13th when he left for Portsmouth. It is not known who he met in London, but Lawless, Doyle, Binns and Bonham were still at large in the city. It seems inconceivable that these men did not meet Cavan. An effective spy would have wanted to meet with these individuals and they would likely have frequented the same locations the spy sought out.

It is known that United English meetings were held at the Nags Head, Clerkenwell: it is assumed that Cavan was one of the attendees. In Portsmouth the spy reported on the troops being assembled for service in Ireland. On 15 March, he 'visited the Club' in Portsmouth: it is assumed the local United Englishmen section. Clearly, his activities in Portsmouth had raised suspicion as our spy was arrested on the 16th: he was released thanks to affidavits by 'Mr Kingsford and Mr Sayer a miner, who provided letters to say I was a resident of the country of Hertford, and they also paid my expenses'. Released on 21 March, our spy headed back to London, which he found in a state of agitation due to the 'terrible situation in Ireland'. From London our spy went to Canterbury where he lodged with a soldier, before heading to Whitstable, from whence he sailed to Flushing. The ship he was travelling on was stopped by the Royal Navy, which boarded the vessel. The English sailors ransacked the vessel looking for letters and parcels being carried to the Netherlands as well as a 'suspicious person'. Clearly, the spy was not as good at covering his tracks as he thought and he was searched, the English sailors going through his clothing, the lining of his hat and his boots to find the 'secret correspondence' he was carrying. Unable to identify a spy and papers, the Royal Navy let the ship go, the spy tells us, but it was shadowed along the coast 'in a game of cat and mouse' before arriving at Flushing. His report was finalized on 4 April 1799 and sent to Louis de Milet de Mureau, the Minister of War.[38]

No doubt aware of this planning process, with sectarian violence pulling Ireland apart, Lewines demanded from the Directory that they act immediately to keep their promise to send troops to liberate Ireland in a terse letter dated 26 April 1799.[39]

All that stood in the way of the French was the British spy network: double agents in the French Ministère de la Marine since the early 1790s were still hard at work informing the British of what the French were planning as well as sabotaging the French Navy.

New Arrivals

Whatever plan was being considered during 1799, it was a year of missed opportunity for the United Irish, in particular because of the creation and rapid loss of a new United leadership in England. Hamburg became a safe haven for those fleeing the tumultuous events at home, and was headed up for a time by Napper Tandy. It was here that William Putnam McCabe had met Napper Tandy and talked about a rebellion and French aid, which Napper Tandy had been dismissive of.[40] Some sort of proposal for an invasion was being discussed as news of the planning got back to London.[41] Rather than head from Germany to Ireland, on hearing of the transfer of the state prisoners rounded up in 1798 being sent to Fort George in Scotland, McCabe and Palmer travelled to Scotland, where they made contact with Arthur O'Connor, who provided them with a letter of introduction to the Directory. They left Scotland in August and arrived in Paris a month later.[42]

In September 1799, a report was sent to Talleyrand, French foreign minister, concerning new arrivals. On the list of refugees were Arthur MacMahon, William Putnam McCabe, George Palmer and William Mount St John among others. The non-refugees recorded included Nicholas Madgett, Patrick MacMahon, Sullivan, O'Keane and Debray.[43] Palmer, McCabe and the others, signing themselves 'The United Irish Directory', were in contact with Talleyrand, who asked for help in a planned insurrection in Ireland.[44]

Right on cue, Cavan was sent back to England but was 'apprehended by a warrant from the Duke of Portland and forcibly rescued by a party of smugglers, two of whom were convicted at the Norwich assizes for the said offence'. Yet, Cavan, despite being a wanted man, made another trip to England in September 1799. Oddly enough, having slipped through their fingers, the Crown 'had judged it necessary to secure him' and he was arrested and gaoled in Norwich and then transferred to Coldbath Fields Prison in London, where he was imprisoned alongside Marcus Edward Despard, William Cheetham and other United Irish leaders. It seems the smugglers who had enabled Cavan's escape in April had 'turned their coats' to evade gaol time. When Cavan was commissioned once more to travel to England via Lowestoft, he used the same smugglers, who promptly told the authorities.[45]

Dr Robert Watson

With Wolfe Tone dead and Napper Tandy in exile in Hamburg, veteran radical Robert Watson comes to the fore. Although he has been mentioned previously, it is worth sketching out a biography of this Scottish radical.

Watson was tried on 11 November 1794 for 'possessing seditious papers' and gaoled for two years in Newgate. Released in October 1796, he planned a Scottish revolution. He had played a role in the Royal Navy mutiny linking the French and the London Corresponding Society, and was arrested again in Biggleswade attempting to get to France. He was tried at the Old Bailey but acquitted. A reward of

£400 was offered to stop him travelling to France. Watson escaped London on a Swedish-registered ship, and the *Le Moniteur Universel* announced his arrival at Nancy as that of 'Lord Walson [*sic*], *écossais libre*' at the start of October that year. He was in Paris by 1 November, and on the 22 he requested aid from the French to land in Scotland. To raise his profile as a leader in exile, he issued an address to the British people, advocating a general rising and to welcome the French Army as liberators.[46] He reported to the French Directory that if the French landed in England or Ireland, 50,000 were ready to rise in Scotland, 200,000 in England and a similar number in Ireland. All that was needed was for the French to land and commented that 'a revolution would certainly soon take place here'.[47] Watson encouraged the Scots to rise in rebellion as the union had sealed the political death of Scotland. He urged all Scotsmen to unite against English corruption 'to claim for their country a place among the free nations of the world'.[48] Lodging with Napoléon's forest-keeper, he was introduced to the consul and gave him lessons in English; Napoléon made him principal of the restored Scots College, with 3,000 francs a year.[49] In Paris he linked up with Thomas Muir.

In an undated letter and memorandum, which was probably written at the end of October at the latest, Muir sketched out a plan of action for Scotland. He requested permission from the Directory for one or two messengers to be allowed to enter France, and whom he could meet outside of Paris. Through intermediaries Muir was confident he 'could give instructions and arrange the plan of operation'. In the same letter, the Scots, Muir reported, unlike the Irish, would not repeat 'the ridiculous and fatal comedy of O'Quoigley and O'Connor'. This was an unmistakable reference to the arrests of the two Irishmen in Margate in February 1798. Muir it seems had no time at all for O'Connor and his faction. In the remaining passages of the letter, Muir outlined a plan to radicalize and foment mutiny in the British Army. Muir noted that that Scots in the British Army were 'deeply tinctured with revolutionary principles', adding that while Scottish sailors 'are unlike the English. As brave in the combat, they are better educated, better informed, more attached to their National Independency and more determined to throw off the yoke'. There could be a decisive uprising in London, he argued, but it would only be by virtue of 'that immense ignorant and debauched populace, fermented by Misery into Insurrection', which given what happened was rather apposite. For revolution to occur in London, he stressed, the radicals needed 'leaders who were men of courage and honesty whose habits had brought them into direct contact with the people who followed "common occupations"'.

161

Muir noted that there was a lack of leadership in England, and if revolution was to occur new leaders were needed.[50]

Clearly, Muir's request for passports for two agents to arrive in France was agreed to and Muir learned from Watson of the impending arrival in Paris of James Kennedy of Paisley and Angus Cameron of Blair Atholl as delegates of the new movement in Scotland. In November 1798, Muir moved secretly to the Île-de-France village of Chantilly to await the arrival of his compatriots. There he died, suddenly and alone, on 26 January 1799. Whether he was assassinated or his death was solely due to natural causes can never be known, but his unexpected demise initially derailed Watson's planning.

Since Muir was by this time the principal intermediary between the Directory and the various republican refugees in Paris, he was aware that his movements were under scrutiny by Pitt's agents. Accordingly, in his last known communication with the Directory in October 1798, he requested permission to leave Paris for somewhere less conspicuous, where his crucial negotiations with the Scots emissaries could be conducted in safety.[51] This implies he knew that assassination by a British agent was possible.

Cameron, who Muir was expecting to travel to France, Muir claimed, had 'organised the Highlanders of Scotland' and 'was the dynamic leader of the United Scotsmen', who hailed from Lochaber. Muir further informed the Directory that Cameron had tried to turn the Militia Riots of 1797 into a revolutionary movement. James Kennedy, Muir wrote, 'is equally well-informed of the state of the low country of Scotland and of England'.[52] Kennedy was a Paisley weaver who supported the idealism of Thomas Paine as synthesised through the lens of French Republican Jacobinsim, and had been implicated in Robert Watt's 'Pike Plot' to seize Edinburgh Castle in 1794.

Nothing more is known about Watson's political activities until the start of July 1799, when he wrote to Minister Reinhard with a lengthy memorandum on fomenting a rebellion in London, to seize the Bank of England and the Tower of London, comparing it to the Hôtel des Invalides in Paris. He reported that the Tower held 120,000 muskets and 200 field guns which were guarded by a garrison of 500 troops who could be easily overcome. Watson reported that he had begun clandestine operations by sending circular letters addressed to all radical societies affiliated to the rump of the London Corresponding Society, which was ostensibly reviving interest in parliamentary reform and peace with France. Once the French had landed, the radical groups in London and the provinces would be summoned to rise on the same day and stage rebellions and disturbances in the major provincial and manufacturing towns. Watson argued that these demonstrations against the British Crown would compel the dispersal of Crown forces to the provinces leaving London vulnerable, and here the radicals could stage the coup against the Bank of England and the Tower, and the landing sites exposed to the French invading army.[53] Watson also wrote directly to Abbé Sieyès, providing him with a lengthy dossier detailing public mood in England as well as London and 'the means to overthrow the monarchy'. Watson in his address to Sieyès described himself as 'President of the Executive Committee of the London Correspondence Company, member of the British Union and representative of the associations of Bath, Bristol'. Watson reported that plans had been made at the time of the 1797 and 1798 invasions to stage a diversion in favour of the operations in Ireland by a general insurrection of the 'Friends of Liberty' across the country via a network of informers and offered the Directory £20 million and the payment of any French forces committed to the invasion. Watson failed to suggest where or how he would obtain the money, but optimistically noted he could organize a coup among disaffected soldiers in London and mentions Colonel Despard as central to his ideas. This plan contains the genesis of the plot that would bear the name of Despard.[54]

Watson's daring scheme was, it seems, flatly ignored – perhaps because he had failed to explain where the money was coming from to pay for the invasion. However, on 22 September, Watson noted that the public mood in England was turning against the war, and that there was growing disaffection with rising food prices.[55] A spy for the British Crown reported frigates departing Brest for Ireland carrying arms at the start of October.[56] If true, clearly someone in France was listening to Watson.

Watson wrote to the Directory on 19 October asking for money to form a coalition among all the 'partisans of liberty' in London and to send a secret agent to the English capital to secure help for those patriots imprisoned in 'English Bastilles' thereby fomenting 'a general insurrection'. Perhaps he was thinking of Marcus Edward Despard and other United Irish leaders in Coldbath Fields Prison, London, or in Scotland. The man for the job, Watson claimed, was his associate James Smith, who was himself known among the leadership of the 'democratic parties'. Smith had been a member of the Edinburgh Convention in 1793 and was, according to Watson, a close friend of Thomas Muir and 'no less attached than he to the interests of France'. Smith had it seems arrived in France with Watson. Come the long-awaited revolution, opined Watson in a rambling letter to the Directory, he imagined that Scotland would be a separate republic and ally of France, along with a free Ireland.[57]

Coup d'État

Whatever Watson and the United Irish Committee were planning it was not the right time. The Directory was 'on its last legs' as rival factions jostled for power. In the final days of the Directory, Abbé Sieyès and Talleyrand – the men of influence and power that the Irish relied upon – were planning a coup to replace Barras with the aid of General Napoléon Bonaparte, who had arrived in France from the ill-fated Egyptian campaign, nevertheless, to be greeted with triumphal cheers. Watson and the committee now became hostages to fate. The conditions in Ireland and England were ripe to exploit – but internal power struggles within France sidelined any discussion of an invasion.

It seems that Watson's October letter never reached the Directory, or if it did, it was never read. Whatever had been planned and agreed was cancelled as factions jockeyed for power. The 'golden moment' to harness Irish bitterness at the repression of the 1798 rebellion and rising levels of unrest due to famine was lost because of the power struggles in France. This was in essence a repeat performance of 1792 under Brissot, when the soldiers, arms and money never left the shores of France, and the coup that toppled Lazare Carnot from power and ended the 1797 invasion.

The new man of the hour was now First Consul Bonaparte.

Chapter 21

FAMINE

With Bonaparte in office for less than a month and not yet secure in his position, on 3 December, Watson wrote again to Talleyrand.[1] During the middle of December, the War Ministry received the details of a new invasion plan for Ireland simultaneous with a landing in Scotland, also from Watson's hand.[2] Once again the letter went unanswered – and little wonder. Hot on the heels of Watson's missive, Lewines wrote to Talleyrand on 11 December about the effect that the Act of Union would have on Ireland.[3] In a separate and longer memorandum Lewines informed Talleyrand, and inter alia Bonaparte, that the 'favourable moment for a new expedition to Ireland' had come, and enquired of Talleyrand what the new government's exact intentions were towards Ireland, and furthermore asked that if plans had been made, that these were 'to be made known to him so that he can warn his fellow citizens'.[4] Lewines was very well aware of the famine that was gripping England and Ireland. A bad harvest in 1799 resulted in food prices increasing massively: in England wheat for making bread had been 53s. a quarter in 1789, by 1795 it was 79s. and by 1800 120s. The other staple foodstuff, oats, was selling at 70s. a quarter. Unable to afford bread or to make a pottage, the poor were starving and, as in 1795, faced a stark choice: starve and pay the rent or eat and be homeless.[5] The famine acted as the 'recruiting sergeant for the United Englishmen'. The link between the famine and radicalism was proved when Lord Eldon was informed that that due to the high price of food many thousands were taking the United Englishmen's Oath in the counties of Cheshire, Derbyshire and Lancashire, particularly in Saddleworth. The informant noted that there would be widespread revolution if the farmers were not forced to bring their produce to market at lower prices instead of hoarding it, adding that: 'a very dangerous conspiracy ... had manifested itself in some parts of the Country ... from all its forms and habits affords the strongest presumption of mutual intercourse between those conspirators and the United Britons'.[6] An underground network between radical groups existed by the end of summer 1800, as the Lord Lieutenant of Gloucester admitted. He informed the Home Office that correspondence was being exchanged between the manufacturing people of Gloucestershire 'with Birmingham, Nottingham, Manchester, Liverpool &c. ... regularly, as to the mode & method they intend to pursue to lower the price of wheat & flour'.[7] A handbill appeared declaring 'NO KING! Buonoparte for Ever!' and urging the masses 'to maintain the noble cause of Liberty ... Death or Liberty must be our Souls Desire!' In Wolverhampton a poster read: 'Damn all the Kings men and damn the King to Hell'.[8]

Despite rising tension and anger, nothing could be done to exploit the situation: Napoléon was not yet established as consul. Talleyrand eventually replied to Lewines on 7 January 1800 and called the United Irishmen massacred in 1798 and those who continued to be murdered 'martyrs for liberty who died to establish freedom for their country'.[9] Yet, Talleyrand made no firm commitments. This was understandable. Franco-English political considerations were important vectors to be taken into account.

Bonaparte's coming to power had been welcomed in England by the Whigs: Earl Fitzwilliam reflected Fox's views that: 'He may continue the use of revolutionary jargon, but he will check all revolutionary practices.'[10] Many on the opposition benches hoped that Bonaparte would bring stability to France: both countries were considering peace, and it would have been foolhardy to undermine any goodwill he may have engendered by planning a coup in London or invasion in Ireland. Both Talleyrand and Bonaparte were astute enough to realize this and put the interests of the state and inter alia consolidation of power before Irish affairs.

Despite French politics putting a stop to officially sanctioned actions of espionage and subversion, Watson and Duckett – and it is assumed Lewines – took little heed of this. Perhaps this was related to the unfolding events in England occasioned by famine. William Duckett – now fully rehabilitated with the French after his arrest and denouncements in 1796 and his cover being blown in Hanover two years later – had travelled to Scotland in late 1799 and submitted a memorandum detailing what he had learned about public opinion in Scotland to the Consulate in February 1800. Duckett, it seems, was now working for Watson and had abandoned Lewines and the Irish factions. In his report he put forward a case for a French landing in Scotland and rather remarkably emphasized the Irish backbone of the United Scotsmen, noting that: 'Scotland is organised on the same lines as Ireland. Societies of United Scotsmen are being organised everywhere. Irish refugees are very active in this organisation. They are very numerous in Paisley and in Glasgow.'[11] The United Irishmen and their allies were once more dreaming of a French invasion. Yet, Bonaparte was not secure in power and would not be until he had conquered the Austrian Army at Marengo.

Napoléon and General Napper Tandy

One of the more pressing issues on Bonaparte's desk – and this explains his reluctance over Ireland – was the diplomatic tussle with England and the authorities in Hamburg over the fate of Napper Tandy and three others. Bonaparte had no hesitation in making the details of this affair available to the public. In response to the excuses offered by the Hamburg Senate, he published a letter on 30 December 1799 directed to the government of Hamburg: 'Courage and virtue preserve states; cowardice and vice ruins them. You have violated hospitality. This would not happen even among the most barbarous desert hordes ... The two unfortunates who you have given over will die gloriously, but their blood will do more harm to their persecutors than an army.'[12] Apart from a public shaming, France punished the burghers of the city for the entire extradition debacle, and probably also as a warning against future collaboration with Britain, with the imposition of a trade embargo until they paid the reparation of several million francs, which they did in April 1801.[13] Peace meant shelving plans for the invasion of Ireland. France was in no position to invade that summer as priority was given to the Haitian Revolution.

As Napoléon negotiated with England at Amiens he strenuously pressed as a condition that the Irishmen be released to France, much as he had worked to free the Marquis de Lafayette from imprisonment by Austria in the Treaty of Campo-Formio in 1797. On 12 February 1800, Napper Tandy was put on trial in Dublin and acquitted. He remained in prison in Lifford Jail in County Donegal until April 1801 when he was put on trial again and sentenced to death, but he was reprieved and allowed to go to France. This leniency may have been partly due to doubts about the legality of the demand for his surrender by the Hamburg authorities. Napoléon succeeded in freeing the four Irishmen in April 1802; he awarded Napper Tandy a sum of 6,000 francs and a pension of 3,000 francs.[14] James Napper Tandy died on 24 August 1803 at his lodgings, 2 rue Moncheuil, Bordeaux; it is supposed that alcohol played a part in his death.

Exploiting Chaos

At this stage, with First Consul Bonaparte about to set off to fight at Marengo, Ireland was very much 'off the radar' for the time being. Nothing more is heard about Ireland until early summer. The famine in England heralded a wave of machine breaking in the north of England as well as riots over food. In Ireland famine and repression made matters go from bad to worse.

At the end of 1799, Humbert had been transferred to the Army of the West, the command of which was vested in the future Marshal Guillaume Brune until 16 April 1800. In May command passed from Brune to another future marshal, Jean Baptiste Bernadotte. Ever the willing ally of the Irish, Humbert had kept 'his ear to the ground' regarding Irish affairs. To this end on 4 July 1800, he reported to the French government that the Act of Union had caused huge suffering and discontent in Ireland. Humbert also noted that the famine and sporadic outbreaks of rioting in England could be exploited as a diversionary element of any attack on Ireland. Now was the moment to send a force of perhaps 12,000 men to Ireland to profit from the division and disquiet.[15]

As Humbert acknowledged, it was important for the French and Irish to resume communications. The French archives contain no information about how this was to be achieved, but the British archives provide an answer. In July 1800, a spy, Turner, who was mentioned previously in relation to the O'Coigly affair, informed the Home Office that two French emissaries had been dispatched to Ireland by France. He identified these men as Edward Carolan and Thomas O'Meara. They arrived at Gravesend in August, having travelled from Hamburg. O'Meara met with radicals in London perhaps to transmit information to them and also to take intelligence back to France. Carolan continued to Ireland to link up with the United Irishmen. Fate took a hand when O'Meara was arrested on 21 September in England, and simultaneously Carolan was apprehended in Ireland.[16] The direct effect of the mission was that Robert Emmet and Malachy Delaney decided to travel to France to gain French military support.

Despite the arrests being made in London, Humbert's enthusiasm remained undiminished. In August and September 1800 several riots about the scarcity of corn and the high price of provisions broke out in Birmingham, Oxford, Nottingham, Coventry, Norwich, Stamford, Portsmouth, Worcester and a number of other areas. Sheffield rioted from 27 August–8 September.[17] Leeds was gripped by rioting from 16–25 September.[18] At the end of September, Dr Robert Watson's envoy from the United Scotsmen reported to Bonaparte that he believed he could muster 50,000 men in Scotland and over 200,000 in England who were ready to aid the French in the event of an invasion to end the famine and bring about a revolution in government and society.[19] Almost immediately General Humbert planned a new wave of 'Chouanization'.

Based on news from his secret agents, Humbert told Bonaparte in a letter of 8 October 1800 that the situation in England was now critical:

> The daily insurrections that erupt in all parts of the kingdom, without excepting the capital, the crowds of workers seeking work and food hunger for work, among which are an infinite number of foreigners and people from whom we can take advantage … in Cornwall, Wales and Ireland the people shout-out for revolution … It would be very easy to organize an insurrection on board the British fleets, by means of the Irish who are there in large numbers.[20]

Humbert planned to raid the Cornish and Welsh coasts and burn Bristol and Liverpool as a diversion to the landing of troops in Ireland. 'Flying columns' of 100 men each would be landed at different points to burn and destroy whatever they found. The army would be divided into divisions of 3,000 men and he hoped that 5 divisions would land at different points and converge, the ranks being bolstered by 15,000 United Englishmen. Learning the lessons from 1798 about the lack of command and control of the men raised by the United Irishmen and United Englishmen, Humbert planned to take with him 3,000 officers to command an army of 6,000 Scots and 15,000 United Britons, who would be armed with the 20,000 muskets he would land.[21]

The following day, Humbert noted that 3,000–4,000 men under his command could sail from Brest, avoid the Royal Navy and land easily in Ireland, and in Plymouth he proposed to land 2,000 men, of which 1,000 would be released prisoners, whose goal was to 'cause chaos'. Humbert noted that similar forces of one or two frigates could be dispatched from Ostend, Dunkirk and Dutch ports to land parties at different points in England – in essence to stage terror raids and burn ports, houses, factories, shops and warehouses. The men conducting the raids would be 'disposable assets' so long as a *coup de main* was struck against the English.[22]

Humbert, who was identified with Jacobin opponents of First Consul Bonaparte, received no response to his letter. Humbert would never set sail. The French victory at Marengo had changed the balance of power. Earl Fitzwilliam, writing on 2 August 1800 in the light of Austria (Britain's remaining ally) making peace with

France, said: 'I am ready to confess that I do not see how war without Continental alliances can tend to produce a counter-revolutionary system in France'.[23] For some in the British Parliament, Bonaparte was in power and it was better to make peace and accept the new mode of government than to continue to wage war to restore the Bourbons. Yet, those who sat on the Tory benches would have none of this, nor would French Royalists in England, such as the Comte d'Artois who exercised a degree of influence over Pitt and later Henry Addington. The comte began plotting almost at once, with both French Royalists and disaffected Jacobins, to depose Bonaparte, funded by British gold.

Chapter 22

ENGLAND AND IRELAND

As 1801 dawned a war for food was underway in England and Ireland. Peace was uppermost in the minds of some in England, and the demand for peace would reach a crescendo at the start of 1801. The failure of government to cap prices of corn and to listen to the grievances of the poor and working class resulted in an unprecedented upsurge in radicalism and anti-establishment politics across the country. On 10 March 1801, a group of recently released state prisoners, freed with the ending of the suspension of the Habeas Corpus Act, met at the Green Dragon in Fore Street, London. Thomas Evans – arrested in 1798 alongside James O'Coigly – upbraided the assembled members of the United Britons for their lack of activity during his imprisonment. Evans was not being totally fair: men such as William Curry, Thomas Pemberton, Joseph Bacon and Richard Oliphant had worked hard at keeping the United Briton movement alive while he along with Colonel Marcus Edward Despard, and William Cheetham were imprisoned. Within days Evans, Galloway and the radical hatter Richard Hodgson, along with Cheetham and John Nicholls, had become part of a shadowy United Britons national committee working towards an overthrow of the government.[1] Despard had not yet been released from prison. A spy had reported to the Home Office that Arthur O'Connor's brother Robert had every intention of returning to Ireland accompanied by Marcus Edward Despard. Without a shadow of a doubt, Despard was an integral member of the O'Connorite faction that sought Irish Home Rule with or without French assistance. In London, the United Irishmen were stirring, this time it was driven by working-class radicals who wanted a say in government. 'The better sort of people … had ceased meeting or subscribing,' reported a magistrate: the abandonment of petitioning and preparations for an armed uprising alienated the moderate middle class. The Black

Lamp was modelled on the United Englishmen with cells of ten run by an eleventh man, the 'conductor', who met other 'conductors' at a meeting of Delegates, who received information and orders from 'The Directory', which in turn passed on information from the Directory in London.[2] It had gained its sobriquet from extinguishing street lamps in Leeds, Manchester, Sheffield and elsewhere.

No sooner had a committee been assembled, than the authorities struck. On 20 April, seventeen members of the United Britons were arrested at the Green Dragon in London, and packed off to Newgate Gaol, among them: John Heron, Charles Pendrell, Wallis Eastbourne, John Blythe, Joseph Patten, Jasper Moore, John and Benjamin Binns and Michael Doyle. These men would all play leading parts in what was to follow. On 31 May, John Nicholls was arrested 'on a vague and undefined charge of treasonable practices' and conveyed to Tothill Fields Prison.[3] Nicholls had been arrested for sedition along with Michael Doyle, his brother, and John Crathorn, and gaoled in Gloucester under the suspension of Habeas Corpus Act.[4]

Simultaneously, Robert Emmet and Malachy Delaney arrived in Paris. With a glowing reference from Talleyrand, in a fractious meeting with Bonaparte, they outlined that this was the United Irishmen's last request for aid, lambasting the French for breaking their promise to assist on 5 occasions, and demanded 25,000–30,000 troops. With discontent rising in England, now was the time to act, they urged.[5] Bonaparte had made peace with Austria with the Treaty of Luneville, and was more concerned with brokering peace with the British Crown. For Bonaparte, the Irish mission, led by General Bernadotte, was a means to an end. The threat of invasion perhaps carried enough weight to bring the British Crown to the negotiating table than an actual invasion. Talleyrand instructed Bernadotte to do nothing to conceal any plans for the invasion, 'the rumour itself might produce the desired effect'.[6] By March British spies in Hamburg and France had informed the Crown of a planned invasion of 15,000 men sailing for Ireland.[7]

The United Irishmen's strategy to achieve Home Rule relied upon three things:

1. France invading Ireland.
2. A major uprising in Ireland.
3. A diversionary uprising in England.

Point 1 was being negotiated, and involved the familiar figure of Humbert. Point 2 was down to the United Irishmen harnessing the anger in Ireland and focusing it into armed rebellion. Point 3 was the problem: for the invasion to succeed a diversion was needed. Recoupling the United Englishmen and Black Lamp to the cause of Irish freedom was the key. That was Marcus Edward Despard's job. Yet, as events show, controlling the simmering anger of the disaffected poor was far harder than he anticipated.

Yet, none of the secret planning was in fact kept secret: Bonaparte and Talleyrand's policy of making 'a song and dance' about the invasion kept the British Crown 'in the loop', as did Royalist secret agents. Prince de Bouillon wrote to Evan Nepean at the Home Office the same month giving evidence of a planned invasion of England and Ireland by the French, thanks to an émigré agent in the Ministère de la Marine.[8]

A key person in the chain between France and Ireland was General Humbert. A spy working for the British Crown reported in March that he was in Brest ordering the repair of flat-bottomed landing barges, preparing for an invasion and that troops were arriving in the port for embarkation.[9] Through his spy network Prince de Bouillon informed the British Crown that General Humbert was in frequent correspondence with Ireland, and gave the Crown an estimated strength of French troops at Brest and also of the Irish rebels.[10] Days later, Bouillon's spies reported that Humbert's destination was Ireland.[11] Nothing can be found in the French War Ministry Archives concerning this invasion scheme, yet, the archives do confirm that Humbert wrote to General Alexandre Berthier, the future marshal and chief of staff, on 29 May asking if his force could be increased to 10,000 men. He stated that he was confident of 100,000 Irish and 100,000 Scots rallying to his cause. He added that he believed the English would rise up 'to take vengeance on their nation', promising a great victory.[12] No reply can be found in archive holdings, and this may explain why in June Humbert wrote to General Bernadotte seeking permission for the grenadier companies from the troops stationed at Brest to be detached to take part in his invasion to bring his invasion force up to the authorized strength of 4,200.[13] It must be assumed Humbert did not get his reinforcements, but by 31 July, Humbert was 'ready to go'.[14] Away he did go, but not to Ireland.

In September, Humbert found out that he was being sent to Saint-Domingue to provide reinforcements for Napoléon's brother-in-law, General Leclerc. Had this been Napoléon's intention all along? Perhaps, as the main force of 25,000 men destined at least in theory for Ireland had in fact sailed to Saint-Domingue in May. Was the pretext of an Irish invasion a cover story for the invasion of Saint-Domingue, to keep the Royal Navy 'out of the way'? It would seem so.

Humbert fought at the action of Cap-Haïtien and then in February 1802 seized Port-au-Prince and Port-de-Paix. Following this action, he was named commander of Môle-Saint-Nicolas, but fell ill and only resumed his command that August. General Brunet accused him of plundering and Humbert was ordered to return to Cap-Haïtien. Humbert refused the order and remained at Môle-Saint-Nicolas until that September when he handed over his command to General Morpas. Humbert never seems to have wanted to be involved with the expedition, and his behaviour in part reflects this, so much so that the commander of the expedition, General Leclerc, sent Humbert back to France in October 1802 over questions about his behaviour. On returning to France, he was stripped of his rank on 13 January 1803. He continued to associate and plan with United Irish exiles in Paris but eventually retired to Brittany, and his persistent and increasingly desperate requests for reinstatement were ignored.

Submarines and Sedition

At the same time as Humbert found himself crossing the Atlantic Ocean, Robert Watson was formulating an ambitious plan to terrorize the Royal Navy. Robert Fulton, the inventor of the submarine, was a close friend and colleague of Watson and hatched a plan to sink the Royal Navy in port. Fulton had begun work on his submarine in winter 1797 and presented his prototype to the French Directory on 17 July 1799.[15] The French Navy accepted it and stipulated that the craft was to be commissioned by April 1800, and had to be able to deliver a torpedo charged with 30kg of explosives. His budget was 60,000 francs. The vessel was finished on 10 April and launched on 30 July 1800, successfully detonating a torpedo which sank a floating jetty in the harbour at Le Havre. On 30 March 1801, Fulton had been granted 10,000 francs to continue his experiments in the development of the submarine. By September he had developed a submarine which when tested operated underwater for 17 minutes in 25ft of water and could deliver a warhead of sufficient capacity to sink an enemy warship.[16] With the weapon, Watson hoped to 'avenge the victims of Aboukir, Naples and Copenhagen who cried for their vengeance'. Watson informed the Minister of the Navy that the republicans in London would rise up to support the invasion forces, and noted that the:

French party are very numerous in the capital ... I have been prudent in discussing my ideas with them ... if it so desired it is possible to procure the means to create a diversion in London, and possibly also in the fleet ... I was present at the executive committee meeting of the London

Corresponding Society during the insurrection in the fleet at Portsmouth and also the Nore, and I know the people who helped organise all this in secret.[17]

A day later, Fulton informed the ministry that with three submarines armed with twenty to thirty torpedoes he could simultaneously attack Portsmouth, Plymouth, Torbay and the mouth of the Thames.[18]

Watson's letter to the Minister of the Navy assuming it was not pure bravado, gives a strong indication of the strength of feeling in London regarding a French invasion. Watson was not the only person thinking of invasion that summer: a memoir dated 10 September reports that the English radicals lacked clear leadership and were 'fighting among themselves' over how to achieve their aims. To accomplish a landing in England a force of 15,000 were to be sent to Ireland, and once the force was landed and had drawn the British Crown to send troops to Ireland, 50,000 French troops would land at designated points in Kent – clearly those identified by DuPont earlier – and link up with the 'French party' in London and overthrow the government.[19]

However, broader political issues intervened. Pitt had resigned in February 1801 as the king refused to countenance Catholic emancipation and the repeal of the Test and Corporation Acts. Henry Addington was now premier, and he was more motivated by the danger of a war with Russia than making peace with Bonaparte. By mid-September, written negotiations had progressed to the point that a draft preliminary agreement was signed on 30 September in London. Allowing Watson and Fulton to build more submarines would have ended any negotiation. Fulton quickly became disillusioned with Watson and the lack of support from France and headed to England and presented his idea to the Royal Navy.

Despard's Coup

France was not coming to the aid of Ireland – at least officially – as Bonaparte had just brokered peace with England. Whatever was happening in Ireland and England was happening spontaneously: the Emmet brothers and the United Irish leadership still had not formulated a cohesive plan, nor had they secured any guarantees of French support. However, one cannot help but suspect that Robert Watson was involved somehow in what happened next. The extensive spy network in the north of England reported that by spring 1802 a major underground revolutionary plot to overturn the government was in operation. Informants confirmed the government's worst fears. The people wanted political, economic and social change: one man one vote, no discrimination on the grounds of religion, an end to war, fixed prices and old-age pensions were some of the demands being made, and studiously ignored by the state.[20]

Ireland wanted Home Rule, and if the French would not help, then with the assistance of the Black Lamp in England the Irish would rise themselves. The problem facing the Irish leadership was containing the English radical groups until plans were in place for the Irish rebels to rise in revolution and France had agreed support. Colonel Despard was the 'man of the hour'. It was probably not his remit to plan and co-ordinate revolution, but more to stop the rebellion 'going off half cock'. It was useless if England rose and Ireland was not ready for revolution. The two events had to be co-ordinated, and Despard was key in 'tempering' the spirit of revolution in England. Since the Treaty of Leoben, the United Irish viewed Bonaparte as a traitor to their cause and Ireland.[21] What was being planned had no support from France.

Senior members of the United Irishmen, who had held field commands in the Army of Wexford in 1798, emigrated to Lancashire and were centred around Liverpool, where secret meetings were held and John Thelwall was reported to attend.[22] The North East became the centre of operations. The Revd Ralph Fletcher told the Home Office that on 9 October a man called Smith, a resident of Ashby de la Zouch, had left Manchester for Sheffield, where he was reported to have ordered 2,000 pikes to be made.[23] It seems the Black Lamp was arming itself. In April 1802, the Jacobin-hunting Ralph Fletcher reported that seditious activity was on the increase. His spy network informed him that the Manchester Committee had sent a man called Cheetham as a delegate to the National Committee, which met in London, in order to obtain orders. The spy noted that the committees in Leeds, Wakefield and Sheffield had contributed to his expenses. Fletcher further commented that a delegate by the name of Winn had travelled to London from Stockport and had been eventually accepted and sent back with instructions. Also involved, the spy network told him, was a schoolmaster by the name of Clegg who taught arithmetic and navigation and gave lectures on the British constitution. More worryingly, Fletcher reported that a delegate from Ireland called Maginnis had attended the London Committee and had told the assembled delegates that there were 36,000 supporters in Dublin who were waiting for the disbandment of the army before they would act. Fletcher also noted that the Sheffield Committee gave one member a pike and an instrument called a cat – a caltrop – that could be used to maim horses. The aim of the committee, Fletcher stated, was to secure a government based on the will of the people, to wipe off the national debt and to disburden the people of taxes.[24] It seems, once roused to action, the Black Lamp's urge for revolution cascaded into an unstoppable force before Ireland was ready to rise: whatever plan was taking shape in England it was happening almost in a vacuum as nothing was 'on the radar' in Ireland.

Paris

A significant factor of the period 1802–4 was the use of secret agents. In London agents of Talleyrand gathered information on public mood. Fortunée Hamelin and Stéphanie-Félicité, comtesse de Genlis, were two women operatives and others were Lieutenant Colonel George Callander, formerly of the 25th regiment of Foot, and Carlo Franciso Baldini, the editor of *Bell's Weekly Messenger*. Their handler was Claude-François André. Callander became a topographical officer as part of the event planning of the Irish invasion, taking the name Beneval, working with Arthur O'Connor and the United Irishmen.[25] Hamburg-based merchant Alexandre Louis de le Chevardière kept Paris informed of news from there and the activities of banker John Thornton and the presence of English officers and merchants, keeping track of who came and went into the city. He reported to Louis Antoine Fauvelet de Bourrienne, the consul. As a merchant, Chevardière had a legitimate reason to be in British waters if stopped by the Royal Navy: he collected packets of information from agents in England and operated in the Thames estuary as well as on the Blackwater and Crouch rivers in East Anglia.[26]

Another was Joseph Fiévée who arrived in London at the start of February: his brief was to identify the motivation behind English political acts, as well as the political mood of England towards France and Bonaparte.[27] Fiévée circulated through Whig society in London, and made contacts with MPs who favoured peace with France. He met with Charles James Fox, and introduced his nephew Henry Vassell-Fox, Baron Holland to Talleyrand, and they dined together on 21 March. He also compiled a lengthy document reflecting on the trade and commerce of England and the advantages that France would derive from a commercial treaty with England. He noted that it was especially important for France to regain its past glory, to restore its greatness and restrict the power of England. The first move towards this, he noted, was that France 'must start by killing Anglomania at home'.[28] In the middle of June, Fiévée reported on the English national debt and the difficult fiscal situation faced by the Bank of England.[29]

Part of the discussions with the Whig leadership, it seems, almost certainly centred on the coming general election. It was under Napoléon's orders that DuPont d'Erval was sent to East Anglia at the end of May 1802. He was instructed to gather intelligence and influence the general election results in favour of pro-peace and pro-French candidates. He distributed £750 in support of Sir Francis Burdett's election in Middlesex, and spent similar sums in the counties of Nottinghamshire, Norfolk and Suffolk, taking care of the election expenses of pro-French members of Parliament.[30] In Middlesex, Burdett stood against William Mainwaring and George Byng. As a committed radical and Foxite Whig, Burdett had the active assistance of a number of Foxite Whigs, and received the votes of others, including Samuel Whitbread. He was personally supported by Charles James Fox and the opposition press, notably *Bell's Weekly Messenger*. The Duchess of Devonshire canvassed for Burdett and there were even rumours, which proved unfounded, that the Prince of Wales was actively interested in his success. At the same time notorious English extremists of the 1790s, who along with Burdett were involved in the Despard conspiracy, such as Frost, John Gale Jones, Fergusson, Bosville and Bonney were prominent among his supporters. Burdett was a man of interest to the French as he was well known to Jean-Baptiste Lechavilie, Talleyrand's librarian, and like Fox sought accommodation with France and to bring down the government of Addington and later Pitt. The decisive stroke in the election was played on the penultimate day, when 375 voters, who had claimed their franchise on the basis of 2-guinea shares in a 'good-intent' mill at Isleworth, which had not yet been completed and had a legal existence of less than twelve months, polled for Burdett (281 of them also for Byng) and not one of them for Mainwaring. This comes as no surprise as French gold was behind the scheme, and thus Burdett was placed with 14 votes less than Mainwaring and on the last day he polled in sufficient numbers to secure second place by 291 votes. Burdett was elected, but the result was contested on the grounds of bribery and corruption, and the election was declared void on 9 July 1804.[31] So concerned about Burdett was the British Crown that a spy, John Moody, who worked for Richard Ford, magistrate of Bow Street and head of the 'Bow Street Runners', was placed in Burdett's office as a clerk.[32] Bonaparte, in interfering with the outcome of elections – this is not just a modern phenomenon – was seeking to destabilize Addington's newly formed administration and bring the Whig opposition to power. A war was being fought by different means, whereby interference and intelligence were the primary weapons rather than muskets and sabres. Nor was this just a French plan of action, as will be demonstrated.

At the end of September 1802, Talleyrand requested that Agent Joseph Eugene de Beauvoison was sent to London to replace agent

Fiévée. Writing from Calais, Beauvoison reported to Consul Bonaparte on 15 October following his secret mission to England and Scotland that public opinion was in favour of war, thanks to the then open hostility of the newspapers.[33] It is not known who he met and what he discussed. Did he talk to English radicals? It would make sense if he did so, but this cannot be proved. Was he aware of other agents? It cannot be said. However, a French secret agent and Despard did discuss event planning.[34] Who that agent was is not known.

Scarcely had Beauvoison reported back, when he was sent to London: his remit was to report on the activity of French Royalists seeking to cause disturbances in France as well as to collect anti-French and anti-Bonaparte newspapers and publications. The newly promoted colonel arrived in London on 20 October.[35] The following day he wrote to Bonaparte concerning the hatred of the English newspapers to France.[36]

Whilst Beauvoison was in London the Despard plot was reaching its climax. In a letter written at the end of November from Calais to Bonaparte, Beauvoison warned of 'the evils which would overwhelm England in the event of war'.[37] He was speaking here, no doubt, of the United Englishmen and the public mood against war away from the media, led by Marcus Edward Despard. For many in England, revolution seemed imminent (see *Fighting Napoleon at Home* by the same author for more detail).

Yet, there was no revolution and Despard was arrested on 16 November. He and fourteen others were tried in February 1803. Although the jury recommended mercy, Despard and John Wood, 36, John Francis, 23, both privates in the British Army, Thomas Broughton, 26, a carpenter, James Sedgwick Wratton, 35, a shoemaker, Arthur Graham, 53, a slater, and John Macnamara, a labourer, were sentenced to be hung, drawn and quartered on 21 February 1803.[38] Many called the execution 'murder'.[39] Ambassador Andreossy wrote to Talleyrand to inform him that the plot was of little value.[40] This letter would have been read by the British Crown before transmission to France, and was probably written more for the benefit of its English readers than Talleyrand's. In the context of the times, the Despard plot is remarkably similar to that of Georges Cadoudal: assassination of the head of state to win a war before it began and winning independence for the instigators' homeland (Ireland or the Vendée).

In the wake of the Despard plot, agent Beauvoison was sent back to London by Bonaparte on 4 December: 'Citizen Duroc will let Citizen Beauvoison know … he will return to England … He will seek different pretexts to travel the entire coast, from the Thames to beyond Plymouth, the Bristol Channel, Edinburgh and the coast of Scotland.'[41] Beauvoison, or one of his immediate circle, travelled around Rye, Winchelsea and Hastings reporting on the local landmarks, the terrain, population centres and local Crown forces. He travelled on to Pevensey, reporting on coastal defence artillery batteries. He also visited Newhaven, Beachyhead, Brighton, Sandgate and Folkestone, and identified Dover and Walmer castles as key targets. He recommended that Rye was an ideal invasion site.[42] Another agent returned to Rye and prepared a plan of the harbour and reported on local landmarks, adding that Camber Sands made a perfect landing ground.[43] Beauvoison was also tasked with uncovering the secret plots being planned by the 'Royal Princes'.[44]

Chapter 23

EMMET'S REBELLION

Contiguous to the Despard plot developing in England, in early summer 1802 William Putnam McCabe returned to Dublin on behalf of the émigré leadership in France, known as the 'Directory'. In July 1802, he left Dublin en route for Paris. He brought news to Manchester that the United Irishmen were ready to rise again as soon as the continental war was renewed. A spy working for Ralph Fletcher, identified as D, reported that McCabe had visited James Napper Tandy in Hamburg – this must have been before the latter's arrest – and noted that McCabe was dismissive of the need for French assistance and encouraged his interlocutors to be ready to act on their own initiative. McCabe argued that the London Directory had been slow in seizing the initiative.[1] It is assumed that the 'London Directory' centred on Wallis Eastburn, John Nicholls, Thomas Evans, Charles Pendrill and by association Colonel Despard. From England, McCabe headed back to France, where in September he was joined by Thomas Russell.[2]

Another key figure liaising between republicans in England and Ireland during 1802–3 was the aforementioned William Dowdall. He travelled to London on United Irish business in July 1802, posing as a clerk in the firm of the Dublin merchant Philip Long.[3] This suggests that whatever was being developed in London was being formulated in co-ordination with Ireland and inter alia the French.

In the aftermath of the collapse of the Despard plot, William Putnam McCabe, who was closely connected with Robert Emmet, persuaded the three former Kildare rebels in Paris – William Aylmer, Hugh Ware and Michael Quigley – to return to Ireland and organize support for a conspiracy in County Kildare codenamed the Louisiana Project. Ware was the recognized leader of the Kildare group and Thomas Russell who was also assisting McCabe gave Ware £30 for expenses and directed him to distribute it equally between himself, Quigley and McDermott. Dr Martin McDermott was a close ally of O'Connor, who had canvassed Protestant gentry in 1796, and was a confidant of Pamela Fitzgerald. This money had come from Robert Emmet for the purpose of conscripting United men in Paris. Ware, however, remained in Paris while Quigley and McDermott set out on the journey back to Ireland.

Over winter 1802, a French agent working for Talleyrand, Pierre Poterat, was in contact with Dr William James MacNeven. Over the intervening months he submitted various schemes for the invasion of Ireland to exploit discontent in England. Ireland was very much 'the poor relation' in Franco-Irish discussions at this stage. MacNeven told Poterat that the Irish would no longer be 'mischief makers'. Indeed, MacNeven told Poterat – and ultimately Talleyrand – that as France had failed Ireland since 1798, that unless France made a firm commitment to land troops in Ireland 'that it would be difficult to bring the people out again'.[4]

On the strength of MacNeven's testimony, in early February 1803, Poterat reported a series of options for invading Ireland to Talleyrand. One of these seems to have been to send a raid à la Humbert comprising 1,830 men: 1,500 NCOs, 300 company officers and 30 senior officers to take charge of the United Irishmen insurgent force. The plan relied squarely on 15,000 United Irish rallying to the French.[5]

The French plans did not suit the United Irish, however. On behalf of the United Irish, MacNeven reported that the Irish would no longer be 'lap dogs' to the French or satisfied with half measures and broken promises. The French had to send a strong invasion force or the Irish would 'go it alone'.[6]

MacNeven left Hamburg for Brussels at the end of February 1803. Here he was joined by Archibald Hamilton Rowan, along with Robert Emmet. Rowan and Robert Emmet assembled around them 'some devoted and resolute men', according to the historian of the United Irishmen, Richard Robert Madden, among whom were Thomas Russell, former lieutenant of infantry, John Allen, cloth merchant, William Dowdall, Phillip Long, William Hamilton as well as 'Mistress Biddy Palmer', the sister of a companion of Lord Edward Fitzgerald who Madden called 'an Irish Madame Roland'. Behind the curtain, Madden adds, there were higher ranking figures who were aware of the conspiracy, knew all its springs and directed all its movements. The conspirators planned to seize Dublin Castle and the city, while forging intelligence with neighbouring counties. For the leadership, it seemed very likely that if the movement succeeded in Dublin, then it would spread to the whole of Ireland.

Russell, the Emmet brothers and MacNeven arrived back in Dublin on 5 March 1803. Quigley and Henry Hamilton arrived in Ireland on the same day: they met Robert Emmet a few days later and planned ways of organizing Kildare dissidents and of getting them to Dublin for a future rising in the city. None of this went unnoticed. A double agent – who the French never suspected – reported to John Reeves in London 'that a great plot against Ireland was being hatched in Paris; that several of the conspirators were known to me, and that every day there was a council of Irish malcontents'[7]; this was centred around General Brune, Bonaparte and Talleyrand. Both France and the British Crown sought to win a war without a battle through the use of information, spies, assassination and provoking internal conflict. For Bonaparte, Ireland offered the best hope of success.

One of the problems that the French faced when dealing with the United Irishmen exiled in France and Hamburg was the lack of clear leadership: an issue that Thomas Muir had noted in 1798. MacNeven clearly led one faction. Arthur O'Connor led another. O'Connor was back in Paris in February, and considered himself to be the legitimate ambassador to Paris from the United Irish. Yet, Thomas Addis Emmet believed he was on invitation from Hamilton Rowan.[8] The continuing feud between the two factions contributed to the failure of any successful uprising or rebellion.

Behind the scenes, Arthur O'Connor in Paris was 'Advising Buonoparte how best to succeed in plundering and desolating this Country', as a British observer commented.[9] O'Connor had, simultaneously with MacNeven, started courting the French about involvement in a rebellion in Ireland.[10] The two men had corresponded, but a conflict of personalities as well as divergent aims meant that any co-ordinated effort between O'Connor and MacNeven – who was a friend and ally of the Emmets – was impossible. Indeed, O'Connor and MacNeven's dislike of each other almost resulted in them fighting a duel.

It seems that O'Connor was endeavouring to rally the scattered United Englishmen and Black Lamp to the United Irishmen's cause. A letter between O'Connor to a known 'United' was intercepted by the British Crown. The recipient was Hugh Bell, a wine merchant of Charterhouse Square, London, who had been arrested in 1798 for harbouring two United Irishmen, Arthur O'Connor and Father James O'Coigley. Yet, O'Connor seemed more concerned about other matters: 'I have been very busy looking out a farm in the neighbourhood of Paris'. He added: 'we are in a state of incertitude about peace or war. I can't think we are to be so soon plunged in war again. I am told many of the English are on their return Home' concerning the exodus of Whigs from Paris. He gave his address as a hotel in Paris.[11]

M. Middleton, a secret agent, was sent to England to report on the political and economic situation. Essentially, his remit was to assess if England was still ripe for revolution.[12] A second agent, by the name of Duverne, reported on 29 September 1803 that the public mood was now in favour of war, and that Addington's administration had begun recruiting for the army and had also mobilized thousands as volunteers.[13]

The French Army Archives hold two reports which may be contingency plans prepared in the wake of Irish hostility. One option for invasion centred on Wolfe Tone's 1796 plans: a French force of four frigates would sail from Rochefort at the same time as twenty vessels from Brest. The French ships would enter the Bristol Channel and land troops in Wales and lead an insurrection to attack Bristol, while the main force, some 12,000 men, would land in Ireland. A force of 5,000 men would depart from Dieppe and Texel and land in Scotland.[14] This document is accompanied by a report on Ireland and England which outlines a plan to invade Ireland with 24,000 French and Spanish troops, landing in different regions to scatter the Crown forces. A force sailing from Dunkirk and landing at Rye in England would act as a diversion. The plan was conceived as 'liberating the Catholics of Ireland from English Protestant slavery', and upon news of the revolution, it was hoped rather naïvely that the Irish sailors in the Royal Navy would mutiny and sail their ships to Ireland.[15]

After two months' deliberation, Napoléon agreed to aid Emmet. On 16 April 1803 Napoléon ordered General Berthier to gather information on the numbers, means and plans for war of the Irish and Scottish chiefs in Ireland.[16] France and England were technically at peace for another month.

Napoléon agreed to invade as long as the United Irishmen could mobilize at least 20,000 men to join the French Army within the first few days of landing.[17] A report reached his desk on 3 June. In the lengthy dispatch, the writer remarked that the Defenders could be relied upon to rise within 24 hours of the landing, but tellingly he did not give any numbers. The writer also felt that 40,000 men would be needed to take control of Ireland with a landing in Gallway Bay and 'the mouth of Kilmain', i.e., off the coast of Belfast and Carikfergus. To prevent the English being able to send reinforcements to Ireland, speed was of the essence once troops were landed. The French would, it was estimated, be able to march 30 leagues in 24 hours and would achieve their objective in two days, thus Belfast would fall almost immediately. However, MacNeven was busy raising rebels in Dublin where the French would arrive four days at most after landing. Could the United Irish hold out that long? The writer again stressed that an invasion in Ireland would trigger the Catholics and Irish in the Royal Navy to mutiny: this begs the question did the United Irish still have agents in the navy over five years after the 1797 mutiny? The author of the paper, an Irish émigré who had been forced to serve in the Royal Navy, concluded with summing up the advantages of launching the invasion from Brest over Rochefort. He glibly assumed that the fleet could easily avoid the Royal Navy – wishful thinking based on Bantry Bay no doubt. 'The enemy are already alarmed by our preparations, our dedication and temerity,' wrote the correspondent, who signed himself 'C'.[18] Who was the mysterious, French-speaking former member of the Royal Navy? It must be assumed that 'C' was involved in the United Irish committee in Paris and aware of the planning being undertaken in Ireland.

Napoléon's formal plans to invade Ireland began on 24 June 1803 when orders were issued to construct sufficient landing barges to accommodate 125,000 men at Brest destined to land in Ireland. The expedition was to be ready to sail in January 1804.[19] By August the scale of the invading army had been grossly reduced: the French task was to assemble 25,000 men under the command of General André Masséna. The French ships were to carry 40,000 muskets, all the necessary artillery and munitions to arm the United Irishmen. Peace was only to be declared once Irish independence were secured.[20]

The Black Lamp

In order to provide a distraction from the events unfolding in Ireland, the United Britons were to stage a rebellion in England. It was hoped that if the British Army was tied down containing the United Britons, then the rebellion in Ireland stood more chance of success.

In Portsmouth forty-two suspected United Irishmen were arrested at the end of March.[21] A month later, delegates from Dublin 'seem to have been sent with the view of enquiring into the reason of the backwardness of the Manchester Citizens which has ... given great uneasiness to their friends'. Despard's arrest and execution seems to have dampened the ardour for revolution, just as the authorities hoped. Fletcher noted, furthermore, that his network of informers reported that three United English delegates had arrived from France, and that an Irish delegate had been in Manchester. Yet, Fletcher commented that Patrick Finney was at large in the north of England and, according to a spy, 'spoke confidently of the French invading Ireland in case of war and should the dispute be patched up between their country and France, the Irish would shake off the yoke themselves'.[22]

When war broke out again in May 1803, Fox blamed Prime Minister Henry Addington for not standing up to the king. The British government had not left Napoléon, sighed Fox, 'any alternative but War or the most abject humiliation' and that the war 'is entirely the fault of our Ministers and not of Bonaparte'.[23] Public opinion was against war, and more importantly the spectre of economic collapse and famine haunted the middle classes and urban poor.[24] The British Crown embarked on an ambitious propaganda drive to once more 'whistle up' nationalism to allow the elites to fight the war they wanted. As in 1794, the government sought to harness hatred of reform, hatred of the French and love of 'king and country' to raise a new force for national defence. By 1804, over 380,000 men were enrolled in the 'volunteer' forces of the country through the Levy en Masse Act. This Act required all men aged between 17 and 55 to be placed into four classes, those of the first class were invited to enrol in the Volunteer Corps if they were to escape the militia ballot.[25] Opposing them were an estimated 50,000 united Irishmen in London, and in Ireland and the remainder of England perhaps 300,000 had joined, or were sympathetic, to the United Irishmen's goal.

In May an informant told the Crown that the United Irishmen were communicating with the French and that the men assembled nightly to practise their drills and could respond to a French invasion at one night's notice. It was their hope, the source noted, that the French would invade and 'then the Irish will join them in overthrowing the British government and the established church'. The informant furthermore mentioned that the United Englishmen would rise at the same time in London and Liverpool.[26] The same month, the Home Office received reports that William Cheetham, the well-known radical Jacobin in Manchester, was sending 'seditious papers and handbills' to Leeds in a consignment of hats.[27] An intercepted letter from Brook Taylor, British Minister to Hesse-Cassel, dated 24 July 1803 informed the Home Office that Napoléon had sent James Napper Tandy and two others named Farqarson and Bolard to Ireland to influence 'the people in favour of France in case of invasion'.[28] The man identified as 'Farquarson' is very likely to have been Glaswegian-born John Farquharson who shows up in the Irish Legion and whom Miles Byrne often refers to as Ferguson.[29]

An informant offered to provide the names of the Irish insurgents then resident in Liverpool in exchange for hard cash.[30] Despard's death, it seems, had changed nothing. Clearly, the United Englishmen were not yet a spent force. Irish agents travelled throughout Nottinghamshire, Lancashire and Yorkshire rebuilding the Black Lamp network in June and July.[31] In the summer came alarming reports from Devon, where handbills were posted which declared:

> You are called upon with others of your country by an oppressive government to be sent on the continent to be butchered – will you tamely submit to this new act of Tyranny & leave your wives & Children to despair & ruin? NO! rouse yourselves, be United – its time to resist those cruel rulers & let them know that you will no longer submit to their will when it is cruel and unjust.[32]

Across England, the Black Lamp and United Englishmen were ready to rise in rebellion. It all depended on Napoléon and Ireland.

Rebellion in Ireland

Emmet had been tasked with raising and training insurgents and keeping the rebellion in check until the French set foot in Ireland. Nothing was to happen until the French landed, at which point Dublin Castle would be seized, followed by a mass uprising in the provinces. When Emmet had left France in October 1802, during the Peace of Amiens, he knew that no French aid had been promised and, even after the rupture of that peace, was sure no such would be forthcoming until early 1804. Ireland, in Emmet's calculation or at least in his imagination, had no need for the French assistance, and he was now unequivocally declaring it unnecessary. Rather than French soldiers, Emmet counted on support from Kildare and Wicklow, but the Wicklow men in particular would not have been very comfortable with street fighting, having been mountain guerrillas in 1798. The Kildare men would probably also have had similar misgivings. Indeed, none of the groups Emmet had hoped to recruit to his cause had never been to Dublin and Emmet, a Dubliner, never understood this.

On the evening of 16 July 1803, one of the rebels inadvertently sparked off an explosion of their stockpile of gunpowder kept in a warehouse on Patrick Street, causing a massive explosion. Believing the police to be on their trail, Emmet and the other leaders decided that the plans must be accelerated, and they advanced the rising to the next week, 23 July. Without French aid or significant organizational unity across the country, and with poor coordination within the capital itself, the rising was limited to skirmishes in Dublin, which the British quickly suppressed. Recriminations quickly followed between the United Irish leadership: yet, it is undeniable that Emmet never gave any signal for Dowdall or Byrne to lead their men forward, as the agreed signal rockets were never fired. Byrne's expectation that a 'thousand armed citizens who would meet in the morning, and the thousands of armed men pouring in from all parts of the country' was not based on any reasonable information, but on the insistence of Emmet.[33]

Yet, the fear of an invasion of Ireland was real enough. Another writer, London resident Thomas Faulder, opined to his friend on 3 August that: 'I HAVE heard … that if the French can land [in Ireland], with some troops, they will immediately be joined by 100,000 Irish … The fact is, that nothing can satisfy them but a separation from this country.'[34] John Lumsden writing from London reported to a friend: 'Discontent may, it is true, manifest itself among the lower classes in London, as well as in our great towns; but I do not think that it can ever be of great consequence. My only fear is for Ireland, where the standard of rebellion has been hoisted a-new.'[35] By 25 August the episode was over, and about fifty people died in all, primarily Emmet's fellow revolutionaries; thirty-two were executed by the Crown. Robert Emmet was captured along with Russell and both were executed.[36] Yet, the United Irishmen were still drilling and expecting the French to come and lead them in a rebellion.[37]

In the aftermath of Emmet's rebellion, it seems that some form of plan of action was put together in France. The plan – which has all the hallmarks of General Humbert – recommended a force of 5,000 Franco-Spanish soldiers land in Ireland. The force for Ireland was increased to 12,000 men and was to land simultaneously with a landing in England. Four frigates accompanied by corvettes were to leave Rochefort and head to Ireland. Concurrently, twenty frigates and corvettes would leave Brest and head to the Bristol Channel. The force would land and lead an insurrection in Wales and into the interior of England. Similar forces would leave Morlaix and Dieppe again carrying 5,000 troops in case the first wave of attack was intercepted. Troops would leave Texel and Oostend and head to Scotland.[38] In England the threat of invasion seemed all too real. On 28 August, a plan was prepared concerning an invasion of Ireland by Alexander Brayer who was: 'aware of the cause and the recent insurrection in Ireland, the energy and character of the Irish and their animosity against the English governments, the talents of their leaders and insurgents' and requested the French send 10,000 men as soon as possible. Brayer outlined that since the Act of Union the Protestants in Ireland had joined the 'cause of the patriots to assure the Independence of their country'. A landing in Ireland would have huge benefits for France and 'shake the foundations till they collapse' of England.[39]

It is not known if this paper was ever presented to the first consul, but the French archives contain a paper on Ireland dated 1803 'commissioned by the First Consul', seemingly in response to the initial invasion plan. The paper explores the economy of Ireland, as well as religious discontent, particularly the lack of rights of Catholics. The paper outlines an invasion force of 24,000 as well as making clear the all-too genuine fears of the Royal Navy.[40] Clearly, in summer 1803, consideration was given to an invasion of Ireland. On 28 August, a spy reported to Bonaparte that an invasion would be hazardous as the British Crown had deployed 60,000 men to Ireland, and feared that upon landing, every Protestant in Ireland would rally to the Crown. The best chance of success lay in a diversionary attack in England and Scotland through supporting an insurrection of the disaffected and mutiny in the British Army.[41] Many in England were convinced that the French were coming.

One British writer reported to Lord William Cavendish Bentinck at the end of August 1803 that:

> They [the Irish] have begun according to their ancient custom. If this country be not attended to, it will be lost. These rascals are as ripe for rebellion as ever. The Government at present is very active. It has seized a great number of rebels and some of their chiefs. A great many Frenchmen, and Irishmen in the service of France, are said to be concealed in Ireland. Parliament has taken the precautions which circumstances required, by authorising the trial of all the rebels by Martial Law, and by suspending the Habeas Corpus. It will be necessary to put in execution the penal laws against the Catholics. If an opinion on the subject were necessary, mine is, that the grand attack will be made upon Ireland, where they (the French) will certainly be joined by a considerable number.[42]

In order to make contact with the Irish leadership, and to find out what exactly was happening in Ireland, John Swiney was dispatched on a fact-finding mission. He travelled to Cork via Hamburg.[43] On landing in Ireland, he learned definitive facts about Robert Emmet's failure, but in his letter to Thomas Emmet, he noted the 'Irish revolution was not yet over'. Based on Swiney's report, Emmet informed Bonaparte on 7 September: 'that help is to be sent as quickly as possible to the Irish who have just revolted against England'.[44] Swiney requested 50,000 muskets be sent to Ireland with all haste. In a second letter to Berthier, Thomas Addis Emmet reported that Swiney had travelled under the pseudonym of Simpson and had landed at Galley Head. From there he travelled to meet the Cork leadership, but was unable to get to Dublin due to increased surveillance by the British Crown.

Swiney reported on the strength of the Crown forces and dispositions of the United Irish, adding that a seventy-six-gun ship of the line and six frigates were on station to defend Ireland from any French invasion force. Due to the threat from the Royal Navy, Swiney counselled that it was impossible to send a large invasion force, and that instead a small force in the manner of 1798 be sent. He urged that it should be dispatched immediately if it was to be any help to the Irish. As well as the disposition of Swiney from Emmet, Arthur O'Connor offered his advice: he reported that Robert Emmet, Russell and others had been at Fort George, and were ardent revolutionaries. Without them, a French-style revolution was impossible, as more prudent men had taken their place who were not Jacobins. For O'Connor the moment of offering direct aid had passed.[45] Bonaparte was more favourable to the views of O'Connor and not Thomas Emmet, and the Irish rebels received no support from France. O'Connor's advice to Bonaparte had been correct. Swiney returned to Paris in October, convinced that any invasion by the French was impracticable given the collapse of Emmet's rebellion and the diaspora of the leadership.[46] Swiney had come to the same conclusion as O'Connor had a month earlier.

The Last-Chance Saloon

The failure of Emmet's rebellion effectively marked the end of French involvement in Irish affairs for the time being. Yet, the United Britons and whatever remained of the United Irish had not given up their activity. At the start of November, a spy reported the French were making active preparations to land in Ireland and England.[47]

Officers from the Collector and Comptroller at Caernarvon informed the Home Office that the ship *Experiment* of New York had docked in Caernarvon having sailed from Dunkirk. The master had given the customs agents information that a force of gunboats and soldiers was being assembled in Dunkirk, to be ready by February to land in Ireland. The master further added that he had been offered £500 by an Irish rebel general to carry 20,000 stands of arms to Ireland.[48] Worrying news came from the Netherlands. A spy for the British Crown reported that: 'Hopwood was at that time employed by the French government as a travelling spy ... knew of certain plans that were contemplated by the French against the English nation, one was a scheme to destroy the shipping on the river Thames ...'.[49]

Simultaneously, a French spy was reported to have arrived from Flushing via Le Havre. The spy is said to have been American Charles Cowing who had been reported at the Cock Inn, Leadenhall Street, London.[50] Flushing was home to a number of British émigrés, among whom, a spy for the Crown reported, was: 'Tom Walker of Manchester ... a serious republican, says he will die in peace when Ireland is separated from England ... he brags of being the oldest member of the Whig Club'. This was Thomas Walker who associated with the Mayor of Paris, Jérôme Pétion de Villeneuve, during 1791, met Talleyrand at the beginning of 1792 and chaired the Revolution Club of Manchester. He had fled to the continent in spring 1793 after Loyalists mobs had destroyed his home and business, burned down two Unitarian chapels and smashed the presses of the radical *Manchester Herald* newspaper to silence free speech. Another man on the Crown's wanted list was: 'Richard Ellis Stone ... a furious republican, he will not take part in any expedition to Ireland. Irishmen and Scotchmen are in great numbers in Flanders, recruiting for the French.'[51] Seemingly the 'ex pat' community was lending its support to the putative invasion.

DuPont d'Erval

As noted earlier, a key part of Napoléon's planning process was the use of secret agents on intelligence-gathering missions. One of the most important of these was Robert DuPont d'Erval, who was mentioned previously.

DuPont d'Erval was named Inspector General of the Compagnie des Guides Interprètes du Premier Consul on 5 October 1803. This organization was formed from Irish, Scottish and English radicals exiled in Paris and Hamburg to act as interpreters – and what else it might be asked? Among the men who were under d'Erval's orders was Henry Jones. He arrived in France from Hamburg in July 1791. He joined the National Guard of Nantes in June 1793, and served in the Vendée with the rank of sergeant major and participated in the massacres that took place during winter 1793/94 during the 'pacification' of the Vendée and also fought at Quiberon in 1795. As a member of the Légion Nantais, he fought 'for the republic and to maintain equality'.[52] By summer 1803 he had been convalescing in Belgium and was lodging in the home of M. Fould, a banker, at 1004 rue Bergere Paris.[53] Judging by the episodes of the war he participated in, one could say he was a 'war criminal' by the time his service in that theatre ended in 1796. Serving alongside Jones were Peter MaCarthy, Charles Max, Peter Bovay and Jack Descourtes, all former British soldiers. Others included Charles Weber, a former soldier of the Austrian Army, Adrian Paridaans, a former officer in the Batavian Army during the revolution of 1786, Francis Moffatt, a United Irishmen from County Wicklow,[54] Peter Murray, a United Irishman exiled from Dublin,[55] and Joseph Murray, a student from

Edinburgh.[56] John Deal, born in Bingley, West Yorkshire, in August 1773, had previously served in the 11e Chasseurs and transferred to the new unit. Pierre Brennan from Saint-Domingue had lived in Philadelphia for twelve years before enlisting on 29 March 1804.[57] Louis Welling asked to join up on 12 October 1803, and stated to Marshal Brune and DuPont d'Erval that despite being a subject of the British Crown, he loved France and had a hatred of England. He was well known to the French secret police for his outspoken political views in support of Jacobinism.[58] M. Jachonon of 17 rue Bertin Poiree, Paris, informed DuPont d'Erval that he was aged 42 and had lived in England thirty-five years, had English customs and habits, and could be of use as a translator as well as 'to gather intelligence about enemies of the government'.[59] Every man in the unit had military experience, perfect English and could pass as 'English'. To what degree DuPont d'Erval utilized his men in his clandestine operations in England and Ireland is not known, but no sooner had DuPont d'Erval taken up his new post, he was back in England.

In August 1803, Fouche had learned from his agents of a plot to kidnap and murder Bonaparte. This was being masterminded in England. The instigators were Georges Cadoudal and Jean-Guillaume Hyde de Neuville. Cadoudal had fought alongside the Chouans of Brittany in 1793 and 1799 and had taken part in the landing at Quiberon in 1795. The Comte d'Artois made him a lieutenant general. Hyde de Neuville, a young man of 24, made a name for himself by organizing a Royalist demonstration in Paris on 21 January 1800 for the anniversary of the execution of Louis XVI. That day, he and his friends draped the facade of La Madeleine Church in black cloth and pasted the king's will on its door. Most of his accomplices were caught and shot, but he escaped. Almost a year passed until 24 December 1800, when Hyde de Neuville and Cadoudal planted a bomb in the rue Saint-Nicaise. The attack killed twenty-two people and injured a hundred others but not the first consul or any of his relatives. After hiding in Germany, Hyde de Neuville and Cadoudal landed in Dover at the beginning of 1803 and travelled to meet the Comte d'Artois. With backing from the British Crown to raise a rebellion in the Vendée, Cadoudal landed in Normandy on 23 August 1803. Days later, DuPont d'Erval returned to London.

On 22 October 1803, DuPont d'Erval was ordered to Scotland for two months, to gather information on public opinion and keep the Comte d'Artois under surveillance. Joseph Murray's intimate knowledge of Scotland and Edinburgh in particular, where the comte resided, would have been essential in these tasks, it can be assumed.

DuPont d'Erval reported on 15 January 1804 that while deliberations were ongoing between the remaining United Irishmen and Napoléon, 'it was essential for the British government to be menaced from several fronts, to keep their attention from our main operation'.[60] The following day, exiled General Pichegru landed in France. On 28 January, Cadoudal and Pichegru met Jean Victor Moreau, the hero of Hohnenlinden. Moreau was sent to the Temple Prison on 15 February. Cadoudal was caught on 9 March. On 16 April, Pichegru was found strangled in his cell. Was it suicide or assassination to prevent him from revealing the names of other accomplices? Cadoudal was guillotined on 24 June. What part DuPont d'Erval played in uncovering all of this is difficult to say, but he was certainly involved given his remit was to observe the ringleader of it all, the Comte d'Artois.

DuPont d'Erval was a key link in Napoléon's intelligence-gathering network. He was named chief of staff of Davout with the rank of adjutant commandant, reporting to the Grand Marshal of the Palace, Duroc, along with the aforementioned Chevardière, who became Consul to Dantzig in 1807, and the spy Schulmeister. He was wounded at Essling and killed at Borodino: all very strange for a 'a trader in information'.

Paris

If Thomas Addis Emmet had been the type of person to reflect on the catalogue of failed French expeditions to Ireland, he would have been far from hopeful in supposing the French would land and the people would spontaneously rise. Belief in the success of a French *débarquement*, as Nicholas Dunne-Lynch says, was 'a triumph of optimism over experience'. Despite the long track record of failure, Thomas Addis Emmet wrote to Napoléon at the start of December 1803.[61] On 13 January 1804, Napoléon sent a lengthy dispatch via Berthier, Minister of War, to Thomas Addis Emmet and Arthur O'Connor. In this he boldly declared that he would not agree peace with England until Ireland was independent:

> Bring MM. Emmet, Thompson and other United Irish Chiefs; let them know, lo that I have read the attached memorandum with the greatest attention; that I cannot make any proclamation before having touched the territory of Ireland; but that the general commanding the expedition will be provided with sealed letters, by which I will declare that I will not make peace with England without admitting the independence of Ireland, however that the army will have been joined by a corps

considerable number of United-Irish; that Ireland will in all things be treated like America in the past war;

2. That any individual who will embark with the French army, forming part of the expedition, will be commissioned as French; and, if he were arrested and not treated as a prisoner of war, reprisal would be made on English prisoners;

3. That any corps formed in the name of the United Irishmen shall be considered as forming part of the French army; if the expedition should not succeed, France would maintain a number of Irish brigades, and would give pensions to any individual who had been part of the government and authorities of the country; these pensions could be regulated according to the pensions given in France under equivalent conditions, when the individuals are not employed; that I would like a committee of United Irishmen to be formed, and that I see no harm in their making proclamations and informing their compatriots of the state of affairs. We would put these proclamations in the Argus and in the other newspapers of Europe, in order to enlighten the Irish on the side to take and the hopes to conceive.

If the committee wished to make a narration of all the tyrannies exercised in Ireland, it would be inserted in the Moniteur.[62]

Yet, beyond Emmet and Lewines, who was actually left to form a committee? Perhaps Napoléon's resurgence of interest in Irish affairs stemmed from the information gathered by the Guides Interprètes. Having a pool of over forty fluent English speakers in Boulogne and Saint-Omer meant that British merchants could be questioned – did they give the information willingly? Did they give the answers the French wanted? Was the information extracted by other means? Thomas Marfawr and five others from the ship's company of the cutter *The George* told the interrogators on 26 December 1803 that: 'the English people and even the soldiers ardently desired peace; that they were preparing to make resistance; but all could see that general discontent, trouble and confusion reigned in England'. Under interrogation, Captain William Weynam was:

Asked if the English feared invasion and if they believed in it, replied that the English were preparing to repel the French. There was great surveillance and a great deal of mistrust; that the batteries were guarded by people from the coast exempt from the press gang; that everyone was enrolled from 15 to 45 years old; that no one was exempted from service, of whatever rank, either individually or by paying. Men were taken from the militias to recruit the regiments of the line where they were put on high pay; that the people very much desire peace and that there would be sedition if the war were to last long.[63]

A week later, on 16 January, Captain William Morrison was questioned at length over several days:

> Asked if he expects to see the French arrive soon in England. He replied that he expects it and that in the island of Wich [*sic* Isle of Wight] where he took on his cargo, there are only a thousand men in garrison who daily are on the move ... Asked where he thinks the French will land. He replied, the general opinion in England is that the French are going to land in Ireland, and if the fleet then lands in England they regard their country as lost. He further adds that there was a rumour in England that a large number of Frenchmen had landed in Scotland. He further states that he anchored for a few days at Dungeness and that there was no camp on the coast, but only a few forts here and there, and are badly guarded ... Asked if the Irish were still unhappy and if we still sent a lot of troops to Ireland? He replied that their revolt is renewed more strongly than ever, that lately an officer of the king was killed in his carriage and his body was mutilated by the people ... Asked if the French descended on Scotland what effect he believed their arrival would have on the inhabitants? He replies that he is convinced that the inhabitants would immediately lay down their arms as they can no longer support the taxes with which they are overwhelmed;[64]

From the questions asked it was clear that Napoléon was planning to land troops in Ireland, Scotland and on the south coast of England. The interrogations were conducted by the French Navy, on behalf of Admiral Bruix, on whose staff, it should be remembered, Henry Jones served.

Buoyed up by the work of his interrogators, on 19 January 1804, Napoléon's thoughts turned to Ireland. The fleet at Texel was to prepare itself for a landing in Ireland in consort with the fleet at Brest. Based on information from his spy network, Napoléon believed: 'we must make a sortie against Cornwallis, who is no less than our numbers, but his troops are scattered on several points because he believes he has nothing to fear.' General Augereau arrived at Brest on 24 January to take command of the *Armée d'Irlande*. In reply to Napoléon's letter, on 25 January 1804, Emmet prepared an invasion plan which was sent to the Minister of War. In his plan, Emmet asked for 25,000 men to invade Ireland. Emmet believed the United Irish in Wexford, Wickford and Dublin were still ready to rise, estimating 6,000 would do so, and recommended that the French land at Drogheda Bay and in Waterford. Both columns were to march on Dublin, the advantage of a quick strike on Dublin being 'incalculable'. The French would land in Waterford and would advance on Clonmell and Drogheda. Emmet made a few fundamental errors: the assumption that rebels would join along the march towards Dublin was not guaranteed. County Kilkenny, for example, had refused to rise in rebellion when the Wexford rebels arrived in 1798. County Wexford had been badly mauled in the '98, with thousands killed. However, a large French army might have encouraged some rebels to join. The other issue with the plans and shows the naïvety of his thinking is that Emmet offered no suggestion on how to combat the Royal Navy. Like the French 1803 plan, it was perhaps little more than wishful thinking. Emmet in a postscript noted that William Dowdall was in Dublin and had assured him of support of the United Irishmen, and that the British garrison was perhaps 70,000, of which 16,000 were militia and 3,500 yeoman 'which posed no threat'.[65]

Amid the planning, the arrest of Cadoudal was announced to the French people: the press demanded vengeance.[66] In reply to the threat, Consul Bonaparte became Emperor Napoléon.

Despite the heightened tension with England, months would pass until 6 September 1804, when an invasion of Ireland once more appeared imminent when Napoléon ordered 16,000 men and 500 cavalry to be readied to embark for Ireland. Three weeks later the force was increased to 18,000 men departing Brest under Augereau and a further 25,000 men under Marmont, with the Grande Armée at Boulogne to head to Kent. Napoléon wrote to Berthier:

Cousin, the Irish expedition is resolved. For this purpose you will have a conference with Marshal Augereau (general-in-chief of the expedition to Ireland). At Brest there are embarkation facilities for 18,000 men. General Marmont (commander of the Utrecht camp), for his part, is ready with 25,000 men. He will try to land in Ireland, and will be under the orders of Marshal Augereau. The Grande Armée de Boulogne will be embarked during the same time, and will do everything possible to penetrate into the county of Kent. You will let Marshal Augereau know that he will behave according to events. If the information I have from the Irish refugees and from the men I have sent to Ireland are verified, a large number of Irish will line up under his colours when he lands; then he will march straight to Dublin. If, on the contrary, this movement was delayed, he will take up position to wait for General Marmont and until the Grande Armée has landed.[67]

Only in English understanding was the Grande Armée solely coming to England. Pitt and his ministers in London created an invasion scare to cement his position in power and to rally the divided country around him. In spreading this misinformation he was successful. Any invasion of England was a diversion for Ireland: the goal was never to invade. A successful invasion of Ireland would cause Pitt's government to collapse and bring Fox to power, who would seek peace terms. Ireland would be a French ally, and the British war effort would be crippled. It was a win-win situation for the Irish and Napoléon. With the French in Ireland, it would only be a matter of time before French boots were landed in Scotland to make Dr Watson and Thomas Muir's dream of an independent Scotland a reality. Lough Swilly was the destination for the troops from Brest, and a further force of 12,000 men and 'no more than 30 ships' was readied to set sail from Rochefort on 29 September. Early in October Napoléon demanded maps of Ireland. For whatever reason the invasion force never set sail.

By summer 1804 more than 70,000 French soldiers, the nucleus of the Army of England under generals Ney and Soult, were encamped at the northern seaports. To prevent the French landing, pre-emptive strikes were made by the Royal Navy against the invasion flotilla. To prevent the fleet sailing, during September 1803, Dieppe, Granville, Le Havre and Calais were all bombarded from the sea by the Royal Navy. However, the number of French vessels at Boulogne was three times that of any other French or Belgian port in October 1804. Pitt met with Dr Watson's protégé Fulton, who proposed a plan of attack on Boulogne using fireships, torpedoes and mines that he had written for the French a few years earlier. The plan was put into action but failed to achieve its objectives. It did, however, overwhelmingly show Fulton's proof of concept for the submarine. Yet, from those northern French encampments came the Grande Armée: the best trained and equipped army in Europe which would triumph at Ulm, Elchingen and Austerlitz. Fulton's attack at Boulogne changed nothing.

A key part of Napoléon's planning process was the use of secret agents on intelligence-gathering missions. Spies were once more dispatched to the English south coast to reconnoitre the best landing ground. Clearly, a diversionary landing was planned. One spy travelled from Rye, Winchelsea and Hastings reporting on the local landmarks, the terrain, population centres and local Crown forces. He went on to Pevensey, noting coastal defence artillery batteries as he went. He travelled to Newhaven, Beachyhead, Brighton, Sandgate and Folkestone, with Dover and Walmer castles identified as key targets. The agent recommended that Rye was an ideal invasion site.[68] The agent returned to Rye where he prepared a plan of the harbour and reported on local landmarks and added that Camber Sands made a perfect landing ground.[69]

However, a month later, Napoléon had changed his plans: 18,000 men would sail from Brest for Ireland accompanied by 25,000 men from Texel as a diversionary attack for a main landing of 125,000 men from Boulogne. Napoléon planned that the French forces would be bolstered by the United Irishmen.[70] The scheme was abandoned as it was feared that British agents had become aware of it. About the intended landing in Ireland, Marshal Berthier as Minister for War approached Arthur O'Connor: he was now de facto leader of the Irish in exile. Muir was dead, Watson was engaged on other activities and Lewines had withdrawn from Irish affairs.

O'Connor told Berthier in a letter, dated 21 October 1804, that: 'being a landing, a landing in Ireland would deal a significant blow to the power of the enemies of France'.[71] A spy identified as 'Mr Smith' – no doubt the associate of Robert Watson who was mentioned previously – noted to be a friend of Arthur O'Connor, reported to Berthier that based on his first-hand experience of travelling in England and Scotland, the Scots and English, due to the press, were favourable to war with France.[72]

The British Crown embarked on arresting known leaders. Identified in 1799 as a 'key person' in the United Irishmen movement in London, Matthew Doyle was considered by the Crown to be a dangerous man. A man named Westermann, 'a member of a seditious Society in Wakefield in the West Riding', was to be apprehended based on evidence from a spy of his involvement with a proposed rebellion in Ireland. The spy reported, furthermore, that Matthew Doyle who had been involved with Emmet's failed rebellion was in Liverpool raising money for a rebellion. The spy stated that it was believed that Doyle was the subject of a £500 reward offered by the Irish government, for his part in the rebellion and had attempted to assassinate Fletcher himself.[73] Magistrate Fletcher had hoped to arrest Doyle and to this end had searched addresses in Liverpool in October. He noted that Doyle had been traced on 9 November 1804 by an informer in Manchester from where he was heading for Hull, determined to die rather than be captured.[74] Doyle seemingly went underground, one spy noting that he had gone to America,[75] but he re-emerged in London and was lodging with a Mr John Nicholls, 'a well-known traitor' and associate of Despard.[76] Nicholls had been a key player in the Despard plot and fled to France. He requested a pension from Talleyrand in 1804 and 1806, but the French state considered him a prisoner of war.[77]

Yet, despite O'Connor's support, no invasion could take place until the French Navy had evaded the Royal Navy. On 11 January 1805,

Missiessy's Rochefort fleet managed to break out of the blockade, and Villeneuve escaped Toulon while Nelson was in Sardinia. However, having bypassed Nelson's fleet, Villeneuve made it to the Gulf of Lyon, where he encountered a heavy storm. At this critical juncture, he turned his fleet around and sailed back to Toulon. The golden moment had passed.

Yet, anger at the British Crown and the Act of Union lingered. In the face of thorough British terror and repression, the Irish were disarmed and the military crushed, their militias disbanded or defeated, and British military presence increased.

With Napoléon's plan to invade failing due to bad weather, the United Irish leadership risked everything in rebellion without French aid. A spy reported to the Home Office in spring 1805 that Doyle planned to go to the west of Ireland to lead the disaffected who were to rise, simultaneously, in three areas – in the west, near Dublin and at Athlone – in order to divide the king's forces and to get possession of a government depot. At the same time, Jacobins in Manchester were preparing an uprising against the Corn Laws.[78] In July, General Marmont was ordered to make ostentatious efforts to foster a rumour that the Texel fleet was preparing to invade Ireland.[79] The ploy was to weaken the blockade of Brest and Boulogne to allow Villeneuve to sail. An intercepted letter from Dublin to a Mr Bibby of Stockport read that a French invasion force had planned to sail for Ireland on 5 August, and that a raid of government depots was proposed to provide the invaders with equipment. Another spy reported that he had heard, also from the Manchester Irish, of the arrival of a man named Downs from Ireland who had noted that the French invasion force was not well provided with clothing and camp equipage and that it was planned to remedy that by raids on government depots. Patrick Finney, recently released from Kilmainham Gaol, was expected to be prominent in the rebellion along with Mathew Doyle, an 'Irish General' in the 1798 uprising.[80] When Villeneuve did eventually set sail, he met his fate at Trafalgar.

This ended once and for all any suggestion of the French landing in Ireland. No invasion force ever left the shore of France for Ireland, and both Doyle and the plot disappear without further trace in history.

Chapter 24

THE INVASION THAT NEVER WAS

Ideas are hard to kill. Irish émigré plans to reclaim their country from the British Crown carried on, more as wishful thinking than actual reality. An officer in the Irish Legion – Fitzhenry – drafted a scheme similar to Emmet's abortive plan for the French to land in Ireland. The plans were dismissed as being unimportant by the French War Ministry.[1] Presumably, the blockade by and strength of the Royal Navy precluded any notion of invasion. The War Ministry received a report dated 5 January 1808 which implied that the Irish were in a state of rebellion and, moreover, as the British economy was increasingly failing, particularly in the manufacture of woollen goods, discontent in England and Scotland was rising. The time was approaching for the French to exploit the situation, the writer informed the French emperor. The Irish and Scots wanted their freedom from the yoke of England, and the writer noted that the religious discontent of the Catholics and Presbyterians excluded by the Test and Corporation Acts could be used to advantage.[2] No consideration was given to such a plan.

At the close of the 1809 campaign, on 28 August, a plan was presented to the emperor for a landing in Ireland and England: the idea was revenge for Walcheren, and ideally to topple the Crown.[3] Napoléon clearly gave this scheme some thought as Arthur O'Connor was summoned to Paris along with Thomas Emmet in the hope of formulating some kind of collaboration between the two men and whatever remained of the Irish leadership.[4] Communication with Ireland was by now non-existent and the network that had been managed by Duckett had ceased to operate. Indeed, Duckett was now retired from Irish affairs and was a schoolteacher, as was Dr Robert Watson. Duckett died in 1848 aged 73 and Watson would return to

England. Lewines was no longer communicating with his compatriots, yet, Napoléon sought information from Lewines in vain.

Hervey Montmorency Morres

Thus, in such an atmosphere where Irish invasion was being discussed once more, at an unknown date in 1809, or early 1810, a Franco-Irish emissary wrote to Napoléon demanding French support for liberating Ireland. The informant was Hervey Montmorency Morres. He was born on 7 March 1767 at Rathailean Castle, County Tipperary, into an impoverished Catholic gentry family from Rathnaleen, near Nenagh, County Tipperary, the eldest son of Matthew Montmorency Morres. In 1782, aged 15, he enlisted as a gentleman-cadet in the Liégeois Regiment of Vierzet in the Austrian Army, seeing service in 1783–4 against the Dutch. He subsequently joined the Regiment of Lacy Infantry and distinguished himself in various campaigns against the Turks between 1787 and 1789, including the siege of Belgrade (1788). Promoted to the rank of lieutenant in 1787 in Lacy's Regiment, he joined Count Kavanagh's regiment of cuirassiers (1790) and fought in the armies of Prince Hohenlohe (1792) and General Wurmser (1793–4) against the new French Republic. After commanding a unit of skirmishers at the siege of Thionville, and earning praise for his conduct in the Army of the Rhine (1793), he was named an aide-de-camp to Prince Charles of Fürstenberg. In September 1794, he married Louise de Helmstadt, from Swabia, and decided to return to Ireland. In November 1796, he joined the United Irishmen and began work on preparing the province for rebellion. He was named a colonel and a county representative for Tipperary. After the arrest of the Directory on 12 March 1798, he was appointed to the new executive and began preparations for seizing the military arsenal at Phoenix Park. He narrowly avoided arrest on 28 April, but his plans were thrown into disarray after the capture of Lord Edward Fitzgerald. He supported Humbert's forces and later claimed to have commanded a rebel army in County Tipperary, although there is no actual evidence to support this statement. In the aftermath of the rebellion, he escaped to Europe but was arrested at Hamburg, one of the 'Hamburg Four' along with James Napper Tandy, William Corbet and James Blackwell, and was incarcerated at Kilmainham Gaol, Dublin, until 1802.

Although Morres had been married twice in Austria, on returning to Ireland in 1802 he married the widow of the executed 1798 rebel John Esmonde, Helen Callan, of Osberstown House, County Kildare. During this period, he pursued his interest in genealogies and antiquarianism, going on a tour of Ireland in summer 1809 gathering material for a projected book on Irish history.[5] In fact this seems to have been a fact-finding mission about the receptiveness of the Irish to a French invasion.

In a letter to Napoléon, Morres noted that the Catholic majority formed an under class of 'inferior citizens' whose rights had been repressed since the middle ages. Worryingly, he noted that since 1798 the leaders of the United Irishmen had been based in Hamburg, which was the conduit for passing information between France and Ireland, but that the flow of intelligence was now frequently intercepted by the British Crown. The people were, however, still ready to rise to gain their liberty, he believed. The enforcement of Catholics to serve in the Irish Volunteers and local militia, to defend a country that oppressed them was 'vehemently hated' and had enflamed 'ancient passions' in the spirits of the Volunteers to fight for a new, liberated Ireland, which was only achievable with help from France. He estimated that 8,000 would rise up, and that at least half of the yeomanry would defect to the Irish banner if the French came, perhaps 14,000 men, all of whom had been trained in the use of arms by the English. Perhaps 20,000 would rise, and if the French landed at Duncannon, they would 'soon be the masters of Waterford and Wexford' where the greater part of the population would rise up. What the Irish needed, however, was 50,000 muskets, artillery and money.[6] Morres was wrong. That Catholics were forced to defend Protestants is not true. Catholic loyalism was widespread.

By the end of 1810, Morres and his family had settled in France where his son, Laurent d'Esmonde, later became an officer in the Irish Legion. Hervey himself joined the French Army on 19 May 1812 with the rank of colonel. Serving on the staff of General Augereau, he was known as Colonel Morres de Latéragh and involved in action in the south-west of France against invading Austrian forces in early 1814. He became a French citizen in 1816 and a Knight of Saint Louis on 25 June 1817, but never achieved his ambition of receiving the *Légion d'honneur*. Retiring from the French Army on half-pay, he spent his final years as a literary researcher. He died at Saint-Germain-en-Laye on 9 May 1839.[7]

Humbert Once More

At some stage, the information that Ireland was ready to rebel was made known to that most interesting of men, General Humbert. Dreaming once again of landing in Ireland to liberate that country and to restore his military prestige, Humbert hastily sent a letter to Napoléon about a plan of invasion, dated 3 July 1810. The Dutch fleet was seen as the ideal tool for the invasion, and Humbert believed that the Scottish Catholics could be induced to rise in support of the French if the French 'put boots on the ground'.[8] A report on Scotland was sent to Napoléon, from the 'Hotel de Prince de Galles, faubourg St Honore 23 Juillet 1810', which advocated landing an invasion fleet in Scotland and noted that the Scots would welcome the French and provide irregular troops to the invasion force. The Isle of Mull and the Hebrides were seen as an ideal anchorage to land troops in the north of Ireland and also into England and Scotland. Humbert planned to lead a raid into England by entering the Bristol Channel and landing troops to attack Cornwall – it is assumed to head to Dartmoor prisoner-of-war camp to liberate thousands of French soldiers and officers – and also into Wales to likely head to Bristol, Chester and Manchester.[9]

By September, Napoléon was interested in the plan. He wrote to Admiral Decrès concerning assembling a fleet to land in Ireland and Scotland:

> Let me know what kind of boats one can build in Dordrecht; I would like to have a flotilla built there capable of carrying to Ireland or Scotland an expedition of four divisions, of ten battalions each of 8,000 men, forming 32,000 men of infantry, 4,000 men of artillery and engineers and 6,000 men of cavalry, total 42,000 men, with 3,000 artillery and cavalry horses and 120 field pieces, making 700 carriages ... Bring me to the council next Friday a report on this expedition, on the species of vessels and their tonnage (the fewer the number, the more advantageous it will be) and on the composition of the stables calculated so as to also have as few as possible.[10]

Napoléon planned a late 1811 or 1812 incursion. Dissatisfied with the emperor's lack of interest in Ireland, and feeling his career was over, Humbert booked passage on a ship sailing to the United States and went to New Orleans. In July of 1812 he was granted permission to enter the service of the Army of the United States and took part in the War of 1812 against Britain. Humbert did not stay inactive, in 1814 he went to Buenos Aires and joined the insurgents there, briefly commanding a corps in their army. Afterwards, he returned to New Orleans and took part in the fighting there in 1815 and was thanked by General Andrew Jackson. He left the army to become a schoolteacher. He died in 1823.[11]

On 5 February 1811, General Clarke was ordered to write to Edward Lewines to inform him that the emperor was giving serious consideration to invading Ireland.[12] Lewines had been out of contact with Ireland for a decade, so what could he actually tell Napoléon that was of use? Lewines would become a knight of the *Légion d'honneur*, and died on 11 February 1828 in Paris and was buried at Père Lachaise Cemetery. Close by lie John Hurford Stone and Helen Marie Williams.[13]

Lewines, it seems, sent some sort of reply to Napoléon, who, on 19 June 1811, wrote to Admiral Decrès proposing an invasion of England and Ireland; with the British Army deployed in Spain, it was felt England was vulnerable to attack. Napoléon envisaged 6,000 men landing in Ireland as a diversionary attack between 1 September and 15 November to give support to the Irish patriots.[14] Days later, on 23 June, Napoléon increased the force to be sent to Ireland to 25,000 men.[15]

The French government had last had any intelligence from Ireland in 1810, and since the failure of Emmet's aborted rebellion in 1803, the Irish republicans – the United Irishmen – had 'dropped off the radar'. The long-established lines of communication via Hamburg had ceased to operate years earlier. To understand the political situation in Ireland, Napoléon made plans to send a United Irish leader to Ireland, Arthur O'Connor:

> Saint-Cloud, July 4, 1811. I want you to bring O'Connor and the other Irish who are in Paris, and that you see a party renewed in Ireland. I have at this moment twenty-five warships in front of the Scheldt and nine in the Texel. I am at all far from making an expedition of 30,000 men and 4,000 horses to Ireland in October, if I am certain of finding a party there … I will make any treaty as the Irish want. I attach great importance to this. I want to have a plan and know what to expect on it within two weeks. Nothing can prevent me from leaving the Scheldt; and the English having few troops in England will be obliged to recall their soldiers from the Peninsula, which will require two or three months. We will have time to arrive in this country before the arrival of these troops.[16]

In essence, Napoléon planned to end the Peninsular War: with Wellington drawn back to England, the French would quickly take complete control of Spain. However, Arthur O'Connor refused to travel to Ireland.

On Bastille Day 1811, Napoléon ordered that 60,000 men with 70,000 muskets to arm the Irish were to be prepared.[17] By August, thoughts had changed to sending 12,000–15,000 men to Ireland and a similar force to England. The emperor was clearly frustrated by the lack of activity regarding an Irish invasion, commenting: 'The Irish expedition does not promise me any results.'[18] Ten days later the emperor demanded that new agents were to be sent to Ireland.[19]

By August Napoléon was impatient for news from Ireland,[20] and demanded that Henri Clarke, the Minister of War, establish communication between Paris and Ireland as a matter of urgency. He was keen to know how a French invasion force would be received by the Irish populus, and, asked furthermore, if the Irish would rise in support. If the Irish would rise, he pledged to send 30,000 infantry and 4,000 cavalry.[21] After months of delay, Luke Lawless was appointed agent on 1 September, and left France ten days later. Lawless was said to have 'gone through a complete course of classical education and served for some time in H.M. navy'. A lawyer by training, he entered Lincoln's Inn in April 1803, was called to the Irish bar in 1805 and was still in Dublin as late as 25 June 1810. In 1810 (the exact date is unknown), he was commissioned as a lieutenant in the Irish Legion of the French Army.

Chapter 25

THE FAILED REVOLUTION
OF 1812

Meantime, events in Ireland meant that Catholic support for a French invasion seemed certain. On 9 July 1811, Dr Edward Sheridan had organized a meeting reviving the Catholic Committee of 1792:

> That a committee of persons professing the Roman Catholic religion, should be appointed, and requested to cause proper Petitions to both Houses of Parliament, to be forthwith framed, for a repeal of the Penal Laws remaining in force in Ireland, and to procure signatures thereto in all parts of Ireland; and to take measures for bringing such Petition under the serious consideration of the Legislature.[1]

On 31 July, Sheridan and five others were arrested. If the Crown felt that the 'Catholic question' could be silenced by this, they were wrong. It was into this ever more volatile Ireland that Luke Lawless arrived. The increased persecution of Catholics by the Protestant Orange Order was a significant driver of the re-emergence of the Defenders of the 1790s in New Year 1811. The 'Ribbonmen', as the re-formed Defenders were known, had begun arming themselves in February 1811. They had begun stealing roofing lead to melt down to make musket balls, and reports were received by Dublin Castle that the 'Catholics wanted to overthrow the Act of Union and British Constitution'.[2] Trouble was brewing in Ireland, and the British Crown once more faced the double threat of a home-grown insurgency and French intervention.

Luke Lawless arrived in Dublin on 24 September. He made contact with his older brother John, who introduced him to the veteran United Irishmen James Ryan, Thomas Dromgoole and Archibald Hamilton Rowan.[3]

Lawless returned to Paris in November and reported to Napoléon on the 23rd. Lawless was promoted captain on 26 November in recognition of his report. He later joined the staff of the Minister of War, the duc de Feltre (who was of Irish descent), but, being too fervent a Bonapartist, was obliged to leave France after the Hundred Days during September 1815. He emigrated to the United States, took up law again and became a judge in St Louis, Missouri.[4]

General Hoche's Ghost

At the close of November 1811, a French agent had landed on the south coast looking for passage to Ireland.[5] For the Home Office, this confirmed their worst fears that French agents were involved in the clandestine planning in Ireland and the north of England: revolution in Ireland and England was, it seems, being planned and sponsored in France. In winter 1811 violence rocked Nottingham, and then West Yorkshire: Luddism appeared. Driven by unemployment, a cost of living crisis and the ideals of the French Revolution and inter alia the United Englishmen, an unprecedented wave of violence gripped the north Midlands and large parts of Yorkshire.

A letter from Ned Ludd written at the start of March provides a good insight into the anti-government feeling at the time and of the broader insurrectionary ideals of the Irish Ribbonmen and Black Lamp:

> ... the Weavers in Glasgow and many parts of Scotland will join us the Papists in Ireland are rising to a so [sic] that they are likely to find the Soldiers something else to do than Idle in Huddersfield and then Woe be to the places now guarded by them for we have come to the easier Way of burning them to Ashes which will most assuredly be their Fate either sooner or later. The immediate Cause of us beginning when we did was that Rascally letter of the Prince Regents to Lords Grey & Grenville, which left us no hopes of any Change for the better, by his falling in with that Damn'd set of Rogues, Percival & Co to whom we attribute all the Miseries of our Country. But we hope for assistance from the French Emperor in shaking off the Yoke of the Rottenest, Wickedest and most Tyranious Government that ever existed; then down come the Hanover Tyrants, and all our Tyrants from the greatest to the smallest, and we will be governed by a just Republic.[6]

Was this possible? Did the Luddites and Black Lamp expect aid from France? It is difficult to say, but, beyond reasonable doubt, revolution was being planned in Ireland. When Joseph Barrowclough – a corporal in the Light Company of the Upper Agbrigg Local Militia – was interrogated in July 1812, he confessed that the 'Lud System' began

207

twenty-two years earlier, i.e., in 1792, the beginning of the United Irishmen movement – and dropped the bombshell that the French were behind Luddism. In the interrogation Barrowclough remarked:

> that it had been mentioned amongst the luddites that on the landing of the French, the French prisoners as well at Chesterfield, as at Plymouth and Dartmoor were to rise and would be joined by the luddites. Barrowclough says he knows where there is a French officer who was at Dartmoor barracks ... he was a General in the French service who had escaped or broke his parole but had been taken again.[7]

He added that of the four local commanders engaged in organizing the arms raid, three were French. A remarkably similar story had been reported to the Home Office from Hull on 1 July that Luddites were sent: 'to different parts of the Country, and especially where French Prisoners are many to some thousands, are already sworn in, to rise on a certain day, appointed in all parts of the Kingdom ... the Luddites mean to rid themselves, of all their Enemys. They reckon on 50,000 French Prisoners, as helpers.' The writer noted that a signal that the revolution had begun was the stopping of mail coaches, and that Lords Castlereagh and Liverpool would be assassinated.[8] The escaped general is likely to have been General Hoche's capable adjutant General Edouard François Simon. He had been made a prisoner of war during the Peninsular War following the Battle of Bussaco. It appears that whatever invasion attempt was being planned, he was involved. The British Crown became aware that Simon was formulating a plan that 'on the landing of the French, the French prisoners as well at Chesterfield, as at Plymouth and Dartmoor were to rise and would be joined by the luddites'. The informant added that three French officers on parole were organizing clandestine arms raids to furnish the Luddites with weapons.[9] From December 1803– July 1812 there were 172 prisoners on parole at Ashbourne and from November 1803–June 1811 there were over 400 held at Chesterfield. Concerning the activities of officers on parole in Chesterfield:

> ... on Wednesday the 6th inst. Dominique Ducasse, Captain and Aide-de-Camp to Gen. Dufour, Tugdual Antoine Kerenor, Lieutenant, and Julien Deslories, Ensign, three French prisoners of war at Chesterfield, were conducted from the house of correction there, by a military escort, on their way to Norman Cross Prison, for having broken their parole of honor. The two former were apprehended at the Peacock Inn, (along with George Lawton, of Sheffield, cutler,) about 10 o'clock on Saturday night, the 26th ult. by the vigilance of Mr. Hopkinson, the landlord, who much to his credit, refused to furnish a post-chaise to carry them to

Derby, and dispatched a messenger to the Commissary at Chesterfield, detaining them until the return of the messenger; the next day they were conveyed back to Chesterfield, and Lawton is now in our county gaol to take his trial for assisting in the escape.[10]

Clearly, Barrowclough's story had the ring of some truth about it concerning officers on parole, and the presence of prisoners of war in Chesterfield. The *St James's Chronicle* reported that 'the traitorous correspondence of General Simon ... with the French government respecting the landing of a considerable number of troops on the coast of Cornwall. General Simon, it is said, undertook to arrange with the prisoners here to join them.'[11] The landing in Cornwall to release French prisoners in Dartmoor had been planned a decade earlier by General Humbert, and clearly the potential of a 'Chouanization' raid to release the prisoners was given active consideration in France. Simon was clearly the 'ringleader' of whatever was being planned. Simon's papers implicated Lieutenant Colonel François Joseph Charles Abraham Vaxoncourt, Assistant Surgeon J.M. Pasquier and two midshipmen, Cornier de Mede and J. Lampo, all on parole at Alresford. At Odiham the conspirators included Captain Flamaud, Lieutenant Dismasure and at Thame Midshipman Lasourdion. Indeed, Vaxoncourt wrote to Simon in congratulatory tones, remarking, 'Thanks to you mon General in this plan the French will finally unite to create one group and through this union will confound our weak but proud enemy...'.[12]

The Admiralty in London reported that Simon was 'carrying on a correspondence with France through the mediation of several Frenchmen resident in London'.[13] These were no doubt French agents working for Talleyrand. Simon's intercepted correspondence with France and co-conspirators demonstrated that the French were contemplating using the French prisoners held in the country to wreak havoc and exploit the already explosive situation that was rapidly developing across the north of England. However, Simon was apprehended in London by the Bow Street Runners and sent to Dumbarton Castle in March 1812 until the war ended in 1814. The threat of an uprising in 1812, led by officers who planned to march on the large camps, free the prisoners and occupy the ports preparatory to a French invasion, forced government to disperse prisoners to more distant locales.[14] Even with Simon apprehended, if Barrowclough is to be believed, the French prisoners remained a potent threat. In July 1812, a bill was passed by Parliament that made the aiding of prisoners to escape a crime punishable with transportation for life. While this measure did not stop smugglers from assisting French officers to escape, it did mean that the bit-part players in the operation such as the messengers, the men hired to row the boats containing escapees across the Channel and those who gave shelter to the prisoners, if arrested, were now likely to turn King's Evidence to escape transportation.

The Revolutionaries

It is undeniable that many thousands saw revolution as the only legitimate option left to them to safeguard community and tradition and to bring about real change. To this end on 9 March, General Ludd addressed the croppers:

> To All Croppers, Weavers &c& Public at Large.
> Generous Countrymen. You are requested to come forward with Arms and help the redressers to dress their wrongs and shake off the hateful yoke of a silly old man, and his son more silly and their rogueish ministers, all Nobles and Tyrants must be brought down. Come let us follow the noble example of the brave citizens of Paris who in sight of 30,000 Tyrant Recoats brought a Tyrant to the ground. By doing so you will be best aiming at your own interest. Above 40,000 Heros are ready to break out to crush the old government & establish a new one.[15]

The writer is exhorting revolution, to bring down the monarchy and government and establish a new form of governance. The reference to the events of the French Revolution is obvious and recalls the United Englishmen's radical activism of 1795–1803, in particular their desire to bring about radical sweeping social changes and the establishment of a republic. Sheffield had re-emerged as a centre of radicalism in Yorkshire with the arrest of Sir Francis Burdett. Some 8,000 gathered in the town to approve a petition condemning the arrest, the conduct of the House of Commons and its composition. This was anti-war and anti-government protest writ large, just as it had been since the heady days of 1799. The societal and economic stress of the late 1790s had not dissipated but grown worse. Radical demands for political reform, an immediate end to war on moral and economic grounds and justifiable working-class anger at the government's continued backing of capital against labour in the Industrial Revolution had not gone away. The Industrial Revolution is more than just the name of an epoch: it was a total change in the nature of society, a revolution that was as real as that in America or France with similar far-reaching consequences for those caught up in it and established very clear battle lines. Yet, these battle lines are literally 'air brushed' from history to brand the

Luddites simply machine breakers, in a battle that was lost in a single year, and is not viewed as half a century of conflict, with far more complex aims and objectives on the part of the radicals than has been considered by most historians. Luddism was simply not standing in the way of technology: it was the desperate cries of the working man who sought to have his voice heard, to get the vote, to have political representation, to preserve his way of life and community. One of the key documents that uncovers the truth about the nature and scope of Luddism is a letter sent by Ned Ludd to a Mr Smith of Hill End:

By the latest Letters from our Correspondents, we learn that the Manufacturers in the following Places are going to rise and join us in redressing their Wrongs Viz. Manchester, Wakefield, Halifax, Bradford, Sheffield, Old-ham, Rochdale and all the Cotton Country where the brave Mr Hanson will lead them on to Victory. The Weavers in Glasgow and many parts of Scotland will join us the Papists in Ireland are rising too ... we hope for assistance from the French Emperor.[16]

Were the Luddites working with the Irish and French? Some thought so. On 6 April, Ralph Fletcher wrote to the Home Office: he was a worried man. The Luddites in Eccles, he was informed, had seized 183 firearms in the space of 2 weeks, and they were pledged 'to put the great man down who had [illegible] them under foot for so long'. Was this a threat against the king or Spencer Percival? Either way, the Luddites in Lancashire were arming themselves and 'were determined ... to seize the arms and ammunition belonging to the Local Militia'.[17] Arms raiding arrived in the West Riding seemingly from Manchester. An informant in Manchester, Humphrey Yarwood, reported that 'something further than the destruction of steam looms or machinery was intended'.[18] Likewise, Thomas Wood of Mottram stated: 'there was to be a revolution, and that all who are not for it would be killed; and those that were for it, were to take the oath'.[19] Across the Pennines in Barnsley, Thomas Broughton informed the magistrates that 'the Luddites have in view ultimately to overturn the system of government by revolutionising the country'.[20] Citizen Bent reported to Ralph Fletcher that he had met an Irish delegate, Patrick Cannovan, in Stockport in April. Cannovan proceeded to relate to them his travels in Scotland and Ireland and dealings with underground committees in Belfast and Glasgow and that a secret committee in Dublin pledged their support for fellow committees in England and Scotland. The Irish plotters hoped to take Dublin Castle in the planned uprising. Bent noted: 'the committee at Glasgow said the ad'on amount of the different towns in Scotland the number attested was about nine thousand seven hundred and that they was determined to persevere in the cause'. He added that the committee in Belfast were in overall command of what was being planned and that:

> ... they would soon make the government wish they had granted them their emancipation ... Ireland was determined to have ... or lose all that was dear to them and all the Cartherlicks [sic] in Ireland was of the same way of thinking ... the Committee at Dublin and is constituents in England and that the Catherlicks of Ireland would do all in their power to shake off the yoke.

The committee in Dublin: 'assure the Citizens in England that there is not a town of [illegible] five score in Ireland [illegible] who will come forward with men & money to support the cause to the uttermost of their power' and continued that the Irish would 'do all in their power to keep good understanding with the Citizens of England and Scotland and do all in their power to forward them some [arms] but arms was difficult things to get as government had taken their from time to time and had scoured the country completely of them'. Bent informed the Crown that: 'eighty two thousand enrolled of Carterlicks [sic] all ready and a few protestants also and that the Kingdom was readyer to shake off the yook [sic] themthe [sic] have been for the last century'. Bent added, moreover, that: 'the citizens of London ... been informed that a delegate would go to Dublin by the way of Glasgow and was returned would go to London ... by the way of Birmingham and return by Derby and take the different towns in his way to establish the business with them'.[21] If the evidence is credible, the Catholic majority in Ireland, despite the failure of Emmet's rebellion less than a decade earlier, was once more planning to rise in rebellion, and to distract the Crown forces had recruited to the cause Luddites and no doubt many thousands who had participated in the failed Despard plot.

Later the same month, Bent reckoned that in Staffordshire: '7,000 men sworn in, as such all will do their duty when called on & they have 2,680 guns, pistols and swords & others are providing themselves with pikes'. He added that in London 14,000 had been twisted-in 'chiefly amongst the Spitalfields weavers'.[22]

Religion, politics and industrial grievances coalesced and, as in the 1790s, external forces hoped to shape the unfolding events in England to their advantage – France. Again, just as in the 1790s, the French hoped to exploit industrial and social unrest for their own purposes. On 12 May, Citizen Bent reported that:

... regular correspondence to and from Ireland, Scotland & many towns in England & particularly those in Yorkshire, Nottingham, Leicester, & Cornwall ... friends in the sister kingdom are doing well & only waiting for England & are ready to start at the same time as Ireland, & by that means the business is to be carried on ... they have more than 400,000 men who can be depended on [illegible] what soldiers come over to join in the cause and that the delegates from Ireland suggested to the Manchester citizens to be as careful as possible.[23]

Yet, by June, no further reports were sent to the Home Office concerning an invasion or revolution in Ireland backed by France.

As in 1801, the French never came and the Irish and English Enragés would be left bitterly disappointed. By spring 1812, Napoléon had ended any pretence of landing in Ireland, yet in re-energising the Black Lamp and de facto United Irish, in the short term, Napoléon had tied down tens of thousands of British regulars who could have been sent into Spain to reinforce Wellington or to the United States. It switched the government's attention from Europe to the home front: maybe this was Napoléon's plan all along? To destabilize the country and thus end the war by other means?

The tantalising prospect remains that as yet uncovered archive documents may shed more light on this episode. Clearly, an underground network of informers existed who spirited away General Lefebvre Desnouettes from his parole. If the network could extract the general, then it is more than reasonable to assume that the network could also organize Luddites into a para-military force and 'Chouanize' the north of England. How much of the Luddite uprising in 1812 was orchestrated and funded by France is difficult to determine, but the links between the Luddites and France are seemingly undeniable. More research is needed on this point. With the French Army largely destroyed in Russia during winter 1812, Ireland slipped away from any focus of event planning.

The French with their Irish and English allies – some would call them traitors, others freedom fighters – never mounted another attempt to invade or destabilize England or Ireland. Napoleon's attention was on the rapidly deteriorating situation in Europe which cost him his throne.

Chapter 26

CONCLUSION

What do we make of these men and women who openly invited a foreign power to invade their country? Were they traitors or freedom fighters hoping to make their own countries fairer and more just places? However uncomfortable it may make some feel, the British Crown was the enemy of the people: in fiction and other genres people love to read stories of how a group of individuals with 'right on their side' overturn a corrupt government and bring about a 'golden age'. Men and women such as John Hurford Stone, Wolfe Tone, William Duckett and Helen Marie Williams considered themselves to be liberating Ireland, Scotland and England from the tyranny of William Pitt and the British Crown. Their demands were simple: Home Rule for Ireland and Scotland, one man one vote and an end to religious tests on participation in public life. This was a direct challenge to the British oligarchy and the notion of empire: many in England, Scotland and Ireland questioned the right of the British Crown to rule Ireland or Scotland and, for that matter, to invade countries such as India for their own benefit.

These ideals were contained in the pages of the works of Jean-Paul Marat's famous political epistle *Chains of Slavery*, the works of the Revd Dr Richard Price and his colleague Joseph Priestley and most famously by Thomas Paine. Samuel Romilly, the Whig MP, succinctly commented in May 1792 to Madame de Genlis – mistress of the Duc d'Orleans – about the impact of Paine's work in Ireland, that it had kindled enthusiasm to such an extent that he felt 'should anywhere break out in acts of violence it will certainly be first in Ireland'. He was perfectly correct. Paine, like the French Republic, declared all men were equal: for those denied the same rights as the man next to them in the street because of religion, the ideals of the Revolution found willing listeners among Catholics and Dissenters – mostly

Unitarians – in England, Ireland and Scotland. The declaration of help by the revolution to all those seeking liberty from oppression stirred in the Irish and Scots dreams of Home Rule. Counter to the views of greater equality, political representation and freedom of religion, the rich oligarchy and Church of England refused to give up their vaunted status as leaders of the country and declared war on those who threatened their power and privilege.

The exclusive nature of 'Britishness' at the end of the eighteenth century precluded perhaps 80 per cent of the country of Ireland from religious equality with those who attended the Church of Ireland – inter alia the Church of England – in England, 20 per cent of the population was discriminated against because of religion, and in both countries, despite paying taxes, over 90 per cent of the population had no vote. The Republic in France, as did the United States, offered one man one vote and equality. Such was the strength of the dream of equality and self-determination that subjects of the British Crown sought the aid of France to export revolution to their native countries, to bring about the changes in society they wished to see. In transmuting idealism to realism, these men and women came close to success: what would have happened if Hoche had landed at Bantry Bay or Hardy had arrived to support Humbert?

The invasion of England which seemed so imminent for two decades remained a 'might have been': the Irish and English Enragés failed because they could not harness more people to the cause. The goal of the Irish struggle was the self-determination of the people of Ireland: however, it quickly became subsumed to the egomania of the leaders and 'the glory of the achievement'. Perhaps it is too idealistic to hold the view that liberation of a country and the self-determination of a people ought to be its own reward. James Hope and Michael Quigley, John Allen and William Dowdall, and the many who have become nameless and faceless with time who played a part in the rebellion, however small, sought no glory.

The lack of a single coherent plan and leader doomed the United Irishmen. Furthermore, another factor that led to the failure of the United Irish was a singular lack of grasping real world politics beyond Ireland. The Irish were dependent on the French: in 1798 Castlereagh asked: 'Will they [the Irish people] do you think, rise again?', to which MacNeven responded without demur: 'Not, I believe, till the French come; and then, most assuredly, whenever they can join them'. That opinion was still firmly held by both MacNeven and Thomas Addis Emmet in 1803, and the precondition 'No French, no rebellion' appears to have obtained throughout Ireland among the leading nationalist cadre, except, it appears, in the mind of Robert Emmet. From 1799, with France beginning peace negotiations with England, the leadership should have realized that any chance of French involvement was 'off the cards'. Bantry Bay had been a fiasco, the three missions in 1798 had failed: with a background of constant failure why should the French send aid, especially when the French had put 'boots on the ground' and the people had not risen en masse in support? Wishful thinking, a desire for revenge and overblown ideas of self-importance meant that the leadership could not accept defeat and continued to plan rebellion. The Irish leadership consistently underestimated the largest stumbling block to the French: the Royal Navy. Bantry Bay taught the Irish the wrong lesson, that the Royal Navy could be easily avoided. Camperdown should have illiminated such thinking, yet it was not until summer 1803 that John Swiney realized the real and present danger the Royal Navy actually presented. When the French fleet sailed in 1804, defeat was the inevitable outcome. No plan ever dealt realistically with the threat from the Royal Navy. If the Royal Navy mutiny was sponsored by the French, it was being handled by Duckett from Hamburg who was working in a vacuum almost entirely independently of what was being concocted in Ireland and Paris: the lack of cohesive planning and co-operation between divergent groups is staggering, and lead inevitably to defeat. Nor did the United leadership ever seem to realize that George Orr, Samuel Turner and others had 'turned their coats' and were aiding the British Crown. For that matter, the French never really grasped that the Ministère de la Marine was totally compromised, and as with Hitler over a century later and the cracking of the Enigma code, never understood that every move the French made was being reported to London. As well as double agents, a highly sophisticated intelligence network for the British Crown based on spies and French Royalist émigrés seeking revenge for the Revolution, effectively sabotaged any hopes of the French landing in 1796, 1797 and 1798. English gold paid for the French Navy to mutiny. Secret agents in the headquarters of General Hoche, and the Ministère de la Marine, ensured that the British Crown knew what was being planned. The French agents by comparison were totally outclassed. French incompetence, infighting between political factions among the United Irishmen and the French government ensured that those planning revolution 'were their own worst enemy' and destroyed their own plans through megalomania and narcissism.

For the French, invading Ireland and England was at first driven by containing the English threat in a looming continental war, and then by 'Chouanization', revenge for the Vendée being uppermost in French minds. 'Chouanization' in league with English, Scottish and Irish groups could, it was hoped, lead to regime change and peace. The shift in English radical protest in winter 1799 to machine breaking and arson attacks has all the hallmarks of 'Chouanization', which led to the mass peace petitions of 1801, and renewed radical anti-government activity did indeed lead to peace and may represent the 'high watermark' of French secret-service activity in achieving its goal through clandestine means.

Sadly, it undeniable that radical underground activity in Ireland and England, sponsored by France in both the long and short term, failed. The government of Pitt was made stronger, the monarchy was not toppled and the execution of James O'Coigly and Despard made it clear the fate that awaited those who contemplated treason. The hopes and aspirations of those who gathered at White's Hotel did not materialize in their lifetime, or that of their grandchildren. England remained largely undemocratic until the middle decades of the twenty-first century. The hated Test and Corporation Acts, which had driven religious Dissenters to seek to topple the Crown, remained in force until 1828 and the last remaining legal impediments against Unitarians were not abolished until 1871.

Robert Watson's aspirations lay dormant largely until the time in which this book is being written, with Scottish independence being openly debated. Thomas Muir, once pilloried for his politics, is now championed as the father of Scottish democracy.

The Catholic Question in Ireland was not successfully resolved during the nineteenth or most of the twentieth century. Only from 1922 did some semblance of Irish Home Rule, the goal of the United Irish leadership, come to pass. It did so at the cost of the Orange Order taking de facto control of the north of Ireland, and the resulting 'troubles' being largely resolved with the Good Friday Agreement in 1998. English aims for working-class emancipation came about largely at the same time as Irish Independence, with women gaining the vote and the demand for free education made by Thomas Paine in 1792 only coming to fruition as late as 1947.

What the United movement did do, and with some success, was to plant ideas and political aspirations in the minds of the people and a new generation of leaders such as O'Connell in Ireland and the Chartists in England to work towards change. Despite a track record of failure, the first steps on the rocky road to Irish independence had been taken, helped by sympathetic groups in England and France.

NOTES

Prologue

1. For more on the philosophical origins of Jacobin thought, see Gregory Dart (1999), *Rousseau, Robespierre, and English Romanticism* (Cambridge and New York: Cambridge University Press), pp. 1–19.
2. Thomas Moore (1935), *The Life and Death of Lord Edward Fitzgerald* (Paris: Baudry's European Library), pp. 73–4.
3. The National Archives (hereafter TNA), Treasurer Solicitor's papers (hereafter TS), 11/959, George Monro, 6 December 1792.
4. Archives Nationales de France (hereafter AN) C11/278/40, pièce 1–3.

Chapter 1

1. Richard Price, 'Observations on the Nature of Civil Liberty, the Principles of Government, and the Justice and Policy of the War with America', *Political Writings*, pp. 28–9.
2. Joseph Priestley (1771), *An Essay on the First Principles of Government* (J. Johnson), p. 36.
3. John Goodchild, personal communication.
4. Richard Price (1789), *Discourse Delivered on the Love of Our Country* (London: J. Johnson), pp. 49–50.
5. Archives Parlementaires de 1787 à 1860; Assemblée nationale constituante, Du 12 novembre 1789 au 24 décembre 1789.

Chapter 2

1. Micah Alpaugh (2014), 'The British Origins of the French Jacobins: Radical Sociability and the Development of Political Club Networks', *European History Quarterly*, 44, Issue 4, p. 594.
2. British Library Additional Manuscripts (here after BL Add MS) 64814.
3. Revolution Society (1792), *The Correspondence of the Revolution Society in London, with the National Assembly, and with Various Societies of the Friends of Liberty in France and England* (London: J. Johnson).
4. Richard Brown (2002), *Church and State in Modern Britain, 1700–1850* (London: Routledge).
5. Michael Fitzpatrick (1995), 'Patriots and patriotisms: Richard Price and the early reception of the French Revolution in England', in *Nations and Nationalisms: France, Britain, Ireland and the Eighteenth-Century Context*, ed. M. O'Dea and K. Whelan (Oxford: Voltaire Foundation), pp. 211–30.

6. Sheffield City Archives (hereafter SCA), Wentworth Woodhouse Munuments (hereafter WWM) F44/32, Address and Declaration, 20 September 1791.
7. SCA WWM F44/45, Handbill from Sheffield, Revolution Club.
8. Albert Goodwin (1979), *The Friends of Liberty. The English Democratic Movement in the Age of the French Revolution* (London and New York: Routledge), pp. 186–8.
9. Ibid.
10. SCA WWM F44/45, Handbill from Sheffield, Revolution Club.
11. Ibid.
12. Ibid.
13. TNA HO 42/32, folio 398, Handwritten copy of a 'club book' containing the rules of the Constitutional Society of Leeds adopted on 14 April 1794 and contribution records for April and May maintained by the district delegate.
14. SCA WWM F45, Riots and Disturbances, United Irishmen of Dublin broadsheet.
15. Ibid., United Irishmen of Belfast broadsheet.
16. Gregory Claeys (2007), *The French Revolution Debate in Britain* (London: Palgrave Macmillan), pp. 20–1.
17. Mark Philip (2017), *Reforming Ideas in Britain: Politics and Language in the Shadow of the French Revolution, 1789–1815* (Cambridge: Cambridge University Press), pp. 119–20.
18. Emma Vincent Macleod (1998), *A War of Ideas: British Attitudes to the War Against Revolutionary France 1792–1802* (London: Routledge), pp. 13–27.
19. Ibid., p. 17.
20. Anon. (1792), *A Letter from His Grace the Duke of Richmond to Lieutenant Colonel Sharman, Chairman of the Committee of Correspondence Appointed by the Delegates of 45 Corps of Volunteers assembled at Lisburn in Ireland, with Notes from a Member of the Society for Constitutional Information* (London: J. Johnson), p. 3.
21. Robert Birley (1924), *The English Jacobins from 1789 to 1802* (London: Oxford University Press), Appendix.

Chapter 3

1. *A Complete Collection of State Trials* (1809–26), various editors (London), Vol. xxiii, col. 414–15.
2. Paul Lindsay Dawson (2023), *Fighting Napoleon at Home* (Barnsley: Frontline), p. 48.
3. https://founders.archives.gov/documents/Jefferson/01-38-02-0510-0002.
4. AN AF VII 4774/70/459.
5. TNA HO 42/32/269, Information of Pauncefort Cooke sworn before William Wickham, 30 June 1794.
6. TNA HO 42/19/4, folio 7, Conclusion of letter to Joseph Priestley.
7. TNA HO 42/21/1, folio 2, Mémorandum de Cruchent, 26 Avril 1792a.
8. TNA HO 42/21/1, folio 3, Mémorandum de Cruchent, 26 Avril 1792a.
9. TNA HO 42/21/1, folio 1, Mémorandum de Cruchent, 3 Mai 1792.
10. TNA HO 42/21/1, folio 5, Mémorandum de Cruchent, 26 Avril 1792b.
11. TNA HO 42/21/1, folio 3, Mémorandum de Cruchent, 29 Avril 1792.
12. TNA HO 42/20/114, folios 257–8, Lettre de Cruchent, 15 Mai 1792.
13. TNA HO 42/20/122, folios 273A–273B, Copy out-letter to John Brooke from Scrope Bernard, 22 May 1792.
14. TNA HO 42/20/102, folio 237, Letter to George Rose (Joint Secretary to the Treasury) from T. Bailey, 7 May 1792.
15. Lewis Stewarton Goldsmith (1895), *Memoirs of C.M. Talleyrand de Périgord: containing the Particulars of his Private and Public Life* (London: H.S. Nichols), Vol. 1, pp. 256–7.

16. AN F7, folio 3688, Lettre de M. Pétion, Maire de Paris, à M. Terrier de Monciel, Ministre de l'Intérieur, 22 juin 1792.
17. Goldsmith (1895), pp. 277–82.

Chapter 4

1. AD CPA 582, folios 72–3.
2. AD CPA 582, folios 73–7.
3. Lewis Goldsmith (1811), *The Secret History of the Cabinet of Bonaparte* (London: H.S. Nichol), p. 286.
4. AD CPA 583, folios 135–55, Noël à Lebrun, 2 November 1792.
5. Marianne Elliott (1982), *Partners in Revolution. The United Irishmen and France* (New Haven and London: Yale University Press), p. 58.
6. This could be Dr Richard Gem, a Worcestershire man, who went to Paris as physician to the embassy in 1762. An avowed materialist, he was enchanted with the Revolution, and was doubtless the 'Ghym, anglais' who in 1792 presented 1,000 francs to the Patriotic Fund. This did not save him from being arrested, like other Englishmen, in October 1793, as a hostage for Toulon. He died in 1800 aged over 80. If this is the case, he seems to have been a link between Paris and London.
7. TNA HO 42/21/1, folio 388, Mémorandum de Cruchent, 1 7bre 1792a.
8. Archives Diplomatique (hereafter AD) Correspondence Politiques Angleterre (hereafter CPA) 588, folio 102, Benjamin Vaughan to Messrs Manning, Anderson and Bosanquet, 2 July 1794.
9. Nicholas Dunne-Lynch, personal communication.
10. AD CPA 588, folios 184–7. See also AD CPA 588, folios 262–4, 268–9, 274–80.
11. TNA HO 42/21/1, folio 391, Mémorandum de Cruchent, 1 7bre 1792b.
12. TNA HO 42/22/12, folios 33–8, Memorandum de Cruchent, 1 8bre 1792.

Chapter 5

1. Nottinghamshire Archives DD/SR/102/213, Letter from John Stephenson of Hull to John Milnes of Wakefield.
2. Thomas Day was a religious and political radical. He married Esther Milnes of Wakefield. Her letters reveal a very self-assured young lady. Her poetry and essays demonstrate her quickness of mind and uniqueness of spirit. Thomas Day was an ardent abolitionist and political writer.
3. Hans Nicholas (1954), 'Franklin, Jefferson, and the English Radicals at the End of the Eighteenth Century', *Proceedings of the American Philosophical Society*, Vol. 98, No. 6, pp. 406–26; JSTOR, www.jstor.org/stable/3143863, accessed 21 August 2021.
4. Benjamin Vaughan (1793), *Letters, on a subject of the Concert of Princes, and the dismemberment of Poland and France. (First published in the Morning Chronicle between July 20, 1792 and June 25, 1793)/by a calm observer [Benjamin Vaughan]* (London: printed for G.G.J. & J. Robinson).
5. https://www.historyofparliamentonline.org/volume/1790-1820/member/vaughan-benjamin-1751-1835.
6. SCA WWM F44/43, Evidence re activities of Thomas Digges, 12 December 1792.
7. 'To Thomas Jefferson from Thomas Digges, 10 March 1793', Founders Online, National Archives, https://founders.archives.gov/documents/Jefferson/01-25-02-0312 (original source: *The Papers of Thomas Jefferson* (1992), Vol. 25, 1 January–10 May 1793, ed. John Catanzariti (Princeton: Princeton University Press), pp. 347–51.

8. Lynn Hudson Parsons (1965), 'The Mysterious Mr. Digges', *The William and Mary Quarterly*, Vol. 22, No. 3, pp. 486–92; JSTOR, www.jstor.org/stable/1920459, accessed 1 June 2021.
9. BL AM 36527, folio 67, John Milnes.
10. https://www.maryhamiltonpapers.alc.manchester.ac.uk/letter/AR-HAM-00001-00002-00019/.
11. SCA WWM F44/43, Evidence re activities of Thomas Digges, 12 December 1792.
12. Very likely David Martin, a Unitarian from Sheffield and central member of the Sheffield Constitutional Society, who traded as bookbinder, printer and engraver.
13. SCA WWM F44/43, Evidence re activities of Thomas Digges, 12 December 1792.
14. *Sheffield Iris*, 15 May 1800.
15. SCA WWM, F46/127, A list of those Luddites who have taken the Oath of Allegiance.
16. William T. Tone (2008), *Life of Theobald Wolfe Tone by Himself, Continued by his Son, with his Political Writings, Edited by W.T. Wolfe Tone*, 5 vols (Cambridge: Cambridge University Press), Vol. 1, p. 136.
17. SCA WWM F44/33, United Irishmen of Dublin broadsheet. See also SCA WWM F44/345, United Irishmen of Belfast broadsheet.
18. SCA WWM F44/35, Revolution Club broadsheet.
19. Service Historique du Armée de Terre (hereafter SHDDT) GR IM 1419.
20. TNA HO 42/21, 'In the Cause of Liberty', 1792.
21. TNA HO 42/23/135, folio 309, Francis Russell to Home Office, 10 December 1792.
22. Lockwood was a shoemaker and became a key personality in political reform in Wakefield. He lived on Silver Street in the 1770s. He was arrested for his part in forming an illegal cordwainers combination in October 1804, and had moved to Nelson Street by 1819. Nelson Street was the centre of the Irish émigré community in Wakefield. He signed a petition for a reduction in taxes and political reform on 23 August 1819.
23. Land Tax records list a Robert Peach living in Robert Milnes' house on Westgate, Wakefield in 1801, and that he was declared bankrupt in 1802. Is this the same man as Digges mentions?
24. SCA WWM F 44/43, Evidence re activities of Thomas Digges, 12 December 1792.
25. Ibid.
26. AD CPA 587, folios 296–300. « Note et mémoire … ».
27. 'To Thomas Jefferson from Thomas Digges, 17 November 1801', Founders Online, National Archives, https://founders.archives.gov/documents/Jefferson/01-35-02-0520 (original source: *The Papers of Thomas Jefferson* (2008), Vol. 35, 1 August–30 November 1801, ed. Barbara B. Oberg (Princeton: Princeton University Press), pp. 681–3).
28. http://shura.shu.ac.uk/4075/1/phdthesisfinalversion16nov2011.pdf.
29. SCA WWM F121111, Charles Bowns to Fitzwilliam, 12 January 1792. Activities of the Sheffield Club; stock of 'Mr Paine's pamphlet' from Crome's Press.
30. F.K. Donnelly and J.L. Baxter (1976), 'Sheffield the Revolutionary Tradition', in *Essays in the Economic and Social History of South Yorkshire*, ed. S. Pollard and C. Homes (Sheffield: South Yorkshire County Council), p. 96.

Chapter 6

1. AN Series C, pièce 242.
2. BL AM 27814, folios 45–6.
3. AN Series C, pièce 242.
4. Goldsmith (1811), pp. 289–301.

5. Goodwin, p. 247.
6. Kate Horgan (2016), *The Politics of Songs in Eighteenth Century Britain 1723–1795* (London: Routledge), p. 141.
7. AD CPA 583, folios 210–12, Lebrun to Noël, 11 November 1792.
8. AD CPA 582, folios 41–52, 'Instructions given to M. François Noël going to London', 29 August 1792.
9. AD CPA 582, folios 133–5, Noël au Lebrun, 2 Novembre 1792.
10. AD CPA 584, Talleyrand to Lebrun, 15 Novembre 1792.
11. TNA HO 1/1, Letters from émigré, 29 November 1792. See also Letters from émigré, 1 December 1792.
12. Goodwin, pp. 507–12.
13. Archives Parliamentaire, Vol. 53, p. 474.
14. Archives Parlementaire, Vol. 53, pp. 635–6.
15. TNA TS 11/959, George Monro, 6 December 1792.
16. Ibid.
17. TNA TS 11/960, George Monro, 21 December 1792.
18. TNA Foreign Office Papers (hereafter FO) 27/41, folio 82, Monro to Grenville, 27 December 1792.
19. Claeys, p. 97.
20. Harry Dickinson (1990), 'Popular Loyalism in the 1790s', in *The Transformation of Political Culture: England and Germany in the Late Eighteenth Century*, ed. Eckhart Hellmuth (Oxford: Oxford University Press), p. 517.
21. Michael Duffy (1996), 'William Pitt and the Origins of the Loyalist Association Movement of 1792', *Historical Journal*, No. 39, p. 943.
22. Thomas Paine (1987), 'Letter Addressed to the Addressers on the Late Proclamation', in *The Thomas Paine Reader*, ed. Michael Foot and Isaac Kramnick (London: Penguin), p. 374.
23. Robert Rae (1961), '"Liberty of the Press" as an Issue in English Politics, 1792–1793', *The Historian*, No. 24, p. 35.
24. Nicolas Rogers (1999), 'Burning Tom Paine: Loyalism and Counter-Revolution in Britain, 1791–1793', *Histoire Sociale*, Novembre, pp. 156–9.
25. AD CPA 584, folios 314–16, Noël au Lebrun, 24 Novembre 1792.
26. AD CPA, folios 314–16, Noël au Lebrun, 22 Décembre 1792.

Chapter 7
1. AD CPA 583, folios 47–50, Noël à Lebrun, 22 October 1792.
2. AD CPA 584, folios 9–11, Benoist à Lebrun, 1 December 1792. Emphasis in original text.
3. SHDDT GR 1M 1420, Projet d'expédition en Irlande.
4. AD CPA 584, folios 9–11, Benoist to Lebrun, 1er Décembre 1792.
5. AD CPA 587, folios 296–300, « Note et mémoire … ».
6. Ibid.
7. AD CPA 587, folio 176, Du Chastellet a Lebrun.
8. SHDDT GR 1m 1419–1420, Memoire sur Thomas Paine.
9. AD CPA 584, folio 401, Paine à Lebrun, 4 Janvier 1793.
10. AD CPA 584, folios 408–11, « Sur l'Irlande ».
11. BL AM 59363, Bruke to Grenville, 16 October 1792.
12. AN AF IV 1961, folios 99–105, Memoire Luines. See also AD CPA 589, folio 48, Madgett a Delacroix, 7 Pluviôse.
13. AD CPA 587, folio 96, Oswald, 11 Juin 1793.
14. Goodwin, p. 424.

15. Elliott (1982), pp. 43–8.
16. AD CPA 587, folio 46, John Hurford Stone au Lebrun, Mars 1793.
17. Liam Swords (1989), *The Green Cocakde. The Irish in the French Revolution 1789–1815* (Dublin: Glendale), p. 56.
18. Nicholas Dunne-Lynch, personal communication.
19. AD CPA 587, folio 20, Magdett au Ministre, 13 March 1793.
20. TNA FO 27/42, Somers to Grenville, 4 March 1793.
21. National Library of Ireland (hereafter NLI) MS 49, 491/2/424L, Letter from Jeff O'Connell to the Privy Council, 12 May 1794.
22. Faulkner's Dublin Journal, 26 June 1793.
23. TNA HO 100/44, folio 184, Edward Cooke, 27 June 1793.
24. Mary Purcell (1978), 'The Strange Story of Richard Ferris', in *The Irish-French Connection, 1578–1978*, ed. Liam Swords (Paris: Collège des Irlandais), pp. 108–10.
25. AD CPA 587, folio 97, Ferris au comité de salut public, Juillet 1793.
26. AN AF III57, dossier 219.
27. AD CPA 587, folio 194, Mémoire sur l'Irlande.
28. AN AFIII 186b, 22 September 1793.
29. AN AFIII 186b, 8 Vendemiaire an II.
30. SHDDT GR 1M 1419, lettre, Cherbourg, 28 Septembre 1793.
31. Ibid.
32. AN AF III 186b, Hoche au Comite de Salut Public, 1 Octobre 1793.
33. AD CPA 588, folios 9–11, Rapport 2 Octobre 1793.
34. AD CPA 588, folio 111, Rapport 11 Vendémiaire an III.
35. AD CPA 587, folios 296–300, Note et mémoire instructif, Août 1793.
36. https://www.historyofparliamentonline.org/volume/1790-1820/member/huskisson-william-1770-1830.
37. Purcell, p. 109.
38. Ibid., pp. 104–7.
39. Ibid., p. 109.
40. Ibid., pp. 108–10.
41. TNA Home Office Correspondence (Scotland) RH2/4/67, folios 393–8, 'Address from the Society of United Irishmen in Dublin to the Delegates for Reform in Scotland', 23 November 1792.
42. Hansard (1818), *The Parliamentary History of England*, Vol. XXXI (London: Longmans), p. 778.
43. National Records of Scotland (hereafter NRS) JC26/276 A, Hamilton Rowan to N. Macleod, 25 July 1793.
44. Ibid.
45. NRS JC26/276.

Chapter 8

1. NLI MS 49,491/2/424L, Letter from Jeff O'Connell to the Privy Council, 12 May 1794.
2. TNA HO 42/32, folios 426–7, Information of Pauncefort Cooke, 30 June 1794.
3. TNA TS 11/555/1793.
4. TNA TS 11/965, J.H. Stone to John Horne Tooke, 15 January 1794, 26 Nivose 2 Year of the Republic.
5. TNA TS 11/555/1793.
6. SHDDT GR 1M 1421, Project d'invasion.
7. TNA HO 42/32/257, folios 395–6, Letter to William Wickham, Home Office, from Edward Gosling, 6 July 1794.

8. TNA TS 11/555/1793.
9. AD CPA 588, folio 262, Rowan to Committee of Public Safety, 2 October 1794.
10. TNA TS 11/555/1793.
11. NLI MS 49,491/2/424L, Letter from Jeff O'Connell to the Privy Council, 12 May 1794.
12. TNA TS 11/965/3510/A3.
13. Ibid.
14. TNA HO 69/29/115, Prince of Bouillon with the Admiralty, March 1794.
15. AN AF II 202, lettre, 12 Pluviose an II.
16. TNA HO 42/30/109, folios 279–80, Samuel Marshall to John Mason, 25 May 1794.
17. Ibid.
18. TNA HO 42/32/273, folios 434A–434B, Letter to William Wickham, 19 May 1794.
19. TNA HO 42/32, folios 420–1, An account of the alleged fabrication of weapons by Josiah Webb of Pamber.
20. Kenneth J. Logue (2002), *Popular disturbances in Scotland 1780–1815* (Edinburgh: Birlinn Ltd).
21. TNA HO 42/30/109, folios 279–80, Samuel Marshall to John Mason, 25 May 1794. Emphasis in the original.
22. AD CPA 588, folios 262–4, Rowan to Committee of Public Safety, 2 October 1794.
23. SHDDT, 2e John Sullivan.
24. AD CPA 588, folios 268–9. See also folios 274–80.
25. AD CPA 588, folio 102, Benjamin Vaughan to Messrs Manning, Anderson and Bosanquet, 2 June 1794.
26. TNA TS 24/1/3, Proclamation reward of £1,000, 2 May 1794.
27. TNA TS 24/3/121, Full Report of the Trial of the Revd William Jackson for High Treason.
28. AD CPA 588, folio 102, Benjamin Vaughan to Messrs Manning, Anderson and Bosanquet, 2 June 1794.
29. AD CPA 588, folio 100, Benjamin Vaughan to M. Otto, 3 July 1794.
30. Clive Emsley (1981), 'An Aspect of Pitt's "Terror": Prosecutions for Sedition during the 1790s', *Social History*, Vol. 6, No. 2, pp. 155–84; JSTOR, www.jstor.org/stable/4285072, accessed 22 August 2021.
31. Emsley, pp. 155–84.
32. Elliott (1982), pp. 43–8.
33. Kent History Centre, U840/O147/4.
34. Edward Palmer Thompson (2013), *Making of the English Working Class* (London: Penguin Classics), pp. 137–8.

Chapter 9

1. *Leeds Intelligencer*, Monday, 3 August 1795.
2. *The Times*, 25 June 1795. See also *The Times*, 8 August 1795.
3. John Bohstedt (1983), *Riots and Community Politics in England and Wales, 1790–1810* (Cambridge: Cambridge University Press), pp. 1–3.
4. TNA HO 42/37, folios 360–1, Anon., 'Address to the Soldiery of Great Britain', n.d. [July 1795].
5. *St James's Chronicle*, 11 July 1795.
6. Dawson (2023), p. 113.
7. AN Fonds Sieyès 284AP/10, dossier 8, Lettre de Duckett.
8. Jenny Graham (2000), *The Nation, the Law and the King: Reform Politics in England, 1789–1799*, 2 vols (New York: University Press of America), p. 754.
9. Ibid.

10. TNA HO 42/43/7, folios 17–20, Two voluntary examinations providing information about Charles Radcliffe.
11. Roger A.E. Wells (1986), *Insurrection: The British Experience 1795–1803* (Stroud: Sutton Publishing), p. 73.
12. Copies of this address to the people of Canada by Edmond-Charles Genêt, Ambassador of the French Republic to the United States, circulated in the British province of Lower Canada in the second half of the year 1793.
13. AN AF III 186, dossier 859, pièces 36–8, Copies jointes des lettres de recommandation du gouverneur général de l'État de Vermont en faveur de l'Américain Ira Allen.
14. AN AF III 186, dossier 859, pièces 33–5, Messidor an IV.
15. AN AF III 186, dossier 859, pièce 39, Mémoire d'Ira Allen.
16. AN AF III 186, dossier 859, pièces 40–1, Mémoire d'Ira Allen sur les moyens d'effectuer une révolution dans les colonies anglaises d'Amérique du Nord afin d'en former une république sous le nom de Colombie réunie et sur les avantages qui en résulteraient pour la France
17. AN AF III 186, dossier 859, pièces 44–5, Note (traduction) sur la situation militaire des Deux-Canada.
18. AN AF III 186, dossier 859, pièces 46–53, Notes (traduction) relative à la date de l'expédition projetée au Canada.
19. AN AF III 186, dossier 859, pièces 56, Marché passé entre le ministre de la Guerre et le major général Ira Allen pour la fourniture de 20 000 fusils à baïonnette, 23 Messidor an IV.
20. AN AF III 186, dossier 860, pièce 9, Lettre en anglais de John Bates (alias Ira Allen) au général Clarke, 9 Vendémiaire an V.
21. AN AF III 186, dossier 859, pièces 12–13, Lettre de Ira Allen au général Clarke, 12 Vendémiaire an V.
22. AN AF III 186, dossier 859, pièce 16, Note de John Bates (alias Ira Allen).
23. AN AF III 186, dossier 859, pièce 17, Note de John Bates.

Chapter 10

1. Edward Smith (1974), *Whig Principles and Party Politics. Earl Fitzwilliam and the Whig Party, 1748–1833* (Manchester: Manchester University Press), pp. 195–6.
2. Earl Stanhope (1867), *The Life of The Right Honourable William Pitt* (London: John Murray), Vol. 2, p. xxiii.
3. Smith, pp. 190–1.
4. Ibid., pp. 193–4.
5. Ibid., p. 199.
6. Ibid. U840/O147/11.
7. Ibid. U840/O147/17.
8. Nicholas Dunne-Lynch, personal communication, 18 January 2022.
9. AN AFIV 1671, pièce 83, folios 357–8, Mémoire anonyme, adressé au Directeur Carnot.
10. AD CPA 589, folio 47, Madgett a Delacroix, 11 Nivôse an V.
11. AD CPA 589, folio 48, Madgett a Delacroix, 7 Pluviôse.
12. AD CPA 589, folio 3, Adet au Comité de Salut Public, 9 Vendémiaire an IV.
13. AD CPA 589, folio 34, Lettre, 23 Frimaire an IV.
14. AD CPA 589, folios 23–4. See also CPA 589, folios 111–15.
15. AN AF III 186, dossier 858, Wolfe Tone, 10 Ventôse an IV.
16. Elliott (1982), p. 87.
17. AN AF IV 1671, folio 66, Lettre de W. Tone au général Clarke, 3 Germinal an IV.

18. AN AF IV 1671, folio 65, Lettre de Wolf Tone, 11 Germinal an IV.
19. AN AF IV 1671, folio 67, Lettre de Wolfe Tone demandant des secours.
20. NRS JC 26/297–8, Examination of Black, June 1798.
21. NRS RH2/4/83, folios 41–9, Narrative of the Arrest, Examination and Imprisonment of George Mealmaker.
22. AD CPA 589, folio 215. See also AD CPA 589, folios 174–88.
23. AD CPA 589, folio 89, Merngaud au Reinhardt, 18 Germinal an IV.
24. AD CPA 589, folio 71 Magdett a Delacroix, 12 Ventôse an IV.
25. AD CPA 589, folio 90, bis Magdett au Carnot.
26. Nicholas Dunne-Lynch, personal communication, 18 January 2022, citing 'Observations' on 'Instructions intended for Eugene Aherne'.
27. AD CPA 589, folio 155.
28. SHDDT B11 1, Instruction pour l'établissement d'une Chouannerie en Angleterre.
29. SHDDT B11 1, Idée pour établir la Chouannerie.
30. Alphonse Frédéric Emmanuel, Marquis de Grouchy (1866), *Le général de Grouchy et l'Irlande en 1796* (Paris: Imprimerie Balitout, Questroy et Ce), pp. 16–24.
31. AN AF III 186, dossier 858, Duckett, 16 Messidor an IV.
32. AN AF III 186, dossier 859, pièce 129, Lettre de l'Irlandais Duckett, 11 Prairial an IV.
33. AD CPA 589, folio 114, Carnot, 8 Germinal an IV.
34. AD CPA 589, folio 93, Note du général O'Shee.
35. AN AF IV 1671, folio 68–9, Lettre de Wolfe Tone, 18 floréal an IV.
36. AN AF IV 1671, folio 70–1, Lettre de Wolfe Tone, 26 floréal an IV.
37. AN AF IV 1671, folio 70–1, Lettre de Wolfe Tone, 27 floréal an IV.
38. AN AF III 373, dossier 1853.
39. AN AF III 186, dossier 859, pièce 132, Mission du général O'Shee à son arrivée en Irlande. Instructions. An IV. See also AD CPA 589, folios 118–19, Instructions l'Envoye.
40. AN AF III 186, dossier 859, pièce 134, 'An Address to the People of Ireland on the present crisis'.
41. AN AF III 186, pièce 140, « Adresse aux matelots irlandais au service de la marine anglaise ».
42. AN AF III 186, pièce 142, « Adresse à la milice d'Irlande ».
43. AN AF III 186, pièce 145, 8 Juillet 1796.
44. AN AF III 186, 144, « Adresse aux Français émigrés en Angleterre par les membres du comité de l'Armée indépendante », 9 Juillet 1796, impr., p. 3.
45. AN AF IV 1671, pièces 73–4, Lettre de Wolfe Tone au Carnot, 15 Prairial an IV.
46. AN AF IV 1671, pièces 75–6, Lettre de Wolfe Tone au Carnot, 26 Prairial an IV.
47. AN AF III 186, dossier 859, pièce 24, Lettre (copie) de François Bartélémy.
48. AN AF III 186, pièce 27, Note jointe remise à Barthélémy par les Irlandais Fitzgerald et O'Connor.

Chapter 11

1. AN AF 193AP/4, Papiers du général Hoche (1789–1875), Minute autographe d'un rapport de Hoche au Directoire sur l'expédition d'Irlande an IV.
2. AN AF IV 1597, Rapport General Hoche, 1 Messidor an IV.
3. AN AF III 186b, au Delacroix, 6 Juillet 1796.
4. SHDDT GR 1M 1420, Rapport, 5 Messidor an IV.
5. TNA WO 1/921/489, folios 489–92, Bouillon to Dundas, 4 July 1796.
6. AN AFIII 186, dossier 859, pièce 57, Minute de l'arrêté du Directoire.
7. AN AFIII 186, pièce 58, Lettre du général Hoche au Directoire, 26 Messidor an IV.

8. TNA HO 100/62/141, 21 July 1796.
9. TNA HO 100/62/144–5, July 1796.
10. AN AF III 186, dossier 860, pièce 110, 12 Fructidor an IV.
11. AN AF III 186, folio 101, Lettre du ministre des Relations extérieures, 5 Fructidor an IV.
12. SHDDT B11 1, Observations sur les Instructions delivrees.
13. AN AF III 186, folio 108, Lettre, 12 Fructidor an IV.
14. AN AF III 186, pièce 75, Lettre de Charles Delacroix, ministre des Relations extérieures, au général Clarke au sujet des frais de mission du général O'Shee, 11 Brumaire an V.
15. AD CPA 589, folios 288–9, Carnot à Berthonneau.
16. SHDDT B11 1, Note pour general Clarke. See Also AD CPA 589, folios 288–9; CPA 590, folio 287.
17. Goodwin, pp. 513–14.
18. AN AF III, dossier 859, pièce 14, correspondance double écrite de Londres par l'agent Berthonneau.
19. Dominic Green (2104), 'From Jacobite to Jacobin: Robert Watson's Life in Opposition', in *Living with Jacobitism, 1690–1788 The Three Kingdoms and Beyond*, ed. Allan I. Macinnes, Kieran German and Lesley Graham (London: Pickering & Chatto), pp. 185–96.
20. SHDDT B11 1, Ministre de la Marine au Citoyen Muskeyen, 25 Thermidor an IV.
21. SHDDT B11 1, pièce 2, folios 15–16, Lettre de l'agent Berthonneau, 23 Fructidor an IV.
22. SHDDT B11 1, pièce 18, Lettre de l'agent Berthonneau, 13 Vendémiaire an V.
23. Elliott (1982), pp. 69–71.
24. Terry Crowdy, personal communication, 15 May 2021.
25. AN AF III 186, pièce 84, folios 359–66, 1er rapport présenté à un Directeur par un agent secret nommé Moyen.
26. AN AF III 186, pièce 85, folios 367–78, 2e rapport présenté à un Directeur par un agent secret nommé Moyen.

Chapter 12

1. AN AF III 186, dossier 859, ordre secret, 30 Fructidor an IV.
2. AN AF III 186, pièce 67, Lettre du général Quantin au général Clarke, 14 Thermidor an IV.
3. AN AF III 186, pièce 86, Lettre du général Quantin au général Clarke, 29 Thermidor an IV.
4. AN AF III 186, pièce 121, Lettre du général Quantin au général Clarke relative au même objet et soulignant son anxiété devant la désertion et la mauvaise volonté des officiers, 21 Fructidor an IV.
5. AN AF III 186, pièces 119–20, Lettre et note du général Quantin au général Clarke pour se disculper d'une indiscrétion par ignorance de l'entreprise Muskeyn, 20 Fructidor an IV. See also AN AF III 186, pièce 127, Lettre du général Quantin au général Clarke sur la situation des déserteurs de Lille et de Péronne et sur les préparatifs de Muskeyn, 28 Fructidor an IV.
6. TNA WO 1/922, folios 21–4, Bouillon to Dundas, 26 January 1797.
7. AN AF III 186, dossier 860, pièce 6, Lettre du général Hoche au général Clarke, 10 Vendémiaire an V.
8. AN AF III 186, dossier 858, Bruix au General Hoche 14 Vendémiaire an V.
9. SHM BBIV, 102, Hoche au Directoire, 11 Brumaire an V.
10. SHM BBIV, 102, Hoche au Directoire, 10 Brumaire an V.

11. SHM BBIV, 102, Carnot au Directoire, 4 Brumaire an V.
12. SHM Project et Expéditions, Tome IV, Rapport Leuins, Brumaire an V.
13. AN F7/4775/52, dossier 2, police files on Bernard MacSheehy.
14. AN AF II 61, Pétition de l'Irlandais MacSheehy, 28 Floréal an II.
15. AN AF III 186, dossier 859, pièce 110, Note jointe sur les Irlandais, 12 Fructidor an IV.
16. Elliott (1982), p. 88.
17. AN LH//1679/77, MacShechy, pièce 3.
18. AN LH//1679/77, MacSheehy.
19. AN AF III 186, dossier 860, pièce 143, Rapport de l'Irlandais Bernard MacSheehy sur sa mission en Irlande, 29 Frimaire an V.
20. AD Mémoires et Documents (hereafter MD), 53, Journal du voyage de MACSHEEHY, capitaine adjoint à l'état-major de Hoche, envoyé en Irlande pour préparer la descente française (novembre–décembre 1796).
21. AN AF III 186, dossier 860, pièce 144, MacSheehy au Hoche.
22. AD MD, 53, Journal du voyage de MACSHEEHY l'état-major de Hoche, envoyé en Irlande pour préparer la descente française (novembre–décembre 1796).
23. AN LH//1679/77, MacShechy.
24. SHDDT 2Yc2620, MacSheehy.
25. TNA FO 27/51-52.
26. TNA FO 33/12/51.
27. TNA WO 1/921, folio 225–8, Bouillon to Dundas, 23 September 1795.
28. TNA FO 95/605/7, Correspondence of Prince de Bouillon with William Windham, 2 March 1795.
29. TNA FO 95/605/7, Correspondence of Prince de Bouillon with William Windham, 27 July 1795.
30. TNA WO 1/921, folios 339–46, Bouillon to Dundas, 16 March 1796.
31. TNA WO 1/922, folios 741–4, Bouillon to Huskisson, 26 October 1799.
32. Jane Ashelford (2008), In the English Service, the Life of Philippe d'Auvergne (Jersey Heritage Trust).
33. TNA War Office (hereafter WO) 1/922/45, folios 45–8, Bouillon to Dundas, 14 February 1797.
34. TNA WO 1/921/513, folios 513–20, Bouillon to Dundas, 14 July 1796.
35. TNA WO 1/921/637, folios 637–40, Bouillon to Dundas, 30 August 1796.
36. TNA WO 1/921/687, folios 687–90, Bouillon to Dundas, 13 September 1796.
37. TNA WO 1/921, folios 703–9, Bouillon to Dundas, 4 October 1796.
38. TNA WO 1/921, folios 723–4, Richard (royalist officer) to Gordon, 8 October 1796.
39. TNA HO 69/27/66, Report 8 October 1796.
40. TNA WO 1/922/5, folios 5–7, Rapport Bouillon, 30 December 1796.
41. TNA WO 1/922/9, folios 9–12, Bouillon, 30 December 1796.
42. SHDDT B11 1, Rapport, 16 Brumaire an IV.
43. TNA HO 42/39/57, folio 124–6, Information received 31 October 1796.
44. AN AF III 186, dossier 860, pièce 75, Lettre de Charles Delacroix, 11 Brumaire an V.
45. TNA HCA 45/43/21, folios 272–4, Case on behalf of the appellant; folio 274, Decree; folios 275–91, Further proofs, 22 February 1804.

Chapter 13

1. AN AF III 189, dossier 859, pièce 32, 19 Messidor an IV.
2. AN AF III 189, dossier 859, pièce 62.
3. AN AF III 189, dossier 859, pièce 63.
4. William Theobald Wolfe Tone (1831), The Life of Theobald Wolfe Tone (London: Whittaker, Treacher and Arnot), pp. 213–14.

5. SHDDT B11 1, Petiet au Directoire, 8 Frimaire an V.
6. TNA WO 1/921/789, folios 789–92, de La Boessière to Bouillon, 15 Novembre 1796.
7. TNA WO 1/921/817, folios 817–20, Bouillon to Dundas, 25 November 1796.
8. SHDDT B11 1, Petiet au Directoire, 8 Frimaire an V.
9. TNA WO 1/921/825, folios 825–8, Bouillon to Dundas, 20 December 1796.
10. TNA WO 1/921/829, folios 829–32, Declaration of Legardes, 20 December 1796.
11. SHDDT 6Yd 26, Emmanuel de Grouchy.
12. T.W. Moody, R.B. McDowell and C.J. Woods (eds), *The Writings of Theobald Wolfe Tone, 1763–1798*, 3 vols (Oxford: Clarendon Press), Vol. 3, p. 306.
13. SHDDT 6Yd 26, Grouchy au Directoire, 12 Nivôse an V.
14. SHDDT GR 1M 1420, Expedition d'Irlande, 1797.
15. TNA WO 1/922/45, folios 45–8, Bouillon to Dundas, 14 February 1797.
16. TNA WO 1/922/45, folios 45–8, Lettre du général Hedouville, 10 Janvier 1797.
17. Ibid.
18. SHDDT B11 1, Correspondence Hoche, Petiet, Hedouville.
19. TNA WO 1/922/37, folios 37–9, Letter à Bouillon, 27 Janvier 1797.
20. AN AFIV 1671, pièce 34, Extrait du rapport fait au Directoire exécutif par le citoyen MacSheehy, 9 Pluviôse an V.
21. AN AF III 186, dossier 860, pièce 56, Copie jointe de la correspondance échangée par Duckett et Hoche.
22. TNA HO 42/40/139, folios 298–301, Letter from Lord Onslow, 27 February 1797.
23. SHM BBIV 112, Journal de Route du chef de Division Castagnier.
24. SHM BBIV 112, Rapport, Capitaine la Vatour.
25. Grouchy, p. 45.
26. TNA HO 42/40/148, folios 318–19, Letter from the Reverend Edward Edwards, 24 February 1797.

Chapter 14

1. West Yorkshire Archive Service (hereafter WYAS) JG001001, Andrew Peterson, Eliza Paine to Andrew Peterson, Dublin 27 January 1797.
2. Smith, pp. 234–5.
3. Clifford D. Conner (2009), *Arthur O'Connor* (New York: iUniverse Inc.), p. 238.
4. Robert Stewart Castlereagh (1848), *Memoirs and Correspondence of Viscount Castlereagh*, ed. Charles Vane, 4 vols (London: Henry Colburn), Vol. 1, pp. 270–1.
5. AN AFIV 1671, pièce 34, Extrait du rapport fait au Directoire exécutif par le citoyen MacSheehy, 9 Pluviose an V.
6. AN AFIV 1961, folios 99–105.
7. AD CPA 592, folios 102–3.
8. AD CPA 587, folio 20, Madgett à Lebrun, 13 Mars 1793.
9. AD CPA 588, folios 480–1, Rapport, 1795. See also AD CPA 589, folios 155–6, Rapport, Fevrier 1796; AD CPA 592, folios 129–30, Rapport, Décembre 1797.
10. TNA FO 27/54, Flint to John King, 13 July 1799.
11. Niklas Frykmann (2020), *The Bloody Flag: Mutiny in the Age of Atlantic Revolution* (Oakland: University of California Press), pp. 176–83.
12. TNA Admiralty Papers (hereafter ADM) 1/1449/105.
13. TNA HO 42/42/145, folios 332–5, Secret information, 12 March 1798.
14. AN AFIII 57, dossier 223, plaquette 1, Réflexions sur les causes de la rébellion des marins de Portsmouth et Plymouth par Madgett, 17 Floréal an V.
15. AN AFIII 57, dossier 223, plaquette 1, Examen des possibilités de débarquement en Angleterre, 25 Floréal an V.

16. AN AFIII 57, dossier 224, plaquette 1, Lettre Noël, 28 Floréal an V.
17. TNA PC 1/43/A 152, Examination of Henry Hastings, May 1798.
18. SHDDT GR 1M 1422, Projet le Gott.
19. SHDDT GR 1M 1422, Projet General Valence.
20. AN AFIV 1671/2, folios 158–60, Memoir given by Lewines to Hoche, 31 May 1797.
21. AN AFIII 463, Lettre du Ministre de la Marine au General Hoche, 3 Messidor.
22. AN AFIV1671/2, folio 40, Letter from Simon to Hoche, 7 June 1797.
23. SHDDT B11 1, Simon au Hoche, 30 Mai 1797.
24. SHM, Vol. 4, 4 Memoires et Projets 103, folio 8.
25. SHM BBIV 103.
26. AD CPA 590, folio 339, 'Official Note from Westminster', 1 June 1797.
27. TNA WO 1/922/241, folios 241–4, Rapport to Bouillon 1 Septembre 1797.
28. AN AFIV1671, pièce 78, Note du citoyen Luines agent secret irlandais au général Clarke.
29. AN AFIV1671, folios 344–5, Note sur l'Angleterre.
30. Moody et al., Vol. 3, p. 81.
31. Castlereagh, p. 272.
32. AN AFIV1671, folios 167–73, Mémoire signé Williams envoyé extraordinaire des Irlandais unis, 13 Juillet 1797.
33. AD CPA 589, folio 115.
34. SHM, Mémoires Tome IV, Rapport, Fructidor an VI.
35. TNA HO 100/70/33, Disposition Samuel Turner.
36. AN AFIV 1671/1, folios 99–105.
37. AN AFIV 1671/2, folio 163, Lettre Simon à Lewines, 21 Thermidor an V.
38. AN AFIV 1671/2, folio 46, Lettre Luyines à Barras, 25 September 1797.
39. AN AFIV 1671/2, folio 176, Verbal response from Barras to Lewines.
40. AN AFIV 1671/2, pièce 47, folio 177, Thompson au Barras, 14 Vendémiaire an VI.

Chapter 15

1. Moody et al., Vol. 3, pp. 164–6.
2. AD CPA 592, folio 43, Project d'invasion Écosse.
3. Moody et al., pp. 167–9.
4. 37 Geo, III, cap. 3 amended by cap. 22, Supplementary Militia Acts (1796).
5. TNA HO 45/39/2, Examinations of Stephenson, Thomas Wallis, William Wallis, and Lough 26, 31 January and 18 August 1797.
6. TNA HO 42/40, folios 373–6, Sunderland to Portland, 11 February 1797.
7. TNA HO 42/39-40, Home Office In-Letters, 1796–7.
8. *Edinburgh Evening Courant*, 18 August 1797.
9. *Edinburgh Evening Courant*, 24 August 1797.
10. Moody et al., Vol. 3, pp. 167–9.
11. Ibid., pp. 170–1.
12. AN AFIV 1671, plaquette 2, folio 49, Thompson au Barras.
13. AD CPA 592, folio 179, Barras au Thompson.
14. AD CPA 592, folio 153, Muir to the Directory, Nivôse an VI.
15. AD CPA 592, folios 144–5, Muir to minister of foreign affairs, 9 Nivôse an VI.
16. Cabotage is the use of small boats to transport people and goods along the coast. He is probably referring to small fishing boats etc.
17. SHDDT GR 1M 1420, folio 36, Project d'invasion Écosse, 26 Nivôse an VI.
18. SHDDT GR 1M 1420, folio 36, Delacroix au Bonaparte, 26 Nivôse an VI.
19. AD CPA 592, folio 161, Muir to the Directory, 13 Ventôse V.
20. *Le Moniteur Universel*, No. 105, 15 Nivôse VI.

21. William Theobald Wolfe Tone (ed.) (1826), *Life of Theobald Wolfe Tone*, 2 vols (Washington DC), Vol. II, pp. 461–2.
22. Moody et al., Vol. 3, p. 205.

Chapter 16

1. Samuel Simms (1937), *The Rev James Coigley, United Irishmen* (Belfast: Quinn).
2. TNA HO 42/45/137, folios 528–9, Examination, before [Bow Street] magistrate Richard Ford, of James Dixon of Belfast, 5 May 1798.
3. Ibid.
4. TNA PC 1/41/A139, Examination of Mary Perrins, 14 April 1798.
5. AD CPA 592, folio 43, James Coigley and Arthur McMahon, 4 October 1797.
6. TNA PC 1/43/A 152.
7. AD CPA 592, folio 61, Tone au Talleyand, 24 Vendémiaire an VI.
8. AD CPA 592, folio 65, Talleyrand au Pierre Sotin, 29 Vendémiaire an VI.
9. AN AFIV 1671/2, folio 176, Verbal response from Barras to Lewines.
10. Moody et al., Vol. 3, pp. 184–5.
11. Ibid., p. 186.
12. SHDDT GR 1M 1420, dossier 91, Rapport Robert Pelleve, 13 Nivose an 6.
13. SHDDT GR 1M 1420, dossier 91, Robert Pelleve à General Desaix, 13 Nivose an 6.
14. SHM BBIV 121, Rapport General Bonaparte.
15. TNA WO 1/922/193, folios 193–200, Bouillon to Dundas, 20 June 1797.
16. Moody et al., pp. 214–15.
17. SHDDT GR 1M 1420, Rapport sur l'Irlande reçu, Germinal an 6.
18. Michael Sydenham (1999), *Leonard Bourdon. The Career of a Revolutionary, 1754–1807* (Waterloo: Wilfred Laurier University Press).
19. Emilie Dréano (1997–8), 'Biographie politique de William Duckett, patriote et espion irlandais sous la Révolution Française', mémoire de maîtrise (Université Lumière–Lyons 2).
20. AN AFIII 58, dossier 28.
21. AN F/7/615/ix, folio 436, Bourdon au Directoire, 1 Ventôse an VI.
22. AN AF III 57 I 226, Bourdon au Directoire, 9 Ventôse an VI. See also AN AF/III/57, dossier 225, plaquette 1, Mémoire sur l'espionnage (9 Ventôse an VI).
23. AN F/7/615/ix, folio 436, 9 Floréal year VI.
24. TNA WO 1/922/297, folios 297–300, Bouillon to Huskisson, 28 December 1797.

Chapter 17

1. Hansard (1818), pp. 642–5.
2. TNA HO 42/45/144, folios 547–50, Deposition sworn on 19 March before Thomas Butterworth Bayley and John Floud, 15 April 1798.
3. AN AFIV 1671/2, folio 176, Response from Barras to Lewines, end of 1797.
4. Moody et al., Vol. 3, p. 198.
5. Nicholas Dunne-Lynch, personal communication, citing Castlereagh.
6. Graham, p. 7551.
7. Kent History Centre U840/O196/2.
8. TNA PC 1/44/A.155, Account of Thomas Conway, undated 1799.
9. TNA HO 100/87/334-5, Examination of Murphy, 2 November 1799.
10. AN AF IV 1671, folios 114–27.
11. TNA FO 33/15/10.
12. Paul Weber (1997), *On the Road to Rebellion: The United Irishmen and Hamburg, 1796–1803* (Dublin: Four Courts Press), p. 94.
13. SHDDT Xab 44, dossier Lanciers de Berg.

14. Graham, p. 753.
15. Kent History Centre U840/O196/2.
16. *Le Bien informé*, n° 170, p. 3.
17. Elliott (1982), p. 171.
18. TNA HO 42/46/173, folio 375, Rev Thomas Bancroft to Home Office.
19. TNA HO 42/46/173, folios 358–76, Papers respecting the Jacobin Societies in England and Ireland, and extracts of letters relevant to French armaments.
20. TNA WO 1/922/297, folios 297–300, Bouillon to Huskisson, 28 December 1797.
21. SHDDT GR 1M 1422, Project General Daendels, Janvier 1798.
22. SHDDT GR 1M 1422, folio 161.
23. TNA PC 1/41/A136, evidence of Robert Gray, 23 March 1798.
24. SHDDT B11 2, Ministre de Guerre au Ministre de Marine, 2 Juillet 1798.
25. TNA HO 42/42/145, folios 332–5, Secret information from an unnamed informant taken by Richard Ford [Bow Street magistrate], 12 March 1798.
26. TNA HO 42/45/138, folios 531–2, Letter dated Liverpool, 20 November 1798.
27. TNA HO 42/42/145, folios 332–5, Secret information from an unnamed informant taken by Richard Ford [Bow Street magistrate], 12 March 1798.
28. TNA HO 42/46/173, folio 363, Copy of Letter by John Waring, 15 February 1798.
29. Ibid.
30. TNA HO 42/46/173, folio 369, Extract of Information Respecting the United Irishmen.
31. TNA HO 42/43/12, folios 33A–33B, Letter from George Cartwright, 6 May 1797.
32. John Gibney (2019), *The United Irishmen, Rebellion and the Act of Union, 1798–1803* (Barnsley: Pen & Sword).
33. TNA HO 42/42/145, folios 332–5, Secret information from an unnamed informant taken by Richard Ford [Bow Street magistrate], 12 March 1798.
34. Graham, pp. 843–6.
35. TNA HO 42/45/114, folios 489A–489B, Information of James Reeves, clerk at the Public Office, Bow Street, 12 April 1798.
36. TNA HO 42/45/136, folios 526–7, Further examination, before magistrate Richard Ford, 5 May 1798.
37. TNA HO 42/61/79, folios 222–3, Letter from the Reverend Thomas Bancroft, 14 March 1798.
38. TNA HO 42/45/147, folios 555–62, Deposition of Robert Gray, Lancashire, sworn on 12 April before Thomas Butterworth Bayley and John Floud.
39. Moody et al., Vol. 3, p. 205.
40. TNA HO 42/42/145, folios 332–5, Secret information, 12 March 1798.
41. Graham, pp. 843–6.

Chapter 18

1. TNA HO 42/47/95, folios 231–3, Minutes of an interview with J.A. Jagerhorn.
2. TNA HO 42/44, folios 260–265C, Unsigned letter sent from Ireland, 31 August 1798.
3. *Le Moniteur Universel*, 4 Prairial an VI.
4. Thomas Pakenham (1997), *The Year of Liberty: The Great Irish Rebellion of 1798* (London: Weidenfeld & Nicolson).
5. SHM BBIV 122, Lewines au Citoyen Directeur, Juin 1798.
6. SHM BBIV 122, Appel des irlandais au Directoire, 16 Juin 1798.
7. SHM BBIV 122, Bruix au Citoyen Bompard, 1 Messidor.
8. Pakenham.
9. TNA HO 42/44, folios 260–265C, Unsigned letter sent from Ireland, 31 August 1798.

10. TNA HO 42/43/40, folios 116–17, Draft letter from the Duke of Portland, 14 June 1798.
11. TNA HO 42/43/36, folios 106–108B, Letter from the Reverend Thomas Handcock, 8 June 1798.
12. AD CPA 592, folio 191, 'Conseil des cinq cents – Corps Legaslitif'.
13. SHM BBIV 122, Instructions au général de Brigade Humbert, 1 Thermidor.
14. Castlereagh, pp. 307–10.
15. TNA WO 1/922, folio 443, Bouillon to Dundas, 16 July 1798.
16. TNA WO 1/922, folio 423, Bouillon to Dundas, 13 June 1798.
17. SHM BBIV 122, folio 26, Bruix, 12 Thermidor an VI.
18. SHM BBIV 122, Instructions au général de Brigade Humbert, 1 Thermidor.
19. TNA WO 1/922/495, folios 495–8, Bouillon to Huskisson, 25 September 1798.
20. SHM BBIV 122, Humbert au Ministre, 13 Thermidor an VI.
21. SHM BBIV 122, Bruix, 12 Thermidor an VI.
22. SHDDT B11 2, Muller au Ministre de Guerre, 20 Frimaire an 7.
23. SHDDT B11 2, Détailles Véritables.
24. SHDDT Xk 31, Guides du Berthier, rapport, 8 Germinal an 12.
25. SHDDT B11 2, Ministre de Guerre au Ministre de Marine.
26. SHDDT B11 2, Rapport General Hardy, 19 Novembre 1798.
27. SHDDT B11 2, John Thompson au Ministre de Guerre.
28. SHDDT B11 2, Declaration Humbert.
29. SHDDT B11 2, Rapport, 11 Fructidor an VI.
30. SHDDT B11 2, Mémoires Militaires Castlebar.
31. SHDDT B11 2, Détailles Véritables.
32. *Saunders's News, Letters, etc.*, September 12, 1798, No. 12198. See also *Saunders's News, Letters, etc.*, September 17, No. 12914.
33. Castlereagh, pp. 306–8.
34. Ibid., pp. 406–7.
35. Ibid., pp. 407–8.
36. SHDDT B11 2, Rapport Citoyen Ameil.

Chapter 19

1. SHDDT B11 2, Rapport General Hardy, 19 Novembre 1798.
2. SHM BBIV 122, Au ministre de la geurre, 12 Messidor an VI.
3. SHM BBIV 122, Ministre de la geurre a général Rey, 5 Vendémiaire an VI.
4. SHDDT B11 2, Rapport General Hardy, 19 Novembre 1798.
5. WYAS JG001001 Peterson Papers, Eliza Paine to Andrew Peterson, 22 October 1798.
6. Tone (2008), pp. 314–16.
7. SHDDT B11 2, Wolfe Tone au Directoire Executif Republique Francaise, Dublin, 20 Brumaire an 7.
8. Tone (2008), p. 316.
9. WYAS JG001001 Peterson Papers, Eliza Paine to Andrew Peterson, post marked 26 October 1798.
10. Ibid.
11. WYAS JG001001 Peterson Papers, Eliza Paine to Andrew Peterson, 22 October 1798.
12. SHM BBIV 123, folio 193, Bruix au Joubert, 8 Messidor an VI.
13. SHM BBIV 122, Agent de la Marine Batave au Joubert, 16 Messidor an VI.
14. Nationaal Archief Nederlands (hereafter NA) 01, Inventaris van de archieven van het Departement van Marine, 1795–1813, dossier 27, Rapport, 12 Novembre 1798.

15. SHM BBIV 123, folio 194, Lettre de Bruix, 13 Messidor an VI.
16. SHM BBIV 123, folio 192, Bruix au Michel.
17. AN AFIII 57, dossier 225, plaquette 1, Mémoire sur l'espionnage, 9 Ventôse an VI, folios 7–32.
18. Ibid.
19. TNA FO 33/16/50, Crauford to Grenville, 7 August 1798.
20. AN AFIII 57, dossier 225, plaquette 1, Mémoire sur l'espionnage, 9 Ventôse an VI, folio 7–32.
21. AN AFIII 57, dossier 225, folio 225, Leonard Bourdon au Directeur, 9 Ventôse an VI.
22. TNA FO 33/15/237-28, Account of Duckett's examination.
23. Castlereagh, pp. 308–9.
24. TNA Adm. 1/5346-7.
25. AN AFIV 1671, folios 114–27.
26. SHM BBIV 123, Joubert au ministre, 30 Messidor an VI.
27. NA 2.01.29.01, Inventaris van de archieven van het Departement van Marine, 1795–1813, folio 27, Instructie van de Schout bij Nacht Story, voor de fregatten Furie en Waakzaamheid, kapteins Pletz en Nierop, Juli 1798.
28. *London Gazette*, 3 November 1798, pp. 1052–3.
29. NA 2.21.046 Inventaris van het archief van H.W. Daendels, Daendels van Corlog, 17 Nov. 1798.
30. TNA WO 1/922/535, folio 542, Rapport Prince de Boullion 16 Novembre 1798.
31. Nicholas Dunne-Lynch, personal communication.
32. TNA WO 1/922/431, Rapport Prince de Bouillon, 18 Juin 1798.
33. TNA WO 1/922/535, folio 537, Rapport Prince de Boullion, 17 Octobre 1798. See also TNA WO 1/922/535, folio 538, Rapport Prince de Bouillon, 20 Octobre 1798.
34. *Le Moniteur: An 8, Vendémiaire à Ventôse, 1799–1800*, No. 77, 17 Frimaire an 8, 303, i.e., 8 December 1799, reports from 21 November 1799 [30 Brumaire an 8] 'Courts martial are still active in many districts', especially in County Meath.
35. WYAS JG 001001, Peterson Papers, Eliza Paine to Andrew Peterson, 12 March 1799.
36. While there is no authoritative source on precise numbers of casualties outside of battle, the general consensus is roughly 30,000. For example, see Adam Zamoyski (1999), *Holy Madness: Romantics, Patriots, and Revolutionaries, 1776–1871* (New York: Weidenfeld & Nicholson), p. 108. Regarding the colonial comparison, it is interesting to note that those who were charged with suppressing Ireland in this period were those who specialized in colonial rule, notably General Gerard Lake, who, apart from leading the British forces in Ireland in 1798, was involved in trying to suppress the American Revolution and later more notably served as commander-in-chief of British forces in India, and General Cornwallis, who, apart from serving as lieutenant general in Ireland from 1798–1801, was one of the key generals in the American Revolution and a governor general of India.
37. TNA HO 42/45/138, folios 531–2, Letter dated Liverpool, 20 November 1798.
38. Ian McBride (2009), *Eighteenth-Century Ireland: The Isle of Slaves* (Dublin: Gill and Macmillan), p. 355.
39. Smith, pp. 250–3.
40. *Le Moniteur Universel*, No. 124, 4 Pluviôse an 8, p. 491.

Chapter 20

1. Síle Ní Chinnéide (1962), *Napper Tandy and the European Crises of 1798–1803* (Dublin: University of Dublin), p. 16.
2. AN AFIV 1671, folios 99–105.
3. TNA WO 1/922/535, folios 535–42, Bouillon to Huskisson, 16 November 1798.

NOTES

4. TNA HO 42/46/1, folios 1–2, Copy of a letter to William Huskisson [Under Secretary for War] from Captain Philippe D'Auvergne, 8 January 1799.
5. TNA 100/85, folios 281–3, Notes on Pollock's intelligence, 15 April 1799.
6. TNA HO 42/46/173, folios 358–76, Papers respecting the Jacobin Societies in England and Ireland, and extracts of letters relevant to French armaments – 13 Inclosure and Schedule.
7. TNA WO 1/922/557, folios 557–60, Bouillon to Huskisson, 8 January 1799.
8. TNA WO 1/922/593.
9. TNA PC1/42/A 161, folio 144.
10. TNA HO 100/85, folios 281–3.
11. TNA HO 42/46/48, folios 105–6, Examination, sworn before Richard Ford, 12 March 1799.
12. TNA FO 33/17/126, Craufurd to Grenville, 12 February 1799. See also TNA FO 33/17/248-248, Craufurd to Grenville, 12 March 1799; TNA FO 1/44/A158, Secret information, 2 May 1799.
13. TNA FO 33/17/245-246, Craufurd to Grenville, 12 March 1799.
14. TNA PC 1/43/A.152.
15. TNA HO 42/46/48, folios 105–6, Examination, sworn before Richard Ford, 12 March 1799.
16. TNA HO 42/55/115, folios 393–406, Observations relative to state prisoners.
17. TNA HO 42/47/148, folios 337–40, Record of a speech, 10 April 1799.
18. TNA HO 42/47/150, folios 342–5, Letter from Joseph White, 15 April 1799.
19. TNA FO 33/19, folios 65–8.
20. TNA 42/47/128, folio 295, Anonymous letter to Home Office, dated 20 April 1799.
21. TNA HO 100/86/2. See also TNA HO 42/47/72, folios 157–63, Document headed 'Proposed General Arrangement for the Defence of the Capital'.
22. Wells (1986), p. 213.
23. TNA HO 100/86, George Orr to John King undersecretary of state, 12 September 1799.
24. TNA FO 33/18/60-1, Craufurd to Grenville, 19 April 1799.
25. SHDDT GR 1M 1420, Project général Humbert, 12 Janvier 1799.
26. Simon Burrows (1998), 'A Literary Low-Life Reassessed: Charles Theveneau de Morande in London, 1769–1791', Eighteenth-Century Life, Vol. 22, No. 1, pp. 76–94.
27. SHDDT GR 1M 1420, folio 97, Temion sur l'Angelterre par Citoyen Thevenau.
28. SHDDT GR 1M 1420, folio 98, Moyen d'execution.
29. SHDDT GR 1M 1420, folio 100.
30. SHDDT GR 1M 1420, folio 101.
31. Ibid.
32. SHDDT GR 1M 1420, Project général Dupont, 26 Ventôse an 7.
33. SHM BBIV 130, folio 8, un projet contre d'Irlande et Écosse.
34. SHM BBIV 130, folio 9, un Project irait en Irlande et sur d'Angleterre.
35. SHDDT GR 1M 1420, Journal de Voyage, Sept Ventôse an 7.
36. TNA HO 42/55/115, folios 393–406, Observations relative to state prisoners.
37. SHDDT GR 1M 1422, folio 85.
38. SHDDT GR 1M 1420, Journal de Voyage, Sept Ventôse an 7.
39. AN AFIII 58, dossier 228, plaquette 2, Demande de Thomson, 7 Floréal an VII.
40. TNA HO 42/65/219, folios 481–2, Ralph Fletcher to John King, 31 July 1802.
41. TNA HO 100/86 301-2, Secret Information from Mr Pollock, 23 July 1799.
42. TNA FO 33/19/50, Crauford to Grenvill, 6 August 1799. See also TNA FO 33/19/56-57, Craufurd to Grenville, 15 August 1799; TNA FO 33/19/71, Craufurd to Grenville 23 August 1799.
43. AD CPA 592, folio 411, report 13 7bre 1799.

44. AD CPA592, folio 409, Le Comite Centrale de Irlandais-Unis a Paris au Talleyrand, 14 Septembre 1799.
45. TNA HO 42/55/115, folios 393–406, Observations relative to state prisoners.
46. AD Memoires et Documents, 53 Watson au Chef du Cabinet, 2 Frimaire an VII.
47. AD CPA 592, folio 220, Rapport Robert Watson, 7bre 1798.
48. TNA PC 1/43/A152.
49. Green (2104), pp. 185–96.
50. AD CPA 594, folios 53–67, Muir to Minister of Foreign Affairs, 29 October 1800.
51. AD CPA 594, folios 53–4. See also AD CPA 594, folios 56–67.
52. AD CPA 594, folios 56–67.
53. AD CPA 592, folios 261–5, Watson au Reinhardt, 22 Messidor an VII.
54. AN Fonds Sieyès (XVIIe–XIXe siècle) 284AP/13, dossier 4.
55. Ibid., Note d'information sur la situation en Angleterre.
56. TNA WO 1/922, folios 749–52, [?] to Bouillon, 7 October 1799.
57. AD CPA 593, folio 18, Watson to the Directory, 27 Vendémiaire VIII.

Chapter 21

1. AD CPA 594, folio 36, Watson to Talleyrand, 12 Frimaire VIII.
2. SHDDT GR 1M 1420, Project d'invasion Ireland et Écosse, 20 Frimaire an VIII.
3. AN AFIV 1671, folios 106–11, Mémoire du même sous le pseudonyme de Thompson, 20 Frimaire an VIII.
4. AN AFIV 1671, folios 112–13.
5. Roger A.E. Wells (1977), *Dearth and Distress in Yorkshire 1793–1802* (York: Borthwick Institute), p. 4.
6. TNA HO 42/49/137, folios 295A–295B, Copy of an anonymous letter to Lord Eldon, 31 March 1800.
7. TNA HO 42/51, folios 168–9, Earl of Berkeley to Portland, 16 September 1800.
8. Wells (1986), pp. 192–4.
9. SHDDT B11 2, Talleyrand au Thompson, 17 Nivôse an 8.
10. Smith, p. 254.
11. AD CPA 593, folios 174–5, William Duckett to Consulate, Ventôse VIII.
12. Napoléon to the Burgomasters and Senate of the Free and Imperial City of Hambourg, 30 December 1799, Napoléon Bonaparte (1858–69), *Correspondance de Napoléon Ier publiée par ordre de l'Empereur Napoléon III* (Paris), No. 4482, VI, 75.
13. Napoléon to Talleyrand, 13 January 1800, *Correspondance de Napoléon Ier*, No. 4520, VI, 107.
14. Decision, 29 April 1802, *Correspondance de Napoléon Ier*, No. 6062, VII, 573 and Order, 26 May 1802, *Correspondance de Napoléon Ier*, No. 6101, VII, 607.
15. SHDDT GR 1M 1422, Lettre General Humbert.
16. TNA FO 33/28/38. See also TNA HO 10/94/143, folios 159–70.
17. TNA HO 42/51/215, Fitzwilliam to Portland, 3 September 1800.
18. TNA HO 42/51, Gott to Portland, 21 September 1800.
19. AD CPOA 593, folio 53, Rapport, Octobre 1800.
20. SHDDT GR 1M 1422, Projet du général Humbert.
21. SHDDT GR 1M 1422, Mémoire général Humbert No. 1, 8 Octobre 1800.
22. SHDDT GR 1M 1422, Mémoire général Humbert No. 2, 8 Octobre 1800.
23. Smith, p. 254.

Chapter 22

1. Iain McCalman (1988), *Radical Underworld: Prophets, Revolutionaries, and Pornographers in London, 1795–1840* (Cambridge: Cambridge University Press), p. 15.
2. Wells (1986), pp. 220–1.

3. TNA HO 42/65/114, folio 300, 4 June 1802.
4. TNA HO 42/62/162, folios 435–6, Petition to Duke of Portland, 19 August 1801.
5. AD CPA 594, folio 173, Talleyrand to Bernadotte, 18 Janvier 1801. See also AN AFIV, folio 204, Rapport sur Bonaparte.
6. AN AFIV 1672, folio 191, Talleyrand to Bernadotte.
7. TNA WO 1/397/117-21, Reports from France and Hamburg January to April 1801.
8. TNA FO 95/612/85, To Evan Nepean, 14 March 1801.
9. TNA WO 1/923/399, folios 399–402, Bouillon, 31 March 1801.
10. TNA WO 1/923/477, folios 477–84, Bouillon, 22 May 1801.
11. TNA WO 1/923/439, folios 439–42, Bouillon, 29 May 1801.
12. SHDDT GR 1M 1422, folio 34, Humbert au Berthier.
13. AN AFIII 572, Humbert au Bernadotte, 27 Prairial an IX.
14. AN AFIII 572, Humbert au Bernadotte, 12 Thermidor an IX.
15. AN AF III, folio 152, Fulton au Comité Militaire pres le Directoire exécutif, 29 Messidor an VII.
16. AN AF III, folio 152, Rapport pour Premier Consul.
17. SHM BBIV 130, Latouche-Treville au minister de Marine citing Robert Watson, 5 Septembre 1801.
18. SHM BBIV 130, Fulton au Monge.
19. SHDDT GR 1M 1422, projet de Monltezun.
20. Wells (1986), pp. 220–2.
21. BL AM 33107, folio 48.
22. TNA HO 42/62/196, folios 535–6, Letter to Major-General Isaac Gascoyne, 31 October 1801.
23. TNA HO 42/62/197, folios 537–8, Ralph Fletcher to Home Office, 1 November 1801.
24. TNA HO 42/65/198, folios 442–3, Ralph Fletcher to Home Office, 3 April 1802.
25. AN AFIV 1598, plaquette 2v. See also AN AFIV 1598, plaquette 2iv.
26. AF/IV/1287-AF/IV/1326/A, dossier 1, pièces 1–78.
27. AN AFIV 1672, pièce 26, folios 63–6, 1re note de Fiévée.
28. AN AFIV 1672, pièce 27, folios 67–70, 2e note de Fiévée.
29. AN AFIV 1672, pièce 28, folios 71–2, Note de Fiévée 17 Juin 1802.
30. SHDDT, 14 Juin 1802, 17 Décembre 1802.
31. David Paget, personal communication, 14 February 2023, citing personal correspondence with Gerald Arboit.
32. TNA PC 1/3117, Ford to Notary, November 1802.
33. AN AFIV 1672, pièce 30, folios 74–5, Lettre du chef d'escadron Beauvoisin, 23 Vendémiaire an XI.
34. BL AM 33112, Rumbold to Hervery, 18 March 1803.
35. Olivier Blanc (1995), *Les espions de la Révolution et de l'Empire* (Paris: Perrin), pp. 219–24.
36. AN AFIV 1672, pièce 31, folios 76–7, Lettre Beauvoisin, 29 Vendémiaire an XI.
37. AN AFIV 1672, pièce 36, folios 91–6, Mémoire, daté après le 29 Novembre 1802.
38. Mike Jay (2004), *The Unfortunate Colonel Despard* (London: Bantam Press), p. 147. See also pp. 232–40, 268, 276, 297–304.
39. TNA HO 42/70/26, folios 74–5, John Gifford to Home Secretary, 20 February 1803.
40. AD CPA 600, Andreossy au Talleyrand, 4 Frimaire an XI.
41. *Correspondance de Napoléon Ier*, No. 6475, 13 Frimaire an XI.
42. SHDDT GR 1M 1422, folio 43, Côtes renseignements sur la côtes des Angleterre.
43. SHDDT GR 1M 1422, folio 63, Rye renseignements sur la bai de Rye.
44. AN AFIV 1597a, plaquette 1, ii–iv.

Chapter 23

1. TNA HO 42/65/219, folios 481–2, Ralph Fletcher to John King, 31 July 1802.
2. Marianne Elliott (1977), 'The "Despard Conspiracy" Reconsidered', *Past & Present* (75), p. 57.
3. Clifford D. Conner (2000), *Colonel Despard. The Life and Times of an Anglo-Irish Rebel* (Pennsylvania: Combined Publishing), pp. 219–20.
4. AD CPA, folio 84, Deuxième mémoire sur l'Irlande, 17 Fevrier 1803.
5. SHDDT GR 1M 1420, folio 63, Aperçu d'une expédition sur l'Irlande.
6. AD CPA 601, folio 60, Rapport sur l'Irlande, 17 Fevrier 1803.
7. BL AM 16,921.
8. AD CPA 601, folio 105.
9. Anon. (1804), *A Full Account of the Proceedings at the Middlesex Election, etc.* (London: M.C. Springworth), p. 11.
10. AD CPA 601, folio 88, O'Connor au Talleyrand, November 1802. See also AD CPA 601, folio 105, O'Connor au Talleyrand, March 1803.
11. TNA HO 42/70/47, folios 133–4, Copy of an intercepted letter from A O C [Arthur O'Connor] in Paris to Hugh Bell, 26 March 1803.
12. AN AFIV 1672, plaquette 2, folios 268–73, Rapport sur le voyage de M. Middleton en Angleterre, 1803.
13. AN AFIV 1672, pièce 78, folios 180–5, Mémoire de Duverne, chargé de mission en Angleterre, 6 Vendémiaire an XII.
14. SHDDT GR 1M 1420, folio 78, Points de départ d'un expédition contre l'Irlande.
15. SHDDT GR 1M 1420, folio 44, Mémoire sur l'Irlande.
16. Napoléon to General Berthier, Minister of War, 16 April 1803, Bonaparte (2004–13), *Correspondance générale, publiée par la Fondation Napoléon* (Paris), No. 7579, Vol. IV, p. 103.
17. AN AFIV 1195.
18. SHDDT GR 1M 1420, Note, projet de décent en Irlande, 14 Prairial an II.
19. AN AFIV 1195.
20. Napoléon to Decrès, Minister of the Marine and the Colonies, 8 August 1803, Bonaparte, *Correspondance générale*, No. 7914, IV, pp. 258–9.
21. TNA HO 42/70/2, folios 223–6, Letter William Goldson, 23 March 1803.
22. TNA HO 42/70/30, folios 249–51, Ralph Fletcher to Home Office, 8 April 1803.
23. Leslie Mitchell (2004), 'Fox, Charles James (1749–1806)', *Oxford Dictionary of National Biography*.
24. SCA WWM Y16/141, Francis Foljambe to Earl Fitzwilliam, 28 June 1803.
25. *Leeds Intelligencer*, Monday, 25 July 1803.
26. TNA HO 42/70/72, folios 230–1, A paper given to Lord Pelham by WH Alexander, 18 May 1803.
27. TNA HO 42/70/66, folios 207–8, John King to John Lead, 24 May 1803.
28. TNA HO 42/68/75, folios 188–91, Letter from George Hammond, 16 August 1803.
29. Nicholas Dunne-Lynch, personal communication, 26 October 2021.
30. TNA HO 42/71/93, folios 250–1, Draft letter marked 'Secret' to Jonas Bold, Mayor of Liverpool, 30 July 1803.
31. TNA HO 42/71/2, folio 179–82, Hornbuckle to Home Office, July 1803.
32. TNA HO 42/71/1, folio 67, Hand bill posted Teignmouth.
33. Nicholas Dunne-Lynch, personal communication.
34. https://www.Napoléon-series.org/research/government/diplomatic/letters/c_letters57.html.
35. https://www.Napoléon-series.org/research/government/diplomatic/letters/c_letters64.html.

36. Alfred Webb (1878), 'Robert Emmet – Irish Biography', www.libraryireland.com, accessed 11 June 2021.
37. TNA PC 30/9/115/5, Lord Castlereagh, 23 September 1803.
38. SHDDT GR 1M, folio 78, Projet de depart d'un expédition contre l'Irlande.
39. SHDDT GR 1M, folio 50, Projet sur L'Irlande, 10 Fructidor an XI, Hotel du Nord, Rue de Grenelle St Germain.
40. SHDDT GR 1M, folio 55, Mémoire sur l'Irlande.
41. SHDDT GR 1M, folio 50, Irlande, 10 Fructidor an XI.
42. https://www.Napoléon-series.org/research/government/diplomatic/letters/c_letters52.html, accessed 11 November 2021.
43. AN AFIV 1962, pièce 84, folio 202, Résumé du rapport.
44. AN AFIV 1962, pièce 86, Mémoire adressé au Premier Consul par Thomas Addie Emmet, 20 Fructidor an XI.
45. AN AFIV 1962, pièce 85, folios 209–16, Rapport présenté par Thomas Addie Emmet au 1e Consul, 20 Fructidor an XI.
46. AN AFIV 1962, pièce 85, folios 203–8, Rapport présenté par Thomas Addie Emmet au ministre de la Guerre.
47 TNA HO 42/74/1, folios 14–21, Rapport. M. Rossollin, 8 Novembre 1803.
48. TNA HO 42/69/30, folios 82–7, Letter from James Hume, 8 November 1803.
49. TNA HO 42/74/3, folios 192–6, Minute of Mr Read's mission to Embden.
50. TNA HO 42/69/2, folios 3–8, Letter from Henry Hutson, 1 October 1803.
51. TNA HO 42/74/3, folios 132–4, No title, December 1803.
52. SHDDT X3 31 Guides de Berthier, dossier An12, Lettre 15 Brumaire an 12. Jones was born in Hamburg 24 July 1769. The Légion Nantais was formed in June 1793. One of Jones' fellow *sous officers* was Pierre-Jacques-Étienne Cambronne, best known for his acts at Waterloo. After serving in the National Guard of Nantes and then in the 1st battalion of volunteers of Maine et Loire, in June 1793, Cambronne enlisted in the Légion Nantais as a *sous officier* in the grenadier company. He was promoted to captain in October 1794. The legion fought at Quiberon in 1795. Jones and Cambronne, it seems, fought side by side.
53. SHDDT X3 31 Guides de Berthier, dossier An12, Lettre 11 Brumaire an 12.
54. Born in Wexford, 24 June 1768, son of Francis Thomas Moffatt and Elizabeth Stafford.
55. Born in Dublin, 15 October 1780, son of Nicholas Morley and Angelica Bouilly.
56. Born in Edinburgh, 25 December 1773, son of Joseph Murray and Mary Walker.
57. SHDDT X3 31 Guides de Berthier, dossier An12, Control Nominatif.
58. SHDDT X3 31 Guides de Berthier, dossier An12, Lettre 29 Vend An12.
59. SHDDT X3 31 Guides de Berthier, dossier An12, Lettre 22 Vend An12.
60. SHDDT 1m 1419, 24 Octobre 1803.
61. AD CPA 602, folio 107, Emmet au ministre de la Guerre, 10 Décembre 1803.
62. AD CPA 602, folio 107, Napoléon au Thompson 22 Nivoise ANXII.
63. AN AF IV 1201, Interrogatoire de l'équipage du cutter anglais Le George; 4 Nivôse an XII.
64. AN AF IV 1201, Interrogatoire de l'équipage du bâtiment anglais l'Actif; 25 Nivôse an XII.
65. SHDDT GR 1M 1420, Emmet au ministre de la Guerre, 4 Pluvoise an 12.
66. *Gazette Nationale ou Le Moniteur Universel*, n° 161, du Vendredi 11 Ventôse an 12.
67. Bonaparte, *Correspondance générale*, lettre n° 9246.
68. SHDDT GR 1M 1422, folio 43, Côtes renseignements sur la côtes des Angleterre.
69. SHDDT GR 1M 1422, folio 63, Rye renseignements sur la bai de Rye.
70. AN AFIV 1195, Berthier to Augereau, 11 8bre 1804.

71. AN AFIV 1962, pièce 82, folios 194–9, Mémoire d'Arthur O'Connor, 29 Nivôse an XIII.
72. AN AFIV 1962, pièce 83 200-201, Résumé des propos tenus par M. Smith.
73. TNA HO 42/79/100, folios 333–4, Ralph Fletcher to Home Office, 24 September 1804.
74. TNA HO 42/77/61, folios 99–100, Ralph Fletcher to Home Office, 17 November 1804.
75. TNA HO 42/82/8, folios 35–7, Ralph Fletcher to Home Office, 16 January 1805.
76. TNA HO 42/80/42, folios 93–4, Ralph Fletcher to Home Office, 16 February 1805.
77. AN 215AP/1, Fonds Talleyrand, dossier 3.
78. TNA HO 42/82/6, folios 31–2, Ralph Fletcher to Home Office, 7 March 1805.
79. SHDDT GR C1 32, Napoléon au Marmont 5 Juillet 1805. See also SHDDT GR C1 32, Napoléon au Marmont, 13 Juillet 1805.
80. TNA HO 42/81/58, folios 94–5, Ralph Fletcher to Home Office, 10 August 1805.

Chapter 24

1. SHDDT GR 1M 1422, Projet d'invasion Fitzhenry.
2. SHDDT GR 1M 1422, folio 44, Angleterre, 1808.
3. SHDDT GR 1M 1422, Rapport, 28 Août 1809.
4. AN pièces diverses entrées en 1992 et 1993 AB/XIX/4190, dossier 4, Note sur un projet d'expédition, 1809.
5. Nicholas Dunne-Lynch, personal communication, 8 December 2021.
6. SHDDT GR 1M 1420, folio 64, Renseignements sur la situation politique et la sur l'esprit des habitants de Irlande. This plan dated to 1797–8 can be found in AD Memoires et Documents 2. – sur un projet de descente en Irlande, par Hervey Morres de Montmoroncey
7. Nicholas Dunne-Lynch, personal communication, 8 December 2021.
8. SHDDT GR 1M 1420, folio 64, Notes particular Gal Humber, 3 Juillet 1810.
9. SHDDT GR 1M 1420, folio 45, Renseignements sur l'Écosse, 1810.
10. Bonaparte, *Correspondance générale*, No. 16916, Napoléon au Decrès, 17 Septembre 1810.
11. Nicholas Dunne-Lynch, personal communication.
12. Bonaparte, *Correspondance générale*, No. 17331 Napoléon au Clarke, 5 Fevrier 1811.
13. Nicholas Dunne Lynch, personal communication.
14. Bonaparte, *Correspondance générale*, No. 17824, Napoléon au Decrès, 19 Juin 1811.
15. Ibid., No. 178446, Napoléon au Clarke, 23 Juin 1811.
16. Ibid., No. 17875, Napoléon au Clarke, 4 Juillet 1811.
17. Ibid., No. 17909, Napoléon au Clarke, 14 Juillet 1811.
18. Ibid., No. 18010, Napoléon au Decrès, 9 Août 1811.
19. Ibid., No. 18050, Napoléon au Decrès, 19 Août 1811.
20. Ibid., No. 18034.
21. Ibid., No. 18123.

Chapter 25

1. Peter Burrowes (1812), *Speeches … on the trials of Edward Sheridan, M.D. and Thomas Kirwan* (Dublin: J.J. Nolan), p. 4.
2. Kyle Hughes and Donald MacRaild (2018), *Ribbon Societies in Nineteenth-Century Ireland and its Diaspora* (Liverpool: Liverpool University Press), pp. 46–7.
3. Elliott (1982), pp. 358–62.
4. Nicholas Dunne-Lynch, personal communication.
5. TNA HO 42/117, folios 491–3, London, 26 November 1811.

6. Leeds University Manuscripts 193, Gott Papers, Vol. 3, 106, letter two.
7. TNA HO 42/125, folios 3–8, Deposition of Joseph Barrowclough, 7 July 1812.
8. TNA HO 42/125, folios 439–40, Letter dated Dyapool, near Hull, July 1812.
9. TNA HO 42/125, folios 3–8, Deposition of Joseph Barrowclough, 7 July 1812.
10. *Derby Mercury*, 14 November 1811.
11. *St James's Chronicle*, 21 January 1812.
12. TNA ADM 98/205, Letters to Agents for Prisoners on Parole, 9 January and 22 January 1812.
13. TNA ADM 98/119, Letters to the Admiralty, 11 January 1812.
14. TNA HO 79/1, Miscellaneous Correspondence. See also TNA ADM 98/119.
15. Leeds University Manuscripts 193, Gott Papers, Vol. 3, 106, letter one.
16. Leeds University Manuscripts 193, Gott Papers, Vol. 3, 106, letter two.
17. TNA HO 40/1/9, folios 4–6, Ralph Fletcher to John Beckett, 6 April 1812.
18. TNA HO 40/1/8, folios 40–5, Statement of H. Yarwood, 22 June 1812.
19. Francis Raynes (1817), *An Appeal to the Public – containing an account of the services rendered during the disturbances in the north of England in the year 1812* (London: J. Richardson), p. 92.
20. SCA WWM F46/122, Deposition of Thomas Broughton, 26 August 1812.
21. TNA HO 40/1/3, folios 90–2, Disposition of Bent to Fletcher, 17 April 1812.
22. TNA HO 40/1/3, folios 100–2, Disposition of Bent to Fletcher, April 1812.
23. TNA HO 40/1/11, folios 45–8, Report Citizen Bent, 12 May 1812.

SELECT BIBLIOGRAPHY

Archive Sources
France
Archives Diplomatique de France
Correspondance Politiques Angleterre
Boxes 582, 583, 584, 585, 586,587, 588,589, 590, 591, 592, 593, 594,600, 601, 602
Archives Nationales de France
C11, F7, AF III, AF IV, AF VII, Fonds Sieyès (XVIIe–XIXe siècle) 284AP/13, Fonds Talleyrand 215AP/1, LH//1679/77 MacShechy
Service Historique du Armée de Terre, Vincennes
Boxes B11 1, B11 2, GR 1M 1419, 1420, 1421, 1422, 1423, 1424. 2Yc2620. MacSheehy, 6Yd 26 Emmanuel de Grouchy
Service Historique de la Marine, Brest
BB^{IV} 122, BB^{IV} 123, BB^{IV} 130

Ireland
National Library of Ireland
MS 49,491/2/424L, Letter from Jeff O'Connell to the Privy Council, 12 May 1794

Netherlands
2.21.046 Inventaris van het archief van H.W. Daendels
2.01.29.01 Inventaris van de archieven van het Departement van Marine, 1795–1813

United Kingdom
British Library
BL Add MS 36527, folio 67, John Milnes; AD MS 27814, AD MS 59363
Cumbria Archive Centre
D SEN 5/5/1/8/36, Threats to Humphrey Senhouse, 1797
East Sussex and Brighton and Hove Record Office
AMS5440/296

Kent History Centre
U840 Pratt Papers
Leeds University
Brotherton Library, Special Collections, Manuscripts 193, Gott Papers, Vol. 3,
The National Archives, Kew
Admiralty Papers 1/1449/105
Home Office Correspondence series 68, 40, 42, 45, 100
Foreign Office papers
Pricy Council Papers
Treasurer Solicitor Papers
War Office Papers
Sheffield City Archives
Wentworth Woodhouse Muniments, Fitzwilliam Papers
West Yorkshire Archive Service
John Goodchild Collection
Quarter Session Records, 1637–1914

Digital Sources

https://www.british-history.ac.uk
https://founders.archives.gov
http://shura.shu.ac.uk/4075/1/phdthesisfinalversion16nov2011.pdf
https://www.historyofparliamentonline.org/
www.jstor.org/
https://spartacus-educational.com
Napoleon Series.

Printed Sources

Alpaugh, Micha (2014), 'The British Origins of the French Jacobins: Radical Sociability and the Development of Political Club Networks', *European History Quarterly*, 44, Issue 4, pp. 593–619

Anon. (1792), *A Letter from His Grace the Duke of Richmond to Lieutenant Colonel Sharman, Chairman of the Committee of Correspondence Appointed by the Delegates of 45 Corps of Volunteers Assembled at Lisburn in Ireland, with Notes from a Member of the Society for Constitutional Information*. London: J. Johnson

Anon. (1804), *A Full Account of the Proceedings at the Middlesex Election, etc*. London: M.C. Springworth

A Complete Collection of State Trials, various editors. London: 1809–26

Ashelford, Jane (2008), *In the English Service, the Life of Philippe d'Auvergne*. Jersey Heritage Trust

Birley, Robert (1924), *The English Jacobins from 1789 to 1802*. London: Oxford University Press

Blanc, Olivier (1995), *Les espions de la Révolution et de l'Empire*. Paris: Perrin

Bohstedt, John (1983), *Riots and Community Politics in England and Wales, 1790–1810*. Cambridge: Cambridge University Press

Brown, Richard (2002), *Church and State in Modern Britain, 1700–1850*. London: Routledge

Burke, Edmund (1780), *Vindication of Natural Society*. London: J. Dodsley

Burke, Edmund (1826), *Speech on the Petition of the Unitarians*. London: C. & J. Rivington

Burrowes, Peter (1812), *Speeches … on the trials of Edward Sheridan, M.D. and Thomas Kirwan*. Dublin: J.J. Nolan

Burrows, Simon (1998), 'A Literary Low-Life Reassessed: Charles Theveneau de Morande in London, 1769–1791', *Eighteenth-Century Life*, Vol. 22, No. 1, pp. 76–94

Chinnéide, Síle Ní (1962), *Napper Tandy and the European Crises of 1798–1803*. Dublin: University of Dublin

Claeys, Gregory (2007), *The French Revolution Debate in Britain*. London: Palgrave Macmillan

Conner, Clifford D. (2000), *Colonel Despard. The Life and Times of an Anglo-Irish Rebel*. Pennsylvania: Combined Publishing

Conner, Clifford D. (2009), *Arthur O'Connor*. New York: iUniverse Inc.

Dart, Gregory (1999), *Rousseau, Robespierre, and English Romanticism*. Cambridge and New York: Cambridge University Press

Dickinson, Harry (1990), 'Popular Loyalism in the 1790s', in *The Transformation of Political Culture: England and Germany in the Late Eighteenth Century*, ed. Eckhart Hellmuth. Oxford: Oxford University Press, pp. 517–20

Dinwiddy, John (1992), *Radicalism and Reform in Britain, 1780–1850*. London: Hambleden Press

Donnelly, F.K. and J.L. Baxter (1976), 'Sheffield the Revolutionary Tradition', in *Essays in the Economic and Social History of South Yorkshire*, ed. Sidney Pollard and Colin Homes. Sheffield: South Yorkshire County Council, pp. 398–423

Dréano, Emilie (1997–8), 'Biographie politique de William Duckett, patriote et espion irlandais sous la Révolution Française', mémoire de maîtrise. Université Lumière–Lyons 2

Duffy, Michael (1996), 'William Pitt and the Origins of the Loyalist Association Movement of 1792', *Historical Journal*, No. 39, pp. 943–62

Elliott, Marianne (1977), 'The "Despard Conspiracy" Reconsidered', *Past & Present* (75), pp. 46–61

Elliott, Marianne (1982), *Partners in Revolution. The United Irishmen and France*. New Haven and London: Yale University Press

Emsley, Clive (1981), 'An Aspect of Pitt's "Terror": Prosecutions for Sedition during the 1790s', *Social History*, Vol. 6, No. 2, pp. 155–84

Fitzpatrick, Michael (1995), 'Patriots and patriotisms: Richard Price and the early reception of the French Revolution in England', in *Nations and Nationalisms: France, Britain, Ireland and the Eighteenth-Century Context*, ed. M. O'Dea and K. Whelan, Oxford: Voltaire Foundation, pp. 211–30

Gibney, John (2019), *The United Irishmen, Rebellion and the Act of Union, 1798–1803*. Barnsley: Pen & Sword

Goldsmith, Lewis (1811), *The Secret History of the Cabinet of Bonaparte*. London: H.S. Nichol

Goldsmith, Lewis Stewarton (1895), *Memoirs of C.M. Talleyrand de Périgord: Containing the Particulars of his Private and Public Life*. London: H.S. Nichol

Goodwin, Albert (1979), *The Friends of Liberty. The English Democratic Movement in the Age of the French Revolution*. London and New York: Routledge

Graham, Jenny (2000), *The Nation, the Law and the King: Reform Politics in England, 1789–1799*, 2 vols. New York: University Press of America

Green, Dominic (2014), 'From Jacobite to Jacobin: Robert Watson's Life in Opposition', in *Living with Jacobitism, 1690–1788 The Three Kingdoms and Beyond*, ed. Allan I. Macinnes, Kieran German and Lesley Graham. London: Pickering & Chatto, pp. 185–96

Marquis de Grouchy, Alphonse Frédéric Emmanuel (1866), *Le général de Grouchy et l'Irlande en 1796*. Paris: Imprimerie Balitout, Questroy et Ce

Hansard (1818), *The Parliamentary History of England*, Vol. XXXI. London: Longmans

Horgan, Kate (2016), *The Politics of Songs in Eighteenth Century Britain 1723–1795*. London: Routledge

Hughes, Kyle and Donald MacRaild (2018), *Ribbon Societies in Nineteenth-Century Ireland and Its Diaspora*. Liverpool: Liverpool University Press

Jay, Mike (2004), *The Unfortunate Colonel Despard*. London: Bantam Press

McBride, Ian (2009), *Eighteenth-Century Ireland: The Isle of Slaves*. Dublin: Gill and Macmillan

McCalman, Iain (1988), *Radical Underworld: Prophets, Revolutionaries, and Pornographers in London, 1795–1840*. Cambridge: Cambridge University Press

Macleod, Emma Vincent (1998), *A War of Ideas: British Attitudes to the War Against Revolutionary France 1792–1802*. London: Routledge

Mitchell, Leslie (2004), 'Fox, Charles James (1749–1806)', *Oxford Dictionary of National Biography*

Nicholas, Hans (1954), 'Franklin, Jefferson, and the English Radicals at the End of the Eighteenth Century', *Proceedings of the American Philosophical Society*, Vol. 98, No. 6, pp. 406–26

Paine, Thomas (1987), 'Letter Addressed to the Addressers on the Late Proclamation', in *The Thomas Paine Reader*, ed. Michael Foot and Isaac Kramnick. London: Penguin

Pakenham, Thomas (1997), *The Year of Liberty: The Great Irish Rebellion of 1798*. London: Weidenfeld & Nicolson

Parsons, Lynn Hudson (1965), 'The Mysterious Mr. Digges', *The William and Mary Quarterly*, Vol. 22, No. 3, pp. 486–92

Pelet de la Lozière, Joseph Claramond (1837), *Napoléon in Council: Or, the Opinion Delivered by Bonaparte in the Council of State*, trans. Captain Basil Hall, RN. London

Philip, Mark (2017), *Reforming Ideas in Britain: Politics and Language in the Shadow of the French Revolution, 1789–1815*. Cambridge: Cambridge University Press

Price, Richard (1789), *Discourse Delivered on the Love of Our Country*. London: J. Johnson

Purcell, Mary (1978), 'The Strange Story of Richard Ferris', in *The Irish-French Connection, 1578–1978*, ed. Liam Swords. Paris: Collège des Irlandais, pp. 97–107

Rae, Robert (1961), '"Liberty of the Press" as an Issue in English Politics, 1792–1793', *The Historian*, No. 24, pp. 26–43

Revolution Society (1792), *The Correspondence of the Revolution Society in London, with the National Assembly, and with Various Societies of the Friends of Liberty in France and England*. London: J. Johnson

Rogers, Nicolas (1999), 'Burning Tom Paine: Loyalism and Counter-Revolution in Britain, 1791–1793', *Histoire Sociale*, Novembre, pp. 139–71

Royale, Edward (2000), *Revolutionary Britannia?* Manchester: Manchester University Press

Smith, Edward (1974), *Whig Principles and Party Politics. Earl Fitzwilliam and the Whig Party, 1748–1833*. Manchester: Manchester University Press

Society for the Friends of the People (1793), *Authentic Copy of a Petition Praying for a Reform in Parliament*. London: J. Ridgeway

Stanhope, Earl (1867), *The Life of The Right Honourable William Pitt*. London: John Murray

Swords, Liam (1989), *The Green Cocakde. The Irish in the French Revolution 1789–1815*. Dublin: Glendale

Thomis, Malcom (1970), *The Luddites: Machine-Breaking in Regency England*. Newton Abbot: David & Charles

Thompson, Edward Palmer (2013), *Making of the English Working Class*. London: Penguin Classics

Tone, William T. (2008), *Life of Theobald Wolfe Tone by Himself, Continued by his Son, with his Political Writings, Edited by W.T. Wolfe Tone*, 5 vols. Cambridge: Cambridge University Press

Vaughan, Benjamin (1793), *Letters, on a Subject of the Concert of Princes, and the Dismemberment of Poland and France. (First Published in the Morning Chronicle between July 20, 1792 and June 25, 1793)/by a Calm Observer [Benjamin Vaughan]*. London: printed for G.G.J. & J. Robinson

Weber, Paul (1997), *On the Road to Rebellion: The United Irishmen and Hamburg, 1796–1803*. Dublin: Four Courts Press

Wells, Roger A.E. (1977), *Dearth and Distress in Yorkshire 1793–1802*. York: Borthwick Institute

Wells, Roger A.E. (1986), *Insurrection: The British Experience 1795–1803*. Stroud: Sutton Publishing

Zamoyski, Adam (1999), *Holy Madness: Romantics, Patriots, and Revolutionaries, 1776–1871*. New York: Weidenfeld & Nicholson

INDEX